cake

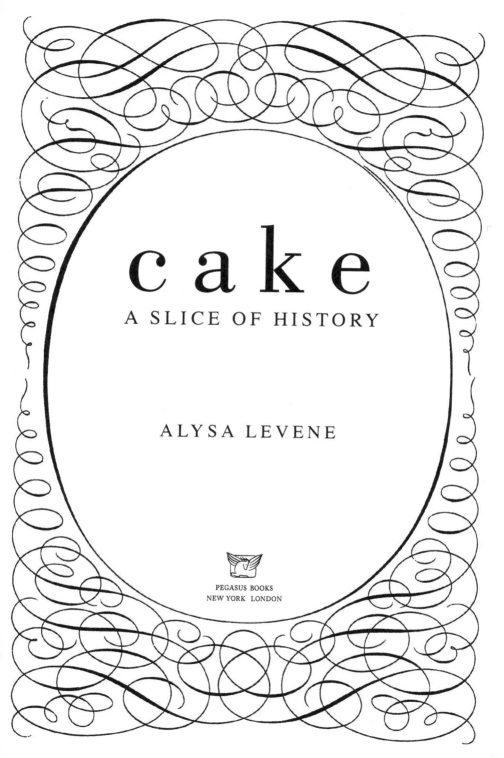

cake

A SLICE OF HISTORY

ALYSA LEVENE

PEGASUS BOOKS
NEW YORK LONDON

CAKE

Pegasus Books Ltd.
80 Broad Street, 5th Floor
New York, NY 10004

ISBN: 978-1-68177-349-0

10 9 8 7 6 5 4 3 2 1

Printed in the United States of America
Distributed by W. W. Norton & Company, Inc.

For Rich, who never licks the spoon, and Alex,
who never misses an opportunity

And for Patricia and all the lessons I learned in her kitchen

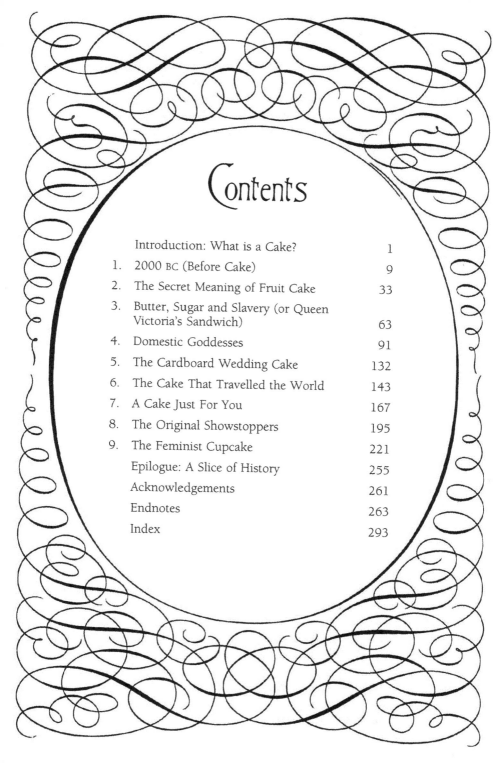

Contents

Introduction

WHAT IS A CAKE?

What is a cake? You might think that the answer is so obvious that we don't even need to ask the question, but this established teatime treat has stirred up more controversy than you might at first imagine. So before we embark on our social and cultural history of cake, we had better get our definitions straight. In 2014 the British tax body HMRC took Tunnock's of Scotland to court. Tunnock's make that beloved British treat, the tea cake: a glossy chocolate-coated dome of marshmallow atop a solid biscuit base, all wrapped in distinctive silver and red foil. On this occasion HMRC were more interested in their Snowballs, however, which are close cousins with the tea cakes and consist of globes of mallow, coated in chocolate and covered in coconut. The problem was that Tunnock's described their Snowballs as cakes. HMRC, meanwhile, felt that they were more properly a biscuit. The reason that this was so contentious is that while chocolate-coated cakes are zero rated for tax (the seller doesn't charge value added tax on sales but can recover any VAT it has itself incurred), a chocolate-coated biscuit is standard rated. One can see how the trouble arose; HMRC had already waded into these waters twenty-three years previously, when it tackled McVitie's over the categorisation of their

Jaffa Cakes (according to the McVitie's website, 'the original combination of light sponge, dark crackly chocolate and the smashing zingy orangey bit' – the latter a layer of firm jelly which can be pleasingly revealed by teasing off the upper chocolate layer with the teeth). HMRC lost on that occasion for three principal reasons. First, the Jaffa Cake's ingredients are those of a cake (egg, flour and sugar), and the batter which is used to make them is thin and not thick. Second, their texture is like that of a cake – they are 'soft and friable' (crumbly, in other words) rather than 'crisp' and brittle. However, the most famous part of the ruling as far as British trivia goes was the third point: that Jaffa Cakes go hard when stale – like cake – rather than soft like biscuits.

HMRC were to lose in 2014 too. This time, however, the ruling was based on a different set of principles and is worth quoting, as much for amusement as for instruction:

A Snowball looks like a cake. It is not out of place on a plate full of cakes. A Snowball has the mouth feel of a cake. Most people would want to enjoy a beverage of some sort whilst consuming it. It would often be eaten in a similar way and on similar occasions to cakes; for example to celebrate a birthday in an office. We are wholly agreed that a Snowball is a confection to be savoured but not whilst walking around or, for example, in the street. Most people would prefer to be sitting when eating a Snowball and possibly, or preferably, depending on background, age, sex etc. with a plate, a napkin or a piece of paper or even just a bare table, so that the pieces of coconut which fly off do not create a great deal of mess. Although by no means everyone considers a Snowball to be a cake, we find that these facts, in particular, mean that a Snowball has sufficient characteristics to be characterised as a cake.

There is something rather wonderful about the picture of a bench of learned appeal lawyers coming to such a precise decision about something as frivolous as a snack (they noted that they tasted a range of similar confections 'in moderation' in the process of coming to their decision). But their words are actually rather interesting. The Jaffa Cake ruling was based on ingredients and the way the cake behaved after baking (whether it went soft or hard). What the judges in the Snowball case chose to dwell on, however, was the *occasion* on which cakes appear: birthdays and other celebrations, as part of a sit-down occasion, not as street food, at a time when they can be 'savoured'. The report of the 2014 appeal at a tax tribunal listed seven key traits which legal precedent had established as important in distinguishing cake from biscuit: ingredients, manufacturing process, unpackaged appearance (including size), taste and texture, circumstances of consumption (including time, place and manner of consumption), packaging and marketing.

However, there is clearly some room for manoeuvre here too. Jaffa Cakes do not have the traditional appearance of a cake: they are flat and, to all intents and purposes, biscuit-like. A Snowball, meanwhile, is not baked, and does not contain flour; meringues have also been accepted as cakes as far as tax law goes. The tribunal judges agreed that Snowballs did not have all of the traits of a cake, but they had enough. So going back to our opening question: what exactly, then, makes a cake a cake?

This book answers that question. Over the course of its chapters we find that the Snowball judges were correct: it's about occasion as much as ingredients. We also see that cake is a treat in some way, not often part of a meal, but central to the ties that bind families and communities together. It signals hospitality and welcome; not offering cake to a guest is a way of keeping a visit short. Even in the long-ago past, sweetness and occasion marked it out in subtle ways from bread.

It's not vital, of course; no one is claiming that cake has a foundational part in the human diet. But that said, if we strip back the layers of icing, if you will, we see that to understand what cake is and what it means to us both now and in the past, we need to deal with a good number of themes which are very important indeed: the spread of international trade and the opening up of the New World (sugar and spices); the transnational migration of people (how cakes travelled and were transformed); the history of female domesticity and emancipation (the gendered nature of baking and how that is breaking down); the importance of appearances – cake as art; and the rise and cementing of national traits and pastimes, to name but a few.

For many people, cakes mean memories, almost always of celebration, family and love. Because they are fairly cheap to buy and easy to make, cakes are both accessible and familiar to most in the Western world. They have played their parts in social occasions and treats for centuries, and in many different forms and tastes. In all these settings, however, cake has always carried a symbolism far in excess of its nutritional importance or, for a long time, its monetary value. For centuries cake has gone hand in hand with weddings, birthdays and funerals; it has accompanied small children to school in lunch boxes and tuck boxes; it has said 'I love you', 'congratulations' and 'I'm sorry'. A be-candled cake carried in to a party marks someone out as special – and its bearer as a nurturing and loving provider. A home-made cake is one of the most nostalgic (and oftentimes unrealistic) emblems of motherhood and domesticity, and one of the reasons that many people feel so attached to family recipes and cakes which are trotted out on regular occasions. Other family memories are built on shop-bought confections – a Battenberg, a Lamington or a Twinkie is less likely to be part of a home baker's repertoire than a simple sponge (certainly the Twinkie, with its list of unfathomable ingredients) – but many people will still sigh nostalgically at the sight of the pink and yellow squares, the coconut covering, or the soft yellowy sponge in its plastic wrapper. Cake is more than a foodstuff: it is the stuff of happy memories and a comfort – as well as a sugar fix to get you through the afternoon.

With its heavy load of sugar, fat and carbohydrates, cake is the archetypal comfort food. The helpings of love and nurture that often accompany it turn that dial a little higher still. For the narrator of Marcel Proust's novel *À la recherche du temps perdu* (published between 1913 and 1927), the buttery, crisp-edged and scallop-shaped French madeleine is a direct line to half-forgotten childhood memories. As he dips his delicate cake into his tea, he is transported back to a place he didn't know he remembered: his aunt giving him a taste of her madeleine on Sunday mornings. This was without even tasting the cake – the simple ceremony surrounding it was enough. As to the madeleines themselves, they are a speciality of Commercy in Lorraine (north-east France) and became fashionable around 1730, although – as we will find time and time again with the genesis stories of different cakes – there are many alternative tales about their origins. One legend attributes them to a pastry cook working for Prince Talleyrand in post-revolutionary France, a culinary patron we will meet again. Another says they were devised by the female cook to King Stanislaus of Poland, who will similarly crop up again in these pages.

Madeleines are speciality cakes; they require their own types of scallop-shaped patty tin for one thing, but that's not putting home bakers off nowadays. The launch of the hugely popular *The Great British Bake Off* in 2010, which led to spin-offs around the world, plus other baking shows like the American *Cupcake Wars*, *Cake Wars* and *DC Cupcakes*, the rise and rise of food bloggers, specialist baking shops and websites, baking books and banks of recipes ('cake' is now the most popular search term on the BBC Good Food database) – have all stoked that interest to new levels of intensity. The trend towards home baking has been on the up since the 1960s but is currently at previously unreached highs, even in countries like France, where baking is traditionally an art practised by master pâtissiers. Market research shows that more than three-fifths of British adults baked at home at least once in 2013 (up from a third in 2011), and a quarter bake at home once a week. More people are making baking their business, and we are collectively buying more cakes too, especially the small individual-sized portion ones which we will meet in Chapter 9. We will consider there what this suggests about our tastes and outlook on life. Meanwhile the market for new baking ingredients and mixes is growing at a dizzying rate, and highly specialised baking books make good sales on Amazon, alongside classic baking bibles by domestic goddesses and *Bake Off* finalists alike. We'll come back to that in Chapter 4.

All of this means that we are increasingly well informed (and well sated) when it comes to cake. Every cake-maker will know that there are four key ingredients in baking most cakes (Snowballs are just one honourable exception), each with a vital part to play in the science of baking. *Fat* – butter, margarine, shortening or oil – lends tenderness and richness to a light cake. This is because it inhibits the formation of gluten, which is what makes bread chewy. It also keeps the cake moist, and allows the crust to colour nicely. Creaming the fat with *sugar* brings in the requisite sweetness and also traps and encases air in the mixture which then expands on baking, yielding a light cake. Sugar does this by carrying air on its rough crystalline surfaces. It also helps to further tenderise the proteins in the flour; adding too much sugar softens these proteins so that they can't hold the shape of the cake. *Eggs* are the butter and sugar's partner in crime for entrapping air in the batter, as well as giving both colour and richness from the yolks. The honeycomb of air bubbles introduced in the whisking of the eggs are what gives cakes their 'sponge'-like appearance. And, finally, *flour* gives cakes their structure. As the oven heats the batter, the gluten in the flour stretches, until finally it and the egg proteins set to form the cake's shape. If the temperature is too cool or too hot, these processes will not occur in the right order, leading to a heavy, sunken exterior, or a too-brown surface and a 'volcano' top. If the flour is mixed in too heavy-handedly it can undo all the good work of introducing air into the batter. Not all cakes are created in the same way, of course, just as they do not all depend on the same ingredients, but again we will come to this later.

In my family, as in many others, cakes are the makers of memories. When my younger sister got married, she asked our grandmother, our mother and our step-mother to make their signature bakes – treats which had a memorable place in our childhood. My grandmother made the rich fruit cake she always baked at Christmas. As children we found it disappointingly heavy and dry, but as we got older we all grew to appreciate it as a part of the family celebration, and now she is now longer with us the recipe is particularly treasured. My mother made a chocolate sponge which we call Queenie's Chocolate Cake, after the great-aunt who gave her the recipe. That cake is light and moist (the secret is the couple of spoonfuls of hot water which are added to the batter), and it appeared at almost every one of our birthdays in one guise or another. It is the recipe we all took away to university with us and now bake for our children's birthdays. And, finally, my stepmother made chocolate brownies, whose sticky, pleasurable unctuousness is fully explained by the amount of butter they contain.

My siblings and I took these ideas about the shared memories of baking into our adult lives. It wasn't until I developed an academic interest in the history of food that I started to think about the deeper significance of these tasty, but nutritionally frivolous foodstuffs. What does cake mean for different people? How have we come to have such a huge variety of cakes? What had to happen historically for them to appear? And what can they tell us about the family and relationships within it? I wrote this book to find out the answers.

1

2000 BC
(BEFORE CAKE)

The alluring sweetness of cake is such an established part of modern life that it is hard to imagine a world in which it didn't exist, but go back four thousand years and you would be very hard pressed to find anything we would recognise as cake today. A world without cake; it's a chilling thought. But where and when did the first cake appear and what would it have tasted like? Let's start our search with a familiar story, a little closer to home.

It is the year AD 878, on the small marshy island of Athelney, in the English kingdom of Wessex. The Anglo-Saxon people have been enduring terrifying raids from Scandinavian Vikings for eighty years and for the last forty of them scarcely a year has gone by peacefully. All of the other kingdoms in England have fallen; Wessex is the last remaining stronghold, but now, in mid-winter, the Vikings are advancing and the small force at Athelney is the last Anglo-Saxon defence. Their leader is the King of Wessex, a man who has gone down in history as Alfred the Great.

At this moment, however, his epithet is far off. An attack has left his men scattered and, with his kingdom under threat, Alfred takes sanctuary in the home of a poor woman. She doesn't recognise him and asks if he can give her a hand by minding the cakes she's baking on her hearthstone. Of course many readers know what comes next: Alfred, lost in thought on how to repel the invading Vikings, lets the cakes burn, and seals his legacy in popular memory for the next 1200 years or so.

We shouldn't leave Alfred in such a state: he collected his men and rode out to meet his enemies shortly afterwards, where he thoroughly routed them. The Viking king submitted to a Christian baptism, a peaceful settlement was reached and Alfred went on to be a great promoter of learning, craftsmanship, common law and religion in Wessex and later across the kingdoms of England. He is the only English king to be known as 'Great'. The burning of the cakes was a rare low point in a distinguished reign. However, this ignoble episode has a lot to tell those of us interested in the early history of cake.

First, we can be sure that Alfred's cakes were not much like the ones we know today. Sugar was not yet available so they would most likely have been sweetened with honey, and probably not too much of that either. The raising power of beaten eggs had not been discovered, so they would have been flat and dense, or alternatively raised with yeast, like bread. And they certainly would not have been baked in an oven – ovens were not to be found in the homes of labouring folk for some centuries to come. Instead, people would have taken items for baking to a communal oven, or baked them over the fire at home. Alfred's cakes were probably more like what we think of as enriched breads today, or perhaps a compressed round of moistened oats. In fact, they were so far removed from what we have in mind when we break out our butter, sugar, raising agents, flour and eggs that we really have to ask whether they were cakes at all.

This question becomes even more pertinent when we find that in some versions of the tale it's not cake that Alfred burns, but bread, and that brings us to the second point: that cake and bread are very close relations indeed. In the ninth century, a Welsh monk named Asser, who was invited to join Alfred's court by the King himself, wrote about the kingly burning of the *loaves* (his *Life of King Alfred* is the main reason we know so much about this particular king). By 1574 and the publication of another *Life of King Alfred*, this time by the Elizabethan Archbishop of Canterbury, the loaves had become cakes. The author Charles Dickens made the cake story even more famous in his *A Child's History of England*, which was published weekly in Dickens' own magazine *Household Words*, between 1851 and 1853. Interestingly, a very similar story to Alfred's is told of another hero at around the same time, but one from the opposing side: the Viking hero Ragnar Lodbrok (otherwise known as 'Hairy Breeches'). His burning of the bread is used in a similar way to the Alfred-and-the-cakes story, to show a moment of weakness in a man of courage and strength, but one which spurred great deeds.

So why did some authors change the bread to cake in Alfred's version? Why not stick with bread, which we could perhaps appreciate needs some element of specialised skill? Cake is, after all, a mere indulgence, and unlikely to be something a warrior king would want associated with his name. Was it a catchier way to show just how preoccupied he was? A better – or perhaps slightly shaming – reflection of his domestic qualities? Or a way of gently poking fun at Alfred and summing up this low point in his kingship before his return to glory? Even if we will never know why or exactly when bread became cake, we can see that later authors felt that they signified different things, and that cake better summed up the traits they wanted their readers to associate with King Alfred. By this stage, of course, cake meant something very different from what it had done in the ninth century.

So the legend of Alfred's cakes tells us about cake, but it also tells us about bread. It does more than that too: it signals how food was differentiated between rich and poor, what ordinary homes and cooking technology were like, and what characteristics were attached to men and women, warriors and cooks. The change from bread to cake in the story makes Alfred's moment of weakness more striking because he is being ordered to do women's work, and by a lowly swineherd's wife at that. What's more, while a warrior would depend on bread, would he really demean himself by eating a treat like cake while he was preparing for battle? Cake might not have been part of the original legend, but it's become a shorthand for us to understand what its authors were getting at.

In terms of the history of cake, then, we have two paths to follow. The first is cake as a form of bread, and the second is cake as something fancy, sweet or special, in the way that we think of it today. The different versions of the legend of King Alfred have essentially moved us from one to the other, but in historical terms, there was only a very fine line separating the two for a long time. Early forms of grain were hard to digest unless they were well cooked in stews. Cracking the hard outer shells, pounding, moistening and forming them into flat cakes for baking was another way to get at their nutriment, like the Scottish bannocks, Derbyshire oatcakes and American corn pancakes (or johnnycakes) we still know today. Another of the Vikings' legacies was a form of oatcake called a haver-cake, while those same oaten cakes lent Scotland, for a time, the name 'Land of Cakes'. The fictional Piers Plowman talks of cakes of oats, and havercakes eaten with curds and cream in the mid-fourteenth-century poem by William Langland, suggesting not only that a cake could be something made from grain, but also that it could be made into a sweetened delicacy. Other flat breads and cakes had extra ingredients added directly to the dough such as honey, fruit or seeds (caraway, fennel, cumin, dill); fat (milk or cream) and eggs. We have many descendants of this sort of cake with us too: the bara briths, stollens, *kugelhopfs* and Bundt cakes we will meet in later chapters. In short, 'cake' in Anglo-Saxon times could mean something very basic, or something quite special.

Dictionary definitions underline that this dual path is of long standing. The first definition given by the *Oxford English Dictionary* for 'cake' is 'a baked mass of bread or substance of similar kind, distinguished from a loaf or other ordinary bread, either by its form or by its composition'. We may suppose, then, that cakes tend to be smaller and flatter than bread and less 'ordinary' in some way, although the dictionary goes on to say that they are 'usually baked hard on both sides by being turned during the process'. This is certainly not true of modern cakes, which are usually far too delicate to be handled while they are baking, and suggests that we are still in the realm of bread. An encyclopaedia published in 1382 makes the same distinction: 'Some brede is bake and and tornyd and wende at fyre and is callyd . . . a cake.' The origin of this cake is clearly bread, but it is baked and handled differently. Biblical references to a 'cake of bread' (Samuel ii, 36 for instance) also suggests a distinction between regular bread and something called a cake, whether that was by shape, taste or function.

The *OED* also gives another definition, however, which boosts cake up into the realm of 'fancy' bread, and that is via the addition of 'special' ingredients: butter, sugar, spices, dried fruits and so on. Anglo-Saxons in Alfred's time would certainly have been familiar with this sort of cake – assuming they had the wealth to purchase the extra ingredients. They would still have been either flat – like our Scottish shortbread, or like the cakes known as hearthstone (halstone), probably in the same humorous tone as British rock cakes, which look like rocks, but hopefully taste rather sweeter; or yeast-raised like an enriched bread. We have a record of a French biscuit or cake called a *gastel* from the twelfth century, which was also flat and round, made from flour, fat and honey (this is where the French word *gâteau* comes from). There were certainly many different words for cakes in Europe at around Alfred's time, from 'cicel' to 'pastillus' (the latter meaning a small cake). It is clear that these had quite a different texture from what came to be known as a cake in later centuries, but they still evidently had the 'sweet and special' qualities which we associate with them today – and existed in some abundance.

To understand what Alfred may have burned on that fateful day, though, we need to appreciate just how important grains were at this time; and not in the fancy form of cake either. It is estimated that at the start of the fourteenth century up to 80 per cent of the calories eaten by a harvest worker came from grains, and even soldiers (whose diets one might think were worth bolstering to give them the necessary strength and stamina) came close to that level. The nobility enjoyed a more varied diet, but still relied on grains for about two-thirds of their calories. The Abbot of Peterborough, who presided over a large house, required bread to be baked more than eleven times per month in 1371, making in excess of four hundred loaves per baking. Fraudulent bakers were treated extremely severely: in 1327 the authorities in London discovered no fewer than ten bakers who had built secret trapdoors into their counters so that dough could be pinched off the bottom of customers' loaves before being taken off for baking. The customer would be charged for a full-weight loaf and the baker gained a stash of dough with which to make extra loaves. All ten miscreants in this case were put in the pillory, and all those who were found with extra ill-gotten dough had to stand with dough hung round their necks. In 1266 the English had passed an Assize of Bread which set out the prices and weights of different loaves, in order to prevent fraud.

Grain in one form or another has been important for so long because it's (a) versatile and (b) filling. It's versatile because there are so many different types: there is a candidate which will grow well in most climates. If more than one will thrive, as it did across much of England, then so much the better, both for nutrition and as insurance in case of crop failure. Once harvested, grain can then be turned into a variety of hefty foodstuffs which fill the belly; an important consideration when food sources and/or income were fairly limited (i.e., for most of our human history). This is fortunate because unprocessed grain is not fit for human consumption, and it takes considerable effort to make it so. To extract the edible kernels, the crop first has to be threshed to loosen the kernels, and then winnowed to separate the useful stuff from the rest: the husks from the stalks, and the kernels within the husks from the waste or chaff. All of this was made a lot easier as crops were domesticated and bred for more convenient characteristics. Wild grains, whether that's corn, barley or wheat (or their antecedents, emmer, which was used by the Ancient Egyptians for bread-making, and einkorn), had evolved in ways which promoted self-seeding and hardiness – in short, survival. They grew tall stems, so that the ear or husk containing the grain was out of the reach of foraging animals. They only had one ear per stem (the word einkorn means 'one grain') to maximise the chances of some surviving and seeding. And while the husks broke open easily to allow the grain to drop to the ground and grow, the grain itself had a hard outer shell or hull. All of these characteristics, however, were highly inconvenient to humans trying to collect enough grain to feed their family, especially when we consider that the early grains also needed soaking or toasting to get through that hard hull before they could be eaten (a trait which, interestingly enough, changed the proteins in such a way to prevent rising, leading to flat and dense breads and cakes).

Once humans started to cultivate grain crops around 8000–7000 BC they started to breed out these unwelcome characteristics in favour of grains which were reliable and easy to grow, harvest and process. Domesticated grains grow tightly packed into one ear, rather than singly. They grow close to the ground, and they ripen at the same time. All of these adaptations were bad news for the crop seeding itself, but they were a big step forward for the cultivators who bred them. Cultivation was a skill perfected by the Egyptians in the Nile valley, an area so fertile that it could produce up to three times more than the local residents needed for their own supplies in all but the worst years of flood or low rainfall. A third of Rome's grain came from Egypt, and tax payments were set according to the amount of grain grown each year.

Even after all this the grain still needed long cooking, and the easiest way to do this was in a pot over a fire: stews and pottages came before bread because they needed much less attention, and the cauldron was for a long time a much more important piece of cooking equipment than a griddle or oven. Turning grain into anything more refined, like flour, requires the kernels to be ground, and if maximum lightness is required, the flour to be sifted or 'bolted' (to use the contemporary term) through a fine cloth. The Egyptians may have been the first to grow grains which didn't need toasting, but skeletal evidence of their worn teeth shows that their flour was still gritty and unrefined. The coarse bread cakes made from grains like emmer would have been painfully hard to eat when cold, like the little rounds made from wheat, hulled barley, wild oats, weeds and seeds which have been found at the English lake village of Glastonbury, dating back to the first century BC.

The last meal eaten by Lindow Man, whose body was preserved in an English bog for 2,000 years after his gruesomely violent death, was a similar, unleavened, griddle 'cake' made of flour ground from spelt, emmer and hulled barley. Lindow Man was deposited face-down in the bog some time in the first century AD, but his last meal reflects the sort of food our ancestors would have been eating for the preceding two thousand years. Here then is our four-thousand-year-old 'cake' –

tasty, isn't it? Analysis of his stomach contents even shows how it was cooked: quickly over a fire made from alder wood. For centuries grinding took place on a quern: a set of stones which broke down the grain by friction. The Egyptians used saddle querns where the top stone was moved over the bottom in a to-and-fro rolling motion. Later, rotary querns were turned with a round-and-round movement, which opened up the possibility of animal power (it is much easier to persuade an animal to go round in a circle than to go back and forth), and eventually water and wind power. By the Domesday Survey of 1086, there were 6,000 water mills in England, although a lot of domestic milling took place using a small hand mill which would be laboriously turned by the women of the household. And this is how grinding took place for centuries to come, despite attempts by the Church and other big landowners to ban home milling in order to preserve their own monopoly: the first biggest advance in terms of milling technology didn't occur until the nineteenth century and the invention of steel roller mills which could grind the flour much more finely.

Once the grains had finally been ground, sifted and bolted, however, the possibilities for making nourishing and filling foodstuffs were almost limitless. The most important has always been bread in its many forms, from raised loaves made from finest white flour and wild yeast, barm derived from brewing, or fermented grape juice (some ale was also made by fermenting part-baked bread), through unleavened tortillas of maize flour or the Mexican speciality *masa harina*, to dense cakes of oat or barley flour. A good grain harvest was so important for the happiness and prosperity of agricultural communities that it took on great cultural significance as a time of feasting and thankfulness. Harvest festivals are still popular around the world, from the moon cakes which form part of the Chinese Mid-autumn Festival through to the more prosaic collection of tins and jars of foodstuffs in British primary schools and churches, although the best known example is, of course, the American Thanksgiving celebration which takes place on the fourth Thursday of November each year, commemorating the bounty of the pilgrim settlers' new land.

Bread has symbolic significance in many other traditions too: bread and salt are traditional symbols of welcome, and breaking bread together is a companionable act (the word 'companion' is from the Latin for 'with' (*cum*) and 'bread' (*pane*). Superstition has it that throwing bread away or placing it upside down on the table brings bad luck. In France it was considered bad luck if a loaf fell to the ground and it had to be kissed. In Imperial Rome, bread (and later grain) was given out to the poor; under Julius Caesar one in three of Rome's population benefited from (or perhaps another way of looking at it is to say 'needed') this charity. One of the best-known facts about the Romans was that they built granaries all over their empire to make sure that there was always enough wheat for everyone.

The Romans, like the Ancient Greeks and Egyptians before them, were also keen bakers of cake. The Egyptians started off by sweetening bread dough to make something fancy, in the way we've already seen, but around 5000–3000 years BC they began making something with a specifically different name and purpose, which was known as a cake. Its ingredients were fairly familiar: wheat flour, honey or dried fruits, yeast, eggs, milk and spices. It was baked on hot stones and had a variety of functions: as tomb offerings for the gods (there are Old Testament references to cakes being made – shamefully – for the queen of heaven by the Jews shortly before their Babylonian exile in the sixth century BC in the Book of Jeremiah); as offerings for the dead to take on their journey to the afterlife; or for communal festivals for the living, like harvest. Over their long period of ascendancy, the Egyptians refined and developed their cake-making into something quite sophisticated. The cakes' shapes became more ornate and decorative, including depictions of birds and fish, and they were baked in ovens rather than on the hearth, which would have given them more 'rise' and a more even bake.

The Greeks and the Romans took up this culinary example and made it their own. Cakes served a similar range of functions in these cultures as they had for the Egyptians: ritual and temple offerings, celebrations and snacks, but everything about them became more diverse and celebratory. The Greeks had hundreds of different types of cakes, distinguished by shape, ingredients and purpose. The most common general name for cakes in Greek was *plakous* (meaning 'flat') – the origin of the word 'placenta', which is literally life-giving and nourishing; in Latin the equivalent label was *libum*. Cakes which were served as temple offerings were known as *popanon* (they were often round in shape in honour of Artemis, the goddess of the moon). The Greeks even started the tradition of putting candles on cakes, again for Artemis and her lunar light, and they discovered that beer could be used to leaven dough instead of yeast. Goat's or sheep's milk cheesecakes were made for the athletes competing at the first Greek Olympic Games to give them energy (cheese was thought to be fortifying), and were soon transported to Rome and across the Roman Empire, gaining their own characteristic ingredients and flavours as they went.

The Old Testament gives further evidence of how cakes were made and used at a similar time: again, some were clearly references to bread, although sometimes made with the best flour; others were used to consecrate newly ordained priests. Their ingredients were many and varied: we see unleavened cakes, cakes of figs and cakes baked with honey or fried in oil. Above all, these references reveal times of community, and of the sharing of local ingredients like honey and dried fruit, which are still prominent in the treats of the Middle East today.

The Greeks and Romans, then, clearly enjoyed their cake (there was a whole book called *On Cakes* by the Greek Iatrocles, but it sadly has not survived), and they were not the only ones: we know that in India sweet cakes were served at important banquets, although they appeared before the savoury items. In China cakes were being baked by the first century BC. Not too many written recipes have survived to show exactly what these early cakes consisted of, but we have a lot of information from plays, paintings and pottery in the last centuries AD. We even have some more immediate evidence from the ash-preserved ruins of Pompeii and Herculaneum, where excavations have turned up individual cake tins and carbonised cakes in several different shapes.

Some of these cakes were for everyday consumption, some were for special occasions. Some clearly had a cheeky side: one author, Heraclides of Syracuse, described festival cakes of sesame and honey called *mylloi* which were made in the shape of female genitals in honour of the goddesses Demeter and Persephone; while the Spartans made cakes called *kribanai* in the shape of women's breasts. The pyramid-shaped *pyramous* (possibly named in mockery of the pharaohs' ostentatious tombs), which were made from toasted wheat soaked in honey, were given as prizes to men who were still awake at the end of the all-night Greek symposia, or drinking festivals, and many other cakes were served at bars as well as at feasts at home, alongside wine, dried fruit and nuts. Others still were more like sweetened bread or pizzas, made using those familiar local specialities like dried figs, dates and sheep's cheese. At this end of the spectrum we can see again the fineness of the line between bread and cake, especially with dainties like the Cretan *glykinai*, which got their sweetness only from sweet wine. Others used a natural leavener derived from winemaking, called must (these were traditionally served on fresh bay leaves, which lent a subtle flavour as well as some extra moistness from their oil). These latter cakes were not necessarily anything very special – the statesman Cato gave them to his farm servants. Cakes like the *gastris*, or nut cake, meanwhile, which were described by the playwright Athenaeus (AD 170–230) in *The Deipnosophists* (or *The Partying Professors* – really a long and mouth-watering dialogue on food), were more akin to flattened rounds of dried figs or dates, spread with ground sesame or poppy seeds. They were apparently so extravagant that they were banned by Roman law. At the other extreme is a cake called *phthois* which was served with the entrails of a sacrificial animal – an unappetising side dish but one with great significance for the Romans who used entrails for divination. Ingredients differed too: many of the recipes of the time used cheese rather than butter or oil (and thus needed larger quantities because cheese contains less fat than butter or oil). Sweetness was mainly from honey, dates or figs, not sugar. And not all cakes were baked: the Greek *enkris* and the Roman *globus* were doughnut-like, deep fried in oil and drenched in honey.

One of the most amazing things about all these cakes is that they were being made at a time when most of Europe was baking unleavened bread on a hearthstone. In fact, many Greeks and Romans were doing this too both for bread and for the simpler cakes, and cutting off the sides and bottom to remove the ashes from the hearth just like the Anglo-Saxon peasantry were to do centuries later. Nowhere were fancy cakes part of the regular diet of most ordinary folk. There were also particular specialities in different places: Athens was particularly famous for its oven-baked bread and cakes, while Mount Hymettus in Attica was said to produce the best honey (it contained the natural flavouring of the wild thyme which grew on the mountainside). The Lydians were famed for their *enkytoi*, or honey cake, which went with their general culture and sophistication.

Much of the fancier cake- and bread-baking in Ancient Greece and Rome went on in professional bakeries. The Ancient Greeks had a strict guild system to regulate their bakers, while the Roman bakers' guild, the Collegium Pistorum (established in 168 BC), was one of the few which presided only over freemen rather than slaves, and even had a representative in the Senate. The richer classes in Rome might frequent one of several hundreds of bakeries several times a week (or send their slaves to do it for them). Not only this; the advance of the Roman army and its followers spread and exchanged baking, milling and cake lore all around its empire – even to its tiny outpost in the British Isles. Unfortunately for King Alfred and his people, even if some of these items and traditions had reached their ancestors, most of this knowledge was lost with the retreat of the Romans from Britain in around AD 400. The Anglo-Saxons retreated back to a diet which was much less colourful and sweet, and much more like the one they had known before the Romans arrived.

Cake in Alfred's Anglo-Saxon times was thus a step back on the foodie timeline in terms of sweetness and sophistication. The Germanic settlers who had followed the Romans had much less-refined tastes in baking, and their cakes were based heavily on wheat or other grains, with little in the way of added ingredients, shaping and decoration. In fact, the little 'cakes' of baked grain eaten by Lindow Man and his compatriots were not much like either our modern breads or cakes. To approach that sort of lightness requires an understanding of aeration and rise, and that in turn requires a certain amount of technology. The almost magical versatility of grain lies in its gluten: a protein which forms stretchy chains when a dough is kneaded. This varies considerably from one type of grain to another, from Canadian wheat at the highest end, to flours like quinoa and buckwheat at the lowest which contain no gluten at all. This is why wheat flours make light cakes and breads, and others like cornflour make dense ones.

Additional rising power comes from yeast which, as the Egyptians realised, could be captured from spores in the air, and which acts on sugars in the dough to create carbon dioxide. Part of the dough would then be saved to 'start' the next batch, like a sourdough. The Germanic lands of Western Europe also gained this expertise early on: most of the early words for yeast in Western Europe are based on Germanic languages. We've already seen that alternative forms of 'lift' came from ale barm or other fermented grains, and most early cookbooks included instructions on how to keep yeast (yeast derived from brewing needed careful washing and could be bitter). Other chemical leaveners derived from soap-making started to appear in the late eighteenth century as we will see in Chapter 3, but commercial yeast was not available until the early nineteenth century, and self-raising flour until the 1870s.

Finally, the dough – whether bread, tortilla or cake – needs to be baked. There is archaeological evidence for ovens at a site in Moravia dating back to 25000 BC, at least 15,000 years before we started the cultivation of crops, and bread ovens have been found in the ancient Near East dating back to 6000 BC. The Egyptians, once again, refined oven baking significantly, first using tall moulds which were turned over the dough on the hearth (making a confined space for steam to circulate and promote rising), and later building round, open ovens like an Indian tandoor, where bread dough was slapped onto an inside wall for baking. These tended to need a hot fire, so in close-packed cities it made more sense to buy your bread ready-made, or take the dough to a communal oven. This was still common practice in Alfred's Anglo-Saxon times, where the lord of the manor would allow his tenants to use the large manorial oven (for a fee). The alternative was baking something simpler on the hearth at home, just as Alfred's hostess did. This was very common in parts of Europe where wood was plentiful; probably more than we will ever know for certain, as hearthstones were too inexpensive to have been worth recording in people's wills or inventories of goods. If no stone was to hand, breads and cakes could be baked on the hot earth where the fire had been, with hot embers piled up around them to give more heat. Baking technology soon moved on, however: by the thirteenth century many people were using iron 'stones' suspended over a fire to bake their bannocks, girdlecakes and oat havercakes – all regional variations on a theme of flat bread – or turning a pot over the dough either on the hearth or suspended above the fire to make a small enclosed 'oven'. There was a significant incentive to make this move as early as possible in the warmer climates of southern Europe where labouring over a hot fire was not an attractive prospect for much of the year. Elizabeth David reported that dough was still baked on a griddle and under a pot, 'kettle' or 'baker' in parts of Cornwall at the end of the nineteenth century. One popular variant was Cornish kettle bread, made from barley flour, which could be as large as a cartwheel for village feasts. The clay ovens built around Barnstaple in Devon (also in Wales, Ireland and parts of America) into the late nineteenth century, meanwhile, had changed little in design since Neolithic times.

Larger institutions, like monasteries and castles, had brick ovens by the time of the Norman Conquest in 1066. These were made from stone or brick, were three feet high and fourteen feet around, or even larger – a man could stand up straight in some of the largest ovens. They would be set into a wall or, more commonly, placed in a separate bakehouse or kitchen (to reduce the not insignificant risk of fire) and heated by lit bundles of wood until the correct temperature was reached (judged by touch, or by the speed with which a handful of flour blackened). The fire would then be swept out and the goods for baking placed inside. First would go the breads, then as the oven cooled, the pies, and finally, the cakes. We can really see here how much making cake was a natural part of the regular process of making bread. It was often made from the same dough, to which extra ingredients were added. This explains the continuing tradition of enriched and sweetened bready cakes which liven British culinary culture to this day: Welsh bara brith, malt loaves, lardy cakes, Cornish saffron cakes, and so on. It also means that we can see cakes as the luxury side of bread-making: the sweet treat baked regularly alongside the staple fare of the household.

Interestingly, while professional bakers were men, at home, it would be the women who did the baking of the hearth breads, just as in Alfred's tale. In fact, the Anglo-Saxon word for 'lady' comes from 'hlaefdige', meaning kneader of bread, while the word 'lord' is from 'hlafward', or the keeper of bread. This is a sign of the vital role women played in making the household's main source of food, and also how valuable it was, that it was part of a lord's duty to 'keep' it. We will come back to this theme of gender divisions in the kitchen later. And in a final piece of veracity for the tale of Arthur's baking disaster: the finest wheat grows best in low-lying areas – just like the area of southern England where his kingdom of Mercia lay.

Not all breads and cakes were, however, created alike. In Western Europe, foods made from white flour have always been more desirable than those made from brown, because white flour took more processing and so was more expensive (this is why the adulteration of flour with whitening products like alum later became a problem). The white colour suggested purity and health, just as we will see it did for sugar. The finest flours required vigorous and repeated sieving to remove the particles of husk and bran; the most refined had been not only sieved but 'bolted' through a fine meshed cloth which would be twisted up and shaken hard so that only the finest particles got through. The best-quality cakes and breads would be made with this type of flour, including 'crompehts' or flat cakes (from the Celtic *crempog* – a type of pancake), and enriched breads like pandemaine and wastel loaves, which may well have been enriched with milk and butter or eggs. The word 'pandemaine' probably comes from the Latin *panem Dominicum* or Lord's bread, which just underlines its status. We will find in a later chapter that the French pastry cooks received extra privileges because they were responsible for baking the Communion wafers. At the bottom end was the least refined, darkest and grittiest flour which still contained most of the outer grain (and thus also more of the vitamins and minerals, although no one knew that at the time). Flour like this was used for trenchers – square breads which were used as edible plates, though they were usually given away after the meal to the poor for eating.

Other flours were dark because they were ground from grains with a higher proportion of bran: barley, millet or rye, for example (all of which were more popular in Eastern Europe, where rye is as culturally important as wheat is in the West). The most common type of loaf in medieval Britain was 'maslin', which was made from a mixture of wheat and rye flour. Derbyshire is still known for its oatcakes; Mrs Beeton of British cookbook fame, who we will meet in a later chapter, spent part of her childhood in Cumbria where she would have encountered barley bread (barley is actually a much more dependable and adaptable form of grain than wheat). Wheat bread would be bought in for Sundays. In Ireland bread was made from potatoes.

These alternative flours made their way into fancier baking too: oatmeal continued to be used in cake-making in the northern British counties of Cumberland, Westmorland and Northumberland in the second half of the nineteenth century (the Yorkshire 33rd Foot Regiment in the American War of Independence were known as the Havercake Lads because their recruiting sergeant always marched ahead with an oatcake impaled on his sword), and chestnut flour is still used to make some traditional cakes in Italy; a custom that arose from necessity, like the breads made from ground peas and even weeds in times of real hardship. In the south-west of France, *farine de maïs* (cornmeal) was traditionally used for cakes. Each type of grain and bread brought its own qualities: wheat for strength, barley for sweetness, and rye for moistness.

The distinctively sweet taste of cake came quite late in the evolutionary journey. Sugar was already known in the first thousand years BC in China, India and parts of Asia, and it was in India that Europeans first encountered it (the word for cane sugar in Greek was *sakkhar*, which comes from Pali, a north Indian language). However, it was not readily available in Western Europe until the time of the First Crusade at the end of the eleventh century when it was carried home from Cyprus, Crete and Alexandria. At this stage it was scarce and novel enough to be an expensive luxury, used in medicines (it was prescribed to the invalid son of the English King Edward I in 1274; sadly it could not prevent his early death at the age of six years), for decoration and in sweets to be served at the end of grand banquets. If you could afford to serve your guests confections like comfits (sugar-coated caraway seeds – hugely time-consuming to make as they needed layer upon layer of clarified sugar syrup to be poured over the seeds), candied fruit, or costly and ornate sculpted 'subtleties' in the shape of castles, flowers, or even scenes from history, you were really someone in the medieval social world.

As might be expected given its cost and scarcity, sugar was highly sought after. Its perils for tooth decay were unknown, and the idea of 'empty calories' was scarcely a problem for people whose activity levels were much higher and calorie intake much lower than our own. In the medical thinking of the day sugar was a valued commodity as it promoted warm and moist 'humours' and was prescribed as a corrective for those whose constitutions were veering towards the cold and dry. It was also thought to be a digestive and good for breaking down food in the stomach. The British didn't need much convincing and adopted a taste for sweetness which soon pervaded their savoury dishes and drinks as well as desserts and cakes. It also came in a number of forms: medieval recipes refer to black, brown and white sugar (representing varying degrees of refinement; after the sixteenth century much refining was done in England), which often had to be carved off a large loaf or cone, and grated into a powder. Fancier forms were rose or violet-scented. The traditional boiled sweets made by pulling out hardened sugar syrup into an opaque rope which could then be twisted up or cut into lozenges, also have their origin in the medieval period, when the delights of sugar were being laid down in the British diet. Some felt that such sweetness was sinful gluttony, but fortunately for those who were tempted the Italian theologian and philosopher Thomas Aquinas declared in the mid-thirteenth century that sweets were not food and were thus exempt from the restrictions on religious fast days.

Sugar did not entirely replace the earlier reliance on honey, though; just like sugar, its sweet taste made it valued and sought after. Honey cakes are still favoured for the Jewish holiday of Rosh Hashanah because it symbolises sweetness and hope for the new year, while the Islamic book the Hadith recommends honey alongside learning to promote health in mind and body. We know from tomb reliefs that the Egyptians practised bee-keeping, and they also made sweet syrups from dates, fig and carob. The Greeks and Romans gathered it from the wild, and we've already seen that the honey which came from Mount Hymettus was particularly prized. Although sugar came to be a mainstay of the British diet, honey remained far more popular right up to the dissolution of the monasteries in the 1530s as part of Henry VIII's birthing of the reformed Protestant church. Much of the know-how and capacity for making honey was lost with the scattering of the bee-keeping monks.

Butter, on the other hand, which was added to cake for richness, was found more commonly in Britain and other parts of north-western Europe than further south. We've already seen that the

Greeks and Romans often used cheese instead of butter in their cakes (their name for butter was *boutyron* or 'cow cheese'), and that's because the warmer climate wasn't conducive to butter keeping well. The cultural divide between oil in the south and butter in the north was set down centuries ago, and extends into baking as well as cooking and early forms of medicine. For the Greeks, the butter eaters of northern Europe were barbarians. In those northern areas, however, the perspective was quite the reverse: butter was venerated as a luxury and had to be renounced in fast periods like Lent and most of Advent. It was introduced into Britain by the Celts during the Iron Age, a period which lasted for perhaps six hundred years before the Roman occupation, and marked the start of written records. The Romans, in turn, brought olive oil with them, but this did not last the occupation (nor, presumably, did the olives fare particularly well in the climate), and the inhabitants of the British Isles soon returned to butter. It was easier to preserve than cream, especially if it was salted or brined before storing. And although it was a luxury, it was one within the grasp of the many people who kept or lived near cows.

The final way that bread doughs could be enriched and made into cake was by adding eggs. Here again, we are talking of a different world from our own, where many more people kept hens and had access to their eggs. Having said that, this was not a year-round supply: hens lay only when there is enough sunlight to stimulate their pituitary glands to produce the requisite hormone (a seasonal influence we have now largely lost sight of with the advent of artificial lighting in poultry houses). This may have increased their worth, but eggs held a special place for more symbolic reasons too. Their combination of cold whites, rich yolks and hard shell made them seem like a microcosm of the world: a combination of different qualities which made them the perfect food. They could be eaten on ordinary fast days in the Christian calendar, although not during Lent. In prehistoric times the eggs of wild birds were eaten simply: roasted, or even sucked raw direct from the shell. Again, it was the Romans who took egg cuisine to a more sophisticated level, using them in custards and to bind other dishes together. Perhaps it was the realisation that eggs made other things richer that led people to try adding them to bread dough. It was an experiment that paid off: the protein in an egg makes for a more tender bread, the fat enriches it, and any degree of whisking traps air which aids rising.

We have several medieval recipes which show these ingredients helping bread on its way to becoming cake, like the one recorded in a sixteenth-century book called *The Widowes Treasure*, which directs the cook to bake and sift some flour and mix it with clotted cream, sugar, spices and egg yolks to form a paste which can be shaped into cakes. These are called 'fine cakes' although they sound more like what we would call a biscuit or a shortbread today. Many other small, fruited, yeasted, sweet buns still remain in the British culinary canon, such as currant buns, fruit buns and wigs – the latter being spiced triangular wedges, now sadly extinct – and all popular as early as the fifteenth century. The light, bready and golden Cornish saffron cake is another example.

Over the next few centuries these types of sweetened breads were to form a distinctive and beloved tradition of local specialities in Britain. The Cornish splits, Devonshire chudleighs, Northumberland singing hinnies (they 'sing' as the fat inside them fries on the griddle) and Ulverston Hiring Fair cakes from the Lake District are distinguished more by their associations with particular places than by their ingredients, although many do look or taste distinctive (the singing hinny, like its cousins, the Sussex plum heavies and the lardy cake which hails from south and south-west England, contain lard as well as butter and are flatter and denser than the bready splits). Others had even more precise associations, such as the Banbury and Eccles cakes (named after towns in Oxfordshire and Lancashire respectively), which are actually based on pastry rather than cake. Eccles cakes are fondly known as 'flies' graveyards' because of the squashed currants in the flaky pastry. This heritage was to be long-lived: an article in the Women's Institute's journal *Home and Country* in 1942 joked that those familiar with the English countryside could navigate their way around the country by their baked goods:

> I shouldn't wonder, in these dark, nameless, perplexing times, when we lose the way to our own front doors, a traveller could identify almost any county in England by its cakes alone. 'Splits for tea!' says the blacked-out wanderer. 'Dear me! I must be in Cornwall.' 'Banbury cakes? Change for the Oxford line.' 'Wigs and cheese cakes. Can this be the noble county of Yorkshire?'

The constituent nations of Great Britain also have their specialities, like the Welsh bara brith (a fruit-studded yeasted loaf, now often made as a simple, not-too-sweet cake by soaking fruit in tea overnight, and adding flour, sugar and eggs. The word *brith* means 'spotted'); and the closely related Irish barm brack.

We also have recipes for dishes which turn bread into a sweeter treat, like the one dating from the fifteenth-century for rastons, which are loaves whose insides have been scooped out, mixed with butter and replaced; the food writer Elizabeth David describes them as being like a sort of ancestor of the vol-au-vent. Another is the 'Wastels Yforced' which is found in the famous recipe collection *Forme of Cury* which is thought to have originated with Richard II's cooks in the fourteenth century. That is also a bread roll with its crumbs taken out and mixed with eggs, saffron, currants – and sheep's tallow (an alternative to melted butter in a more carnivorous age perhaps), all bound together and boiled. Simpler versions were the popular enriched toasts: bread which had been browned, soaked in wine and reheated to crisp up or, alternatively, spread with sweetened pastes. These were the ancestors of cinnamon toast, which is a popular favourite in America today. We are also still familiar with a recipe called *pain perdu* (literally, 'lost bread'), which is bread dipped in beaten egg, and fried with sugar in butter.

We will never know exactly what Alfred was supposed to have burnt on the hearthstone that fateful day on Athelney in AD 878, but the story is a useful introduction to the history of cake. It makes us think about the common origins of bread and cake, and the dividing lines: the forms, ingredients and functions that mark cake out as special, sweet or celebratory. It is clear that while their base ingredients are the same, cake was soon differentiated into something more luxurious, and something which denoted specific occasions – generally ones which involved ritual, feasting and communal ties. As we continue on our journey through its history, we will see that these remain some of its most defining characteristics today. We've also seen very clearly that as soon as bakers had the know-how and wherewithal to start enriching bread and shaping it into special forms, customers were keen to eat it. The astonishing array of different cakes baked by the Greeks and Romans shows us this very clearly. Put simply, as soon as they knew what it was, consumers wanted more. In the next chapter we will see how these early cakes developed into something even richer, sweeter and more special, and how vital they became in the annual calendar of feasting and ritual.

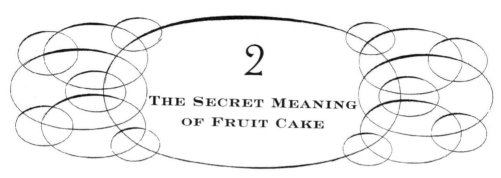

2

THE SECRET MEANING
OF FRUIT CAKE

In 1714 a young Englishman wrote a letter to the British satirical magazine the *Spectator*. He wanted to report that he had made a test of a popular proverb by sleeping all night with a piece of 'Bride-Cake' under his pillow. This was supposed to bring on dreams of great significance, and he had fasted all day just to make sure that the cake's charm had a good chance of working. Unfortunately, he wrote, he remembered nothing in the morning except a vague recollection of eating some cake, and under his pillow he found only crumbs. This is clearly a lesson in not putting cake in temptation's way, even of our sleeping selves. It also introduces the theme of this chapter: the special rituals associated with cakes, and especially spiced and rich fruit cakes which were the next stop down the line from Alfred's enriched breads.

This evolution was made possible by the great expansion in international trade through the medieval period and after, and specifically the sugar, dried fruit and spice it brought to Western Europe. Thanks to the expeditions of men like Christopher Columbus and Vasco Da Gama, whom we will meet again shortly, a great exchange triangle started to open up in the late fifteenth century, with sugar eventually coming from the Americas to Europe, finished goods travelling from Europe to Africa, and in the leg we today find the most troubling, slaves being transported from Africa to man the sugar plantations in the Americas. Another triangle took molasses – a by-product of sugar refining – from the Caribbean to America to make rum, the money from which was used to buy slaves from Africa who were, in turn, carried to the sugar plantations. The sugar that these triangular trades brought to European ports sweetened all parts of the diets of the rich from sauces to meats to wines, and (to return to our main theme) made cake look – and taste – a lot more like what we think of as cake today. Sugar was so highly prized that loaves of it were given as gifts and used as bribes.

If this was true for sugar, it was doubly so for spices like ginger, cloves, nutmeg and cinnamon, which all attracted staggering price tags thanks to their exoticism and fragrance. They were thought to come from Paradise itself – an indisputable justification for their high prices. Gradually they became more affordable and started to lend the cakes of the time the flavours and scents which are still familiar today in our modern fruit cakes. For the first time, baking hoops started to be used to give the cakes a more regular shape and a softer crust than a loaf or bun, and ovens became more common, which meant that more households could bake cakes and breads.

By the fourteenth and fifteenth centuries, then, European cakes were starting to look – and taste – a lot more like our idea of a cake (and a lot less like bread). They were sweeter, more regularly shaped, and more likely to be baked in an oven. The enriched breads we met in the previous chapter were still popular (even in the late seventeenth century spiced breads were regularly eaten for breakfast among the better off), but something more distinctly akin to cake had emerged alongside them. Many of these also featured another still-popular ingredient: dried fruit, which brought moisture, sweetness and heft.

Dried fruits – known generally as 'plums' – hence 'plum' or 'plumb' cake – only arrived in Britain in the thirteenth century although the trading centres of Portugal and the eastern Mediterranean may have known then earlier. They were expensive so, like spices and sugar, they were a luxury ingredient. Given that they made up fully half of the weight of the finished cake in some recipes, the fruit cake as we know it now could not really have existed prior to this. Dried fruits also make a cake keep well, an advantage when cakes were large and not to be wasted.

This chapter will examine how these new fruit cakes were made, but it is also concerned with the uses they were put to. As we move through the medieval period, we see festive and symbolic cakes really come into their own, as sugar and spice become more plentiful, and as communal feasts and customs settled into regular places on the calendar. Every country in Europe has a glorious array of local traditions centred around these fruited cakes, some now half forgotten, others elevated to national favourites. For such a small land mass, however, the United Kingdom had a particularly rich proliferation. In this chapter we will meet not only the rich and imposing fruited wedding cake, whose first cut represents the first joint act of the new couple; but also the hugely popular Twelfth Night cake, which gradually migrated from January into December and became our much-loved Christmas cake; the Shrewsbury cake; the Cornish saffron cake; and the bitter tansy cake. We will also see how many of these cakes were taken overseas and adapted to their new surroundings. The black cake of the Caribbean, for instance, is a direct descendant of the north-west European plum pudding, with the addition of rum and a dark sugar syrup. The gingerbread spices so beloved of coffee vendors in North America hearken back to the gingerbreads sold at medieval fairs across Germany, and taken to the New World by migrants keen to preserve their familiar seasonal rituals. The original

First Lady, Martha Washington, had a handwritten family cookbook which included a recipe for thin Christmas gingerbreads.

By the medieval period and the early modern one which followed, we can also see that cake had definitely come to mean something sweet and desirable, as evidenced by its appearance in proverbs and popular tales as such. A sixteenth-century collection of English proverbs gives us 'wolde ye bothe eate your cake, and haue your cake?' which is the original (and more sensible) version of our 'you can't have your cake and eat it'. Geoffrey Chaucer put cake in the mouths of his Canterbury pilgrims many times (so to speak) in his fourteenth-century *Tales*. The gluttonous and corrupt Pardoner, for example, puts off telling his tale until 'heer at this ale-stake / I wol both drinke, and eten of a cake'. (Another character, the Summoner, carries a bread 'cake' instead of a shield, so there was evidently still considerable cross-over between the two categories.) Shakespeare's merry-making Sir Toby in *Twelfth Night* cries in scorn at the virtuous Malvolio, 'Dost thou think, because thou art virtuous, there shall be no more cakes and ale?' This would be a sorry prospect indeed for a culture intent on joyful celebration whenever an opportunity arose. And to introduce the first type of celebratory cake we will consider we can turn again to Shakespeare, this time *Love's Labours Lost*: 'An I had but one penny in the world, thou should'st have it to buy gingerbread . . .'

Gingerbreads (though as will soon become apparent, they were variously bread-, cake- or biscuit-like) were a medieval invention and start to appear in the records of several European towns in the middle of the fourteenth century. Originally made by monks and popular from the outset at Christmas and other feasts, they also became quite a luxury good and featured on menus for banquets through to the middle of the seventeenth century thanks to their expensive ingredients. Every town which made gingerbread had its own speciality, but they were not, on the whole, the soft cakes we think of today; nor were they entirely like the British ginger 'snap' biscuits, which are brittle and crunchy. Instead they were probably quite flat and chewy, their texture living on in the German *lebkuchen*. Their name is something of a misnomer as they were, according to the *A to Z of Food and Drink*, originally called *gingerbras* which meant 'preserved ginger' in Old French, and had little to do with bread itself. By the middle of the fourteenth century, however, we find recipes which included bread as a key ingredient. Early British recipes directed the baker to first take some stale manchet (one of the fine white breads we met in the previous chapter), grate it finely, and mix it into a stiff paste with honey, ginger, cinnamon, pepper and saffron before shaping and slicing it. Here is a recipe by one of the first women to make her living from cookery writing, Hannah Woolley, published in her 1670 work *The Queen-Like Closet*:

> To make Ginger-bread. Take three stale Manchets grated and sifted, then put to them half an Ounce of Cinnamon, as much Ginger, half an Ounce of Licoras and Aniseeds together, beat all these and searce [sieve] them, and put them in with half a Pound of fine Sugar, boil all these together with a quart of Claret, stirring them continually till it come to a stiff Paste, then when it is almost cold, mould it on a Table with some searced Spice and Sugar, then bake it in what shape you please.

With all those exotic spices, gingerbread was an expensive luxury and this was reflected in its decoration: we have moulds from this period which are several feet high and ornately detailed, turning out a slab depicting, for example, a saint pressed into the surface. The finished gingerbread could be made yet more luxurious by painting it with gold leaf, making it a suitably grand gesture of a host's wealth and hospitality. Just as today, ginger was thought to be good for settling the stomach too; Benjamin Franklin recorded buying gingerbread while shipwrecked off Long Island in 1727 for this reason, although we can be fairly sure that this was a good deal less ornate than its medieval ancestors and more like the small ginger 'fairings' sold at fairs around medieval Europe.

Gradually, the breadcrumbs in the British version of gingerbread were replaced with flour, although they do live on in its close relation, parkin, which is another ginger-spiced chewy cake traditional as a Bonfire Night treat in Yorkshire. The sharp spice from ginger and pepper was softened with honey and soon afterwards the cheaper sweetener, treacle (known in the Americas as molasses), and by the end of the seventeenth century gingerbread had become the soft cake we know today. A little book published in 1854 by a professional gingerbread baker named George Read, titled *The Complete Biscuit and Gingerbread Baker's Assistant*, gives dozens of variants being sold in England at that time. 'This is a favourite article with many nations', the author says, from Holland, France and Germany, through to India, where gingerbreads were sent over from England. Smaller cakes and biscuits like gingerbread nuts, doll nuts and laughing or fun nuts (cut from a long rope of dough), or biscuits shaped like horses, men and women, were bought for children and lovers to curry favour; they could be purchased for a penny or two from shops, itinerant sellers and fairs, where customers could also buy embossed and gilt-painted biscuits like the ornate banqueting items of earlier days. Thicker gingerbreads were sold for a shilling, and others included preserved peel, caraway seeds, orange, honey and other spices.

On the Continent, however, gingerbread had remained more

cookie-like than cakey, and hadn't diverted to crumbled bread rather than flour. Two of the most popular and enduring specialities are the French *pain d'épices*, and the German *lebkuchen*, both still firmly associated with Christmas, probably because their exotic spices made them too expensive to eat every day (perhaps their warming tang also made them appealing in the cold months!). The French *pain d'épices* (literally, 'spice bread') has a very cake-like appearance, with a close texture, and is baked in a loaf tin. It is also an excellent example of how cakes evolve to make the most of local ingredients and traditions. The most traditional *pains d'épices* are made with local rye rather than wheat flour, and are sweetened with honey, making them close descendants of the Egyptian and Greek honey cakes, although other tales put their ancestors in China (where ginger originated). They might not have contained bread but they did have bread-like roots; they were originally made using a sourdough bread starter which over time has been replaced with chemical leavening agents (thin slices of *pain d'épices* are still sometimes served with savoury foods like *pâté de foie gras*). Reims, in the Champagne-Ardenne region of north-east France, became particularly famed for its *pain d'épices*: in 1571 the bakers who made them were awarded their own separate charter, and except at Christmas, no one else was allowed to make and sell the cakes. When the Académie Française published its famous *Dictionnaire* in 1694, it referred to the residents of Reims as '*mangeurs de pain d'épice*'. In the early nineteenth century their prominence was challenged by bakers from the city of Dijon in Burgundy, and *pain d'épices* remains a speciality of that town too (although it is quite different from the Reims variety, whose professional tradition, sadly, ended with the First World War). The Francophile American cook Julia Childs noted that every region in France had their own version of this special spiced cake; her own contained no eggs or fat, and was based on rye flour, honey, baking soda, ground almonds and the ubiquitous mix of ginger, cinnamon, cloves and nutmeg, livened with candied fruits.

In fact, the 'ginger' in gingerbread was not necessarily a given. In Germany, another name for the soft, chewy *lebkuchen* cookies are *pfefferkuchen* (pepper cookies), referring to the family of spices to which ginger and pepper both belong. Some of the recipes for English gingerbreads from the fourteenth and fifteenth centuries also contained pepper, alongside cinnamon and sandalwood. Nonetheless, the German gingerbreads which are still such a feature at Christmas markets all over the world are decidedly gingery. *Lebkuchen* originate at least as early as the thirteenth century when we know that they were being made by monks. They soon became more widespread, but they were a speciality of places with good trade connections and access to honey. The Bavarian town of Nuremberg, and Aachen, on the border with Belgium, were both particularly favoured in these respects and both became famous for their *lebkuchen* (both still ship their special cookies around the world, especially at Christmas time of course). Again, their specialities are distinctive, with *Aachener printen* being generally heftier and crisper than the Nuremberg variety. Both have official status as foods with 'protected designation of origin' meaning that the name can only be attached to goods made in that place.

Many of the crisper German gingerbreads are formed into shaped biscuits, which can then be assembled into ornate houses (popularised by the early nineteenth-century publication of the folk tale of Hansel and Gretel, who were fatefully enticed into eating parts of a gingerbread house). The gingerbread man or boy has also gone down in folk tales (in France he is called a *bonhomme de pain d'épices*), while in England gingerbread men were supposed to signify a girl's future husband. In Germany the *honigkuchenpferd* ('honey cake horse') is a popular treat. The tradition of baking gingerbread houses was taken to

America with German migrants and remains particularly popular in Pennsylvania, where many of them settled.

Gingerbreads have developed in other directions too. In New England they are sweetened with the local speciality maple syrup, and many other North American recipes use molasses. In Italy, the panforte, a speciality of the Tuscan town of Siena, is another traditional spiced and chewy cake, originally featuring pepper, and now, like many of its cousins, softened and sweetened with cinnamon, nutmeg and ground coriander. In Poland, the town of Toruń is as famed for its soft gingerbread (*piernik*) as Nuremberg is in Germany, and holds an annual gingerbread festival. Napoleon Bonaparte is among the many noted people who were presented with a gift of the local sweet treat by the town's authorities. In the UK too, particular towns have put their own stamp on a local variety of gingerbread: Market Drayton in Shropshire calls itself the Home of Gingerbread, while the Lake District town of Grasmere sells a shortbread-like cake whose recipe has been closely guarded for centuries. Further afield, the Jamaicans stand proudly by their tradition of ginger cake (which inspired a much-loved British teatime favourite, the stickily topped McVitie's Jamaica Ginger Cake), Jamaica being one of the earliest exporters of ginger to Europe.

Gingerbread, then, has a much-loved place both in the history of cake and in modern cake traditions, especially in Western Europe (and by extension North America), where it is intimately associated with Christmas. And Christmas and all its sweet treats is where we turn next.

There has been feasting and festivity in late December for much longer than Christianity has been with us. It was a natural time of year in the northern hemisphere to hunker down against the cold and dark and enjoy some good cheer while food stores were relatively full from the autumn harvest. It was also the time to mark the passing of the shortest day of the year and to pay tribute to the gods and the sun to ensure that light and fertility returned for another season. Part of that involved communal celebration with festive foods and drinks, and those which were sweet and warming soon came to play a special part. This is a tradition with growing numbers of followers today who prefer to mark the turning of the seasons rather than the birth of Christ. Having been brought up in a Jewish family, I always refer to the festive cake I make every year as a 'Solstice cake', and we make the first cut on 21 December. Unusually for the Jewish calendar, the December-time Festival of Lights (Chanukah) does not have a traditional cake, but is celebrated instead with oily doughnuts to commemorate the miracle which kept a tiny vial of oil burning in the temple for seven days.

The Romans were not the first to believe in celebrating the passing of the shortest day but, as with so many other things, they did it in style. They started with a lavish period of feasting in mid-December, known as Saturnalia, paused to mark the Birthday of the Unconquered Sun (not coincidentally on 25 December) and finished it with the Kalendae in the first few days of January, and which marked the returning of the sun. Both Saturnalia and the Kalendae involved much feasting and exchanging of gifts, including candles. Further to the north the Scandinavians and Norse people were even more aware of the value of the gradually lengthening days and also celebrated the winter solstice with traditions of fire and feast.

The Christian celebration of the Nativity of Christ was deliberately built on the timing and customs of these earlier festivals, part of a strategy by the Church to make new practices appear familiar and appealing to the people (it is very unlikely, after all, that shepherds would actually have been in the fields in midwinter, as they are supposed to have been at the time of Christ's birth). The celebration was not confined to the Nativity of Christ alone – in fact, for a culture which did not celebrate birthdays in any particular style, Christ's birth was for several hundred years a less-important occasion than the Epiphany, when he was revealed to the Wise Men or Magi. Christmas wasn't established as an official Christian festival until the fourth century AD. Just as for the Romans, Norsemen and Scandinavians, the early Church commemorated a series of events around this time which spanned twelve days in total: the martyring of St Stephen (26 December); the commemoration of St John the Apostle and Evangelist (27 December); Holy Innocents' Day (otherwise known as Childermas, on 28 December, remembering the killing of male children ordered by King Herod); Christ's circumcision (1 January); and Epiphany on 6 January – still remembered now as Twelfth Night when the packing away of the Christmas decorations marks the end of the festive period. This day is also sometimes commemorated as Christ's baptism. The notable absence from these dates was the celebration of the new year, which did start on 1 January in the classical Roman calendar, but did not move from 25 March in Britain until 1752 when the Gregorian calendar was adopted (leading, incidentally, to protests over the eleven days 'lost' in the process of realignment). The high points over the Twelve Days may have brought a more muted style of commemoration than the Saturnalian feasts which preceded them, but they still marked the passing of the darkest time of year and made space for celebration. It is no coincidence that they became particularly beloved in the northern parts of Europe which experienced the longest periods of dark and cold.

It is hard to tell exactly how quickly or otherwise the earlier midwinter festivals morphed into the Christian Christmas. The historian of religion and folklore Ronald Hutton has found that in AD 1038 the Nativity was still being described as 'midwinter' in

Anglo-Saxon chronicles, but for the first time in that year it appeared as 'cristes Maessan', or Christ-mass. Our friend King Alfred had already attempted to protect the long period of feasting between the Nativity and Epiphany in his law code of AD 877 which granted all servants the right to be free of work during that time (it is said that he lost that famous battle of Chippenham to the Danes which drove him to the swineherd's cottage on Athelney in 878 because he refused to fight during the Twelve Days). This was, of course, the quietest period of the year when it came to agricultural work in any case.

All of these occasions brought big communal feasts, bonfires and merriment, but cake was likely quite a latecomer to the party. Feasts were usually richer versions of the usual fare; that is, meats and wines. The closest antecedent of the fruited Christmas cake was probably a boiled porridge or frumenty of grains, milk and egg which was gradually spiced and sweetened until it became the boiled Christmas pudding which is still brought to the table, aflame with brandy, at the end of the Christmas Day meal. In my extended family, no doubt like so many others, the awe on the children's faces when the pudding is set on fire is matched only by their complete lack of interest in eating it. Much ritual still surrounds the making of the Christmas pudding, which is traditionally made on Stir-up Sunday, the last Sunday before Advent. Each person present takes a turn at stirring the mixture and makes a wish for the year ahead. In America, meanwhile, the Christmas baking season starts the day after Thanksgiving, making it the last Friday in November. Another sweetmeat which still graces our Christmas tables is the mince pie, which in medieval times formed part of the tradition of 'wassailing' from door to door for alms and good cheer. Wassailing sometimes involved small cakes, too, although there is no evidence that these were a special Christmas variety. The thickened and boiled Christmas pudding at some stage started to be baked, where it set off on its own trajectory as a traditional heavy and dark cake.

This new baked cake (often still contained yeast or ale barm) was not originally made for Christmas, but instead for Twelfth Night on 6 January. This was a time of joyous feasting and 'misrule' in many parts of Europe with much cross-dressing, feasting and the election of 'boy popes' and 'Lords of Misrule' to direct their courtiers in ribald dance, drama and song. The cake played a significant role in Twelfth Night festivities from at least the sixteenth century onwards as it held the token – a bean or a coin – which would confer the role of 'King of the Bean' on whoever found it, and give him licence to order his subjects as he pleased. The tradition proliferated in lively fashion until cakes were being stuffed with an array of items denoting not only a king, but his queen and all their courtiers too. In 1838, a man was indicted at the Old Bailey in London for forging a request for a Twelfth cake, complete with 'characters' from a baker in the city. In the Victorian period the tokens mutated into objects which predicted the finder's future, and cakes made for modern American bridal showers still continue this theme, with small trinkets on ribbons baked into a cake. A Twelfth Night cake is still provided every year at the Drury Lane Theatre in accordance with the will of an eighteenth-century comedian and one-time pastry chef, Robert Baddeley. The custom has only ever been abandoned on thirteen occasions, principally during the world wars. It was also carried across the water to America, where we will find it propping up festivities from Epiphany to the decidedly non-Christian revelry of Mardi Gras.

Another traditional Christmas cake has even more distinctly pre-Christian origins: the yule log. Today, the yule log, or alternatively, *bûche de Noël* in French, or *Kerststronk* in Flemish, is a simple Swiss roll: a large shallow sponge cake, spread with cream, or in France sometimes a sweetened chestnut puree, and rolled up into a log shape. Its name comes from its distinctive decoration, which consists of chocolate buttercream or ganache, patterned to look like the bark of a tree. A third of the log is then sliced off, using an angled cut, and positioned adjoining the larger remaining part, so that it looks like a forked branch. The log is sometimes given further veracity with meringue mushrooms, leaves or a festive robin, making it a much lighter and more child-friendly treat than the traditional fruited Christmas cake. It does not have the same revered place at the Christmas festivities as the Christmas cake, the mince pies or the Christmas pudding, but it is a popular addition, especially for those who do not care for the spiced and fruited theme of the other Yuletide desserts.

The modern, butter-creamed appearance of the yule log belies its long history. The word 'yule' arrived in England from Scandinavia, and one theory holds that it originally meant 'wheel', and signified the turning of the year. The original yule log was literally as the name suggests: a large log of wood which would be kept burning through the night of the winter solstice to keep light in the house and to keep evil spirits away. The tradition has its own twist in different parts of Europe, from the type of wood used (which varied according to the local forest: oak in England, birch in Scotland, cherry in France and so on), to the period over which it is burned – some say it must remain lit through the Twelve Days of Christmas. The log's burnt ashes were meant to protect the house from lightning, and in Somerset, the young men would compete to stay astride it as it was dragged home, earning themselves hot cakes and ale if they managed to stay on. Part of the log was traditionally kept back to start the fire the following year, heightening the symbolism of the light which burned through the darkest part of the year. Gradually, hearths became smaller, and a cake seemed like a more manageable tribute to the original log. One story has it that the *bûche de Noël* became popular when Napoleon banned wood-burning fireplaces because their chimneys brought in cold air and ill health. It was transported with French settlers to Canada where it is still popular in this festive season, and served at family gatherings after midnight mass on Christmas Eve. In Shetland, meanwhile, the traditional yule celebration endured into the eighteenth century as did a yule bread or yule bannock, which was a large, round cake.

All of these traditions took a severe hit in the middle of the seventeenth century, when the Puritan government which had ordered the execution of the English King Charles I, banned all the trappings of Christmas – special church services, evergreen decorations, carols – and festive sweetmeats. This was actually at the behest of the Scottish Church, which had already abolished Christmas feasting in their own lands a century earlier. The English Puritans had wished only to lower the status of Christmas so as to heighten that of the regular Sunday worship, but in order to cement Scottish support, they signed away all official sanction for the holiday. In 1642, Parliament remained in session on 25 December, churches were ordered only to give their regular services, and people were expected to work. Unsurprisingly this proved to be an unpopular move; the authorities were faced with riots in some parts of the country, many churches did still allow the traditional evergreen decorations, and no doubt there was much unauthorised carolling, carousing and feasting too. In 1660, to much popular relief, the newly restored Charles II swept away all attempts at asceticism and Christmas returned with some vigour, although probably not at the level enjoyed in the decades before the Civil War. The Scots remained more sober about Christmas, and their high jinks and feasting gradually moved towards New Year's Eve and Hogmanay, as it remains today. This is when the Scots eat black or Scotch buns which also originated in the medieval period. They were another spiced bread cake, but by the late nineteenth century they had become a spicy fruited filling wrapped in pastry. Another name for Hogmanay is 'Cake-day', with one traditional children's rhyme declaring 'My feet's cauld, my shoon's thin, / Gie's my cakes, and let's rin'.

It was the mid-Victorian period which saw the real reinvigoration of Christmas. Charles Dickens' tale of cheer and goodwill, *A Christmas Carol*, was published in 1843 and was immediately enormously popular, sparking a new enthusiasm for the festive period and a sense of nostalgia for old traditions. In one year the book sold a phenomenal 15,000 copies and was soon turned into a stage sensation too, being dramatised at nine different London theatres in the following year. Queen Victoria's consort, Prince Albert, also popularised many of his native German Christmas customs, like the evergreen tree and the sending of cards. Depictions of Victoria's large family all celebrating Christmas happily together, like the engraving of them delightedly examining a Christmas tree in 1848, cemented the family aspects of the season. And in the States, Washington Irving's tales of traditional British Christmases (as observed in his travels) did much the same for the transformation of the season there, even inspiring the cult of the flying sleigh driven by Santa Claus. The Victorians were, after all, living through a period of huge and often unsettling social and economic change, and they were happy to exchange a sense of anxiety about the fragmentation and industrialisation of modern society for one of nostalgia about communal customs, deference and good times. From 1847, the Poor Law Board famously permitted a special Christmas dinner to be served in all the workhouses in England and Wales, which in some institutions included cake. Gradually the period of rest around Christmas lengthened, with Boxing Day also declared as a day off under the 1871 Bank Holidays Act. In America Christmas was recognised as a public holiday by one state after another over the period from 1836 (Alabama) to 1890 (Oklahoma).

Dried fruit and spices are a common characteristic of Christmas cakes around the world, but beyond that similarity there is considerable variation (except in the Far East, where European-style sponge cakes are eaten at Christmas). Take the Italian panettone, for example (not to be confused with the solid Sienese panforte). This is a tall, bread-like cake with a soft, bready texture, lightly studded with dried and crystallised fruit. Another bready cake (much beloved in my family, though usually purchased at our annual pilgrimage to a Christmas market rather than made at home) is the German stollen, but this one is flatter and heavier, dusted with icing sugar and with a roll of marzipan running through it. (Tradition says that the shape of the cake and the marzipan encased in the middle represent the infant Jesus in his swaddling clothes; the cakes are often specifically known as *Christstollen* during the Christmas period.) We know they were being baked as early as 1329, when Bishop Henry of Naumburg allowed the bakers' guild new privileges as long as they undertook to provide the bishop's office with two stollen every year. This cake also travelled with German migrants to Chile where it became the round *pan de pascua*. In the United States, meanwhile, a traditional brioche-like 'President's cake' has been eaten at midnight on Christmas Eve in the White House every year since the time of Abraham Lincoln.

Other cultures extend their sweet, festive fare up to New Year. In Brittany the antler-shaped *kornigou* cake represents the god of winter shedding his horns in a type of rebirth. We have already noted that the Scottish Hogmanay was a time for cakes, while in the English town of Bury St Edmunds in Suffolk, 'cakes and ale' used to be given out to mark the recommencement of agricultural work on the first Thursday after 'Plough Monday' (the first Monday after Epiphany). Sadly, the cakes have now been replaced by cash presents. And the British 'Tunis cake' which is an alternative to the traditional Christmas offering, is a chocolate-covered Madeira, which shares much more with the pound cakes we will meet in the next chapter than the fruited variety. The only fruits you will meet in a Tunis cake are the marzipan ones adorning the top.

Another key point in the annual cycle of cake falls at Easter. Just like Christmas, Easter is a festival of huge significance in the Christian calendar, but with much older origins. For Christians, Easter marks the time when Christ died and rose again. It is preceded by the forty days of Lent when feasting is proscribed, so Easter Sunday, when the Resurrection is remembered, is a day of considerable celebration, feasting and release. Alfred the Great, liberator of the working man for the Twelve Days of Christmas, also directed that all servants should be free from work during the week on either side of Easter. In the natural annual cycle, Easter coincides with a period of new life, as crops are planted, animals give birth and hens start to lay eggs again. The latter is almost certainly the most practical reason behind the adoption of the egg as a symbol of Easter (and also, of life and rebirth in the Jewish festival of Passover, which falls at around the same time). It is probably no coincidence that the timing of Easter is determined by the timing of the first full moon after the Spring Equinox, when the hours of daylight at last start to outlast those of darkness. Eggs are also a star in the traditional Greek sweet Easter bread, *lambropsomo*, which is ring-shaped and has a hard-boiled egg baked into the top.

The joyful return of new life and spiritual rebirth are not the only reasons why sweet things have long had a special place at Easter. There is also a Christian tradition of celebrating baking at this time: one of the stops Christ is said to have made on his painful road to Golgotha was by a woman baking at the roadside. In contrast with a washerwoman who threw her dirty water at him, the baker gave him bread and water to drink. This gave rise to the tradition that baking at Easter is especially appropriate, aided, no doubt, by the ban on eating eggs during Lent and their plentiful abundance with the return of hens to laying. It also led to a belief that items baked at Easter have special properties, producing many legends about long-surviving and talismanic hot cross buns (lightly fruited, sweetened, and cinnamon-scented buns, glazed with an egg wash and decorated with a characteristic cross on the tops). One pristine specimen has apparently been kept in the same Lincolnshire family since it was baked on Good Friday in London in 1821, while the Widow's Son pub in East London has a collection of hot cross buns which commemorate a sailor who left for sea in the early nineteenth century and told his mother to save him a hot cross bun for his return. He did not come back, but his mother, whose cottage stood on the site later occupied by the pub, set aside a bun for him every year. The tradition is continued to this day, when every year a sailor solemnly presents a new offering to the landlord.

The most traditional Easter cake, however, is the Simnel cake. A little lighter than a Christmas cake, this is a fruit cake – originally yeasted but rarely so today – covered with marzipan, with a second marzipan layer in the middle, and decorated on top with the twelve marzipan balls representing the apostles (minus Judas). The term Simnel cake was certainly in use by 1267, and it is thought that the name means 'fine', as in the fine flour which was used to bake it. Originally boiled and then baked (like the modern bagel, or the early Christmas cake), it gradually became richer with fruits and spices as these started to infiltrate the market. Several English towns claim to be the originators of Simnel cake, including Shrewsbury in Shropshire and Devizes in the West Country. The two cakes are quite different though: those from Shrewsbury are heavy and dark with a saffron-yellow crust, while the Devizes cakes are star-shaped and have no crust. The cake we know today is apparently based on the one made in Bury, in Lancashire, which was presented to Queen Victoria in

1863, although the Victorians were fond of placing crystallised flowers and fruits on the top rather than the marzipan balls. Simnel cakes also have a close association with Mothering Sunday – the fourth Sunday in Lent, when the rigours of the fast were relaxed and servants traditionally went home to visit their mothers (or alternatively, when people made a pilgrimage to their 'mother church', which was usually the local abbey or cathedral).

Not all Easter cakes were sweet and joyful though; the now-unknown tansy cakes were bitter with the tansy herb to commemorate Christ's suffering, while pax cakes were small, hard biscuits handed out at church on Palm Sunday. Scripture cakes meanwhile, are a real brain-teaser which require a good knowledge of the Bible to interpret the recipe (example: cream together 200g of Judges v, 25 ['she brought forth butter'], 250g of Jeremiah vi, 20 ['the sweet cane from a far country' – i.e., sugar], and 3 tablespoons of I Samuel xiv, 25 ['and there was honey upon the ground']).

All of these early fruit cakes were luxuries; the dried fruit alone took care of that. But it was the spices – the ginger, cinnamon, cloves and pepper – which put them really beyond the bounds of the ordinary. These were just part of a palette of spices which took Europe by storm in the medieval period. They were introduced by Crusaders returning from their pilgrimages to the Holy Lands in the eleventh century and became among the most traded commodities in the world. (The Crusaders brought back many foodstuffs to Europe, potentially causing considerable improvement to the diets of the time; it is possible that they conveyed the recipe for gingerbread too, but that may be wishful thinking.) Many of the spices that we think of today as having a principally culinary function, like ginger, were sought after in the medieval period also because of their medicinal properties. Ginger, for example, was thought to aid the digestion and neutralise poisons (pregnant women still swear by its stomach-settling properties today), and was also used as a preservative. In times of plague many people wore fragrant spices around their necks or in masks across their faces to prevent them from breathing tainted air. Spices also featured in incense and perfumes long before they made the transition to food under the Ancient Greeks, and the Egyptians used them in embalming. In fact, 'spice' was for a long time probably understood to be anything with a strong scent.

It is hard to imagine how unfathomably remote the places where these spices originated were to Western Europeans in the eleventh and twelfth centuries, and even later: places like China, Sri Lanka, India and the Spice Islands off Indonesia. To them, these fragrant and expensive spices seemed literally to have come from Paradise, a place which was believed to lie somewhere down river of the Nile – ginger and cinnamon were allegedly trawled from that great river in nets. They were happy to believe the legends put about by spice traders that these rare substances were guarded by mythical creatures, the outwitting and killing of whom added more and more to the price tags. Flying snakes, huge man-eating birds and giant bats were all said to lie between the intrepid spice hunter and his bounty. In fact, cinnamon, nutmeg, mace and cloves all came from southern India and Sri Lanka; cinnamon is the dried bark of the *cinnamomum verum* tree which is native to Sri Lanka; and ginger originated in South-East Asia, with almost half of the total coming from India (where it is a common savoury ingredient in its fresh form).

Whatever their provenance, spices soon became extremely popular in all types of European dishes. The suggestion that they were used to disguise the smell or taste of rotten food is now generally dismissed; instead they seem to have genuinely changed people's palates – or the palates of those who could afford them, anyway. Spices (including sugar in the thinking of the day) were added to meat dishes, to fruit and to drinks; they were presented as gifts and treasured like investments. Later, they were joined by another familiar baking flavouring: vanilla, which came from the tropical forests of Central America where it grew as the seed pod of a type of orchid. Like the Aztecs, the seventeenth-century British used it to flavour their new favourite drink, chocolate, which they had finally learned of from the Spanish – it had been secretly drunk at the royal court there since the early sixteenth century.

The trouble for consumers was that the spice trade was reliant on a long and risky journey which bumped up the price and made supplies limited. The Romans had learned how to utilise monsoon winds in their larger ships to make a direct trip to southern India, but the journey still took almost a year; prior to that it had involved a much longer trip across open sea from China, Malaya and Indonesia, around the northern coast of Africa. It was also such a lucrative business that it was subject to a constant battle for influence, and at various points virtual monopolies were in operation, first from Mongol traders and later Ottoman Turks, who had taken the key gateway cities of Constantinople and Athens. With ever-increasing taxes and a highly restricted supply, Europeans decided that they would be better off finding their own route to the Spice Islands. Christopher Columbus and Vasco Da Gama stood in the wings; the age of great European exploration had begun.

The problem was that they were labouring under several significant misconceptions as to where the coveted source of the spices actually was and how best to reach it. Christopher Columbus (a Genoese, though he sailed on behalf of the Spanish government) was convinced that the best way to find 'the Indies' was to sail west, significantly underestimating how large the globe was. He did indeed find land when he set sail in 1492, and momentous was his discovery: no less than the Americas. He brought back turkeys, pineapples and tobacco, but no spices. His Portuguese rival Vasco Da Gama, sailed south and then east around the coast of Africa and reached India in 1498. On a subsequent voyage the Portuguese founded a strategic stronghold in southern India, and soon a scramble for the spices had begun. Most of the trade was divided up between the Spanish and the Portuguese, with the former controlling the western part of the new sphere of influence, and the Portuguese the east. It was another Portuguese, Ferdinand Magellan, who finally reached the coveted Spice Islands in 1521, and the Dutch and the British also claimed outposts in strategic areas, eventually breaking the Spanish/Portuguese stranglehold on the trade in the late sixteenth century. By this time, however, falling prices and changing fashions in food meant that spices were no longer the treasures that they had been. Their place had been taken by a new range of alluring foodstuffs: coffee, tea, tobacco, and ever more abundant sugar. We will meet the story of how this made the tradition of afternoon tea possible in the next chapter.

We can see nonetheless that the fragrances and tastes of some of our most beloved and traditional cakes and buns were in effect flavoured with the scents of a newly expanded world. By the time a cook had cut and powdered his or her sugar, measured out the cloves, cinnamon or ginger (which would not have been as strong as they are today, partly because of the long voyages they had been on before their arrival, and partly because of the high chance of adulteration by sellers), and weighed, washed and stoned the dried fruit, he or she had participated in a world of trade which was previously unimaginable. No wonder that many of these cakes were out of the reach of ordinary people for so long. Meanwhile, the trade and communication which had been opened up by the scramble for spices introduced travellers to the sweet goods of other lands: the citrus, cardamom and rosewater of the Middle East, the flaky pastry and fried sweets of the Arabs, and the steamed rice buns of the Chinese, which are round to symbolise the moon. It is no overstatement to say that the growth of the spice trade was responsible for the opening up of the world, with all its mix of tastes, languages and cultures.

On a slightly less momentous level, but no less important as far as this book is concerned, it brought the wherewithal for Germany to produce its *lebkuchen*, Italy its panettone, and the Netherlands its *kruidkoek* (spice cake). In the United Kingdom it brought a new era of spice to the already rich tradition of yeasted breads, like the hot cross bun, which also, of course, features dried fruit. A rare example of a coveted spice which took well to English cultivation is saffron, which lent its name to the town where it was principally grown: Saffron Walden in Essex. It was used in Cornish saffron cake, as well as in wigs and Sally Lunn cakes. A seventeenth-century recipe for 'Spice Cake' by the cookery author Gervase Markham featured a mix of warmed milk, butter, sugar, saffron and ale barm (for leavening), to which was added eggs and flour spiced with aniseeds, cloves, mace and cinnamon. This produced a stiff dough, to which was added rosewater and currants – all flavourings brought from thousands of miles away. English baking, like the Scandinavian tradition, also favoured savoury spices like caraway, seen in the solid seed cake which was still popular for shooting parties and luncheons in the early twentieth century, and the sugary comfits which were strewn over the top of cakes.

Many of the newly spiced and fruited yeast cakes we met in the last chapter also came to be associated with communal and special occasions, where they cemented hospitality and community bonds. Wakes, for example, which were local celebrations to commemorate the founding of the parish church, often included cakes. British poet and clergyman Robert Herrick captured the occasion in a poem entitled 'The Wake', written in the seventeenth century, which invites a companion to 'Go to feast, as others do, / Tarts and custards, creams and cakes, / Are the junkets still at wakes.' The nineteenth-century rural poet, John Clare, described a village feast in his native Northamptonshire which included stalls selling gingerbread, as well as trinkets, bows and ribbons. The rush-bearing festival in Ambleside in the Lake District, which marks the rush harvest – an important local crop in times past, and used to make items like baskets – included a procession for the children, after which they all received a gingerbread cake (perhaps from neighbouring Grasmere, which was famed for its gingerbread, and had its own rush-bearing celebration in early August). And harvest was often marked with feasting to celebrate the earth's bounty, including fruit cakes, cheesecakes and honey cakes. Meanwhile 'groaning cakes' were traditionally made for birthing mothers, to sustain them through labour (the dried fruit would certainly have been a good source of energy and iron). If the mother-to-be broke the eggs herself it was meant to shorten labour. Pieces of the cake were often handed out when the mother was 'churched' or readmitted into the church after childbirth.

Cakes had a different function again on All Hallows', or All Saints' Day, the feast of the dead which took place on 1 November (Hallowe'en is the day – or 'eve' before All Hallows' Day). It was traditionally marked with spiced 'soul cakes' or 'soul mass cakes' which were given to the poor, eaten to celebrate the lives of the dead, or handed out to children going 'souling' from door to door, much like our trick-or-treaters. One traditional children's song went 'A soule-cake, a soule-cake, / Have mercy on all Christian soules for a soule-cake' (prayer, commemoration – and eating special cakes – were all thought to shorten a soul's time in Purgatory). In certain places the tradition of going a-souling continued well into the twentieth century, with anything handed out to the children still called 'soul cakes' even if they were really coins or other treats. Like the perennial favourites, hot cross buns, they were often marked with a cross to indicate that they were baked as alms. Similar traditions existed in other countries too, including the *pan de muerto* which is eaten for the Mexican Day of the Dead (2 November, which is All Souls' Day) and widely celebrated in parts of the United States with large Hispanic communities. These cakes are often decorated with bones or skulls to commemorate the dead. In China and Singapore, pink ghost cakes (steamed rice cakes encased in a pink shell) are made for the Hungry Ghosts festival, when the dead return to visit and must be fed to keep them from doing mischief. In Victorian England, meanwhile, when mourning was elevated to an art, cakes decorated with images of cherubs would be handed out after the funeral of a loved one. The Dutch, in their turn, serve shortbread at funerals; a tradition still popular in Dutch areas of America in the nineteenth century.

The final symbolic event for the fruit cake which we will consider here is the wedding. Simon Charsley is an expert on the history of the wedding cake, and points out that while it is highly symbolic, it actually has very little specific meaning of its own. When quizzed, couples can rarely say *why* a cake is a requisite part of a wedding, only that it is one. It stems from the same tradition of feasting and show what we have already encountered, with the cake itself closely linked with the sugar subtleties and Twelfth Night cake of earlier times. Recipes for 'bride cakes' which were similar to Twelfth Night cakes, appear from the mid-sixteenth century, though the term wedding cake was longer in coming, and the modern tradition of white embellished icing did not become popular until the middle of the nineteenth century, as did the tiered height. Queen Victoria's wedding cake in 1840 was still one layer, although it was a very large and highly adorned one, featuring Britannia blessing the couple, along with dogs, cupids, doves and flowers. It was 300 pounds in weight, 3 yards around and 14 inches deep, and caused a sensation. Eighteen years later, when Victoria's eldest daughter got married, things had changed. Her cake was a tiered one, standing over five feet high, although the top layers were made from sugar rather than cake. By this time, fine dining had taken on architectural aspirations, and the preferences of the royal family sparked a big following.

The average bride and groom could not afford a fancy tiered wedding cake for another century or so; even in the 1930s two tiers were common. Even the single layer cakes were historically very large though: Elizabeth Raffald, a cookery author and professional cake-maker who we will meet again over the next few chapters, published a recipe for bride cake in 1769 which called for 4 pounds each of flour and butter, 2 of sugar, 36 eggs, 4 pounds of currants, a pound each of almonds, citron, candied orange and lemon, and half a pint of brandy. The sugar had to be beaten into the creamed egg for at least quarter of an hour, and the eggs were beaten for another half hour. She was also the first to suggest the now customary double layer of almond paste and white icing, although this did not catch on for another century or so. And her cake was also notable because it contained neither yeast nor ale, both of which were still commonly used to give the bake more 'lift'.

Clearly these cakes were – as they are now – only for very special occasions; but significantly, they are *not* now part of the main wedding feast – they sit to one side, and the act of cutting it is more important than ensuring it is eaten. Cutting the cake became the first act performed together as bride and groom, and the top tier started to be saved for the christening of the couple's first child. And as height and white icing became more customary, the cake started to take on its symbolism as a reflection of the purity of the bride herself.

The fruited wedding cake is still traditional in Britain, but it is not so in other countries. Nor is the tradition of the symbolic first cut by bride and groom a common one. In fact, in America it is often joked that tiers of the fruited sort of wedding cake are preserved because no one wants them. Indeed, *Tonight* host Johnny Carson once quipped that there is just one fruit cake in existence which is passed on and on and on . . . As a result, they do not take centre stage at American weddings and, if they appear at all, are demoted to the lesser status of 'groom's cake', which is a dark and heavy counterpoint to the light, white offering which symbolises the bride. Nowadays the dark colour is often achieved by chocolate, and even in the UK, many couples now substitute a chocolate or vanilla sponge for one of the layers of their wedding cake. Incidentally, although the groom's cake tradition is almost unknown in the UK, Prince William famously had his own cake at the royal wedding of 2011: a very British McVitie's Chocolate Biscuit Cake, which is not really a cake at all but a mix of crushed biscuits, golden syrup, butter, cocoa and sugar, topped with melted chocolate. Another tradition associated with the American groom's cake is that it is not meant for eating, but is instead given out to unmarried female guests to put under their pillows to bring dreams of their future spouse – just like our unlucky *Spectator* reader.

America is not the only country to eschew the heavy, fruited wedding cake. In Norway the much more light-hearted *kransekake* is traditional: a stack of biscuity marzipan rings, each reducing in size to form a pyramid. These are not made exclusively for weddings, but when they are, the rings often conceal a bottle of wine or aquavit (at Christmas they can be decorated to look like Christmas trees). The guests take it in turns to break a piece off the cake until the bottle is revealed and a toast is made to the newlyweds. Alternatively, the happy couple remove the top layer and see how many come away with it: this signifies the number of children they will have. Similar cakes are made in Denmark and Norway. The New England Appalachian wedding cake is not a million miles removed from the *kransekake* either, consisting of a stack of molasses-flavoured cookies or shortbreads (sorghum molasses was the traditional sweetener in the area), sandwiched together with an apple filling made from dried apples, apple sauce or apple butter. Traditionally each guest brought a layer, so that the height of the cake was a marker of the couple's popularity. We will meet the traditional tall French wedding cake, the *croquembouche*, in a later chapter. If the couple can kiss over it without knocking it over, their marriage will have good luck. The height of the wedding cake is also important in Greece, China and Indonesia, probably reflecting the status of the two families, while in Germany the cake is often a single, large sponge, heavily decorated with piped cream, chocolate and sugarwork. Although these traditions have diverged from their fruited past, all of these cakes continue to carry a hefty weight of symbolism and sweetness.

In this chapter we have traced a story of growing sweetness and richness in the cakes of the medieval period. They became more uniform, and more differentiated from bread; but their role as markers of celebration and luxury grew apace. Not only this, the fruit cake also tells a tale of a world which was becoming ever more tractable and comprehensible. Its exotic spices, dried fruits and sugar are a shorthand for an unprecedented growth in world trade and communication. We have seen how this affected the spicing of some of the most traditional cakes from Europe; it also brought vanilla, coffee beans, new and exotic fruits – and, of course, chocolate. The growth of trade gradually meant that the ingredients – and thus the cakes themselves too – became more affordable. By 1600, most European towns had a bakery in every neighbourhood. And as we will see in Chapter 6, these cakes travelled with European migrants as they spread around the globe, adapting to new tastes as they went. This is how traditional Welsh fruit cake ended up in Patagonia and the French *bûche de Noël* in Quebec.

The cakes we've been discussing here were mainly dense and heavy affairs, sometimes still relying on yeast for their rise. Towards the middle of the eighteenth century something started to change. Sugar became more plentiful, so recipes could dial back on sweet dried fruit. And bakers who wanted something lighter began to realise the raising power of well-beaten eggs – we have seen that Mrs Raffald's weighty 'bride cake' eschewed yeast for the frothiness of eggs. The next step on the cake timeline was the realisation that these developments could be harnessed to produce something altogether newer and lighter, and that is where we go next.

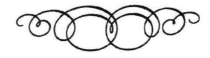

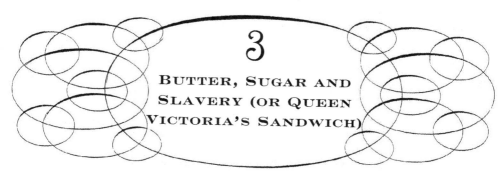

3

BUTTER, SUGAR AND SLAVERY (OR QUEEN VICTORIA'S SANDWICH)

The legendary American cookery writer Julia Child is said to have declared that 'with enough butter anything is good'. This is a popular view: butter is one of those foods which is seen as luxurious and 'natural'. Anyone in this camp will probably pick a rich and buttery pound cake over the dark fruit cake. Even the name pound cake sounds solid and weighty – it derives from the fact that the cake was traditionally made from a pound of butter, a pound of flour, a pound of sugar and a pound of eggs (weighed in their shells). Although it is now a classic of American bakeries, the pound cake is not a native: it originates from Europe. In France it is called a *quatre quarts*, or 'four fourths', also in reference to its ingredients, and in Germany a *sandkuchen* because of its sand-like texture.

The pound cake became popular in Britain in the eighteenth century as cake moved away from its heavy, fruity incarnation towards something lighter and more golden, eventually becoming the iconic Victoria sandwich cake (also known – erroneously – as a Victoria sponge). It is not hard to see how such an easy-to-remember recipe caught on, although as the calibration for a pound in mass changed at various points in time it was not the greatest guarantee for success (perhaps this is where the alternative measurement of matching the other ingredients to the weight of the eggs in their shells came in). The formula doesn't make much sense any longer in North America, where bakers use calibrated cups of sugar and sticks of butter instead of scales. Nonetheless, our affection for this pleasingly sturdy, golden and simple cake remains, as does its name; in Britain many bakers still use the basic pound cake formula even in the age of metric measurements (today more usually four ounces of each ingredient and two eggs).

So why did we go from the fruit cake of the previous chapter to the pound cake? The simple answer to this question is that we could. It was not a straightforward passage, though: it took until the late eighteenth century for the technology, ingredients, processing and tastes to coincide to produce a light and spongy cake. For it was not until then that we had, firstly, improved flour processing, which produced a lighter product and in turn a lighter cake batter (think of the difference between white and wholemeal bread today). Secondly, imperial trade brought sugar to much of Europe and North America, and, like flour, it became far cheaper and whiter thanks to better refining. Thirdly, stove technology was also starting to forge ahead, bringing more precise temperature control and enclosed ovens to many more families. Meanwhile, the adoption of the whisk by the end of the seventeenth century made it much easier to harness the leavening properties of beaten eggs, and, finally, by the end of that century chemical raising agents had been discovered too. Because these new products and foodstuffs were available, people's tastes changed to take up the new, the fashionable and the light on the tongue: dried fruit and dark sugar were gradually dropped, and the amount of butter and sugar rose as a proportion of the cake batter. For all of these reasons: fashion, technology, food processing and trade, the transition from fruit to pound cake represents nothing less than a social and culinary revolution.

There is also a psychological point to be made here about the appearance of the two types of cake. In the history of food, lighter colour has always meant more refined (that is, more processed), and more refined has meant more expensive. Therefore, to be able to eat whiter breads and whiter sugars you had to be well off, and hence lighter colours in food have come to be a marker of affluence and desirability. We see these associations in butter, too; as Julia Child pointed out so memorably, it is – in all its glorious sunshiny yellowness – a luxurious and 'natural' product, which makes other foodstuffs taste richer. To understand why the pound cake is so popular, then, and why it knocked the dark fruited cakes off their cake stands, we need to examine how golden butter and white sugar came to be widely available, and how they entered the pantries and cookbooks of the domestic baker.

The first published recipe for a cake which looks recognisably like our modern pound cake was written in 1615 by an author we met briefly in the last chapter: the farmer, cookbook writer, poet, one-time London courtier and (perhaps unexpectedly) one-time soldier, Gervase Markham. It contained a pound of flour, a pound of sugar, and eight eggs which were beaten for a horrifying full hour. Markham was really more of an editor than a deviser of original recipes, which suggests that cakes like this probably weren't new; they certainly contained vestiges of earlier baked goods with their inclusion of aniseed and coriander seeds. 'Portugal cakes' had become popular in Britain after the marriage of Charles II to a Portuguese noblewoman, Catherine of Braganza, in 1662, and they were similarly golden and unfruited, but still featuring the traditional rosewater and sack (sweet wine). In fact, the Spaniards were among the first to develop sponge cakes: the Italians, who perfected them, called them *pan de Spagna* and it is possible that it was they who brought them to Britain.

In fact, Markham did not label his recipe a cake at all, but instead called it a 'Bisket-bread' – unless it was rolled thin, in which case it *was* referred to as a 'cake' – or rather, several small cakes, as the mixture was divided into a number of different tins. In many other ways, however, Markham's cake had claim to something new. It was baked in a tin, in an oven rather than on a griddle or hearth, and all that beating must have introduced some air as he directed that the cook flatten the cakes, or 'thrust them down close', with her hand halfway through baking. Another suggestion is that the small versions were more akin to what we would think of as cookies today (perhaps explaining the linguistic connections between that word and the Dutch name for cake, *koekje*). The most obvious difference from later recipes was that Markham's cake contained no butter. This makes it closer to our modern fatless sponge, in which beaten eggs are still the principle form of raising agent.

The savoury, spicy note of Markham's cake – which we saw in the earlier seed cakes and some of our yeasted buns – remained a common feature for some decades more, although the simple 1:1 ratio of the ingredients also became a recurring characteristic. Meanwhile, an explosion in print culture brought published recipes for a huge variety of cakes to those who had the means to buy books. One very popular British cookery author and ex-cook, Eliza Smith, included a chapter on 'all sorts of cakes' in her 1727 *The Compleat Housewife*, which contained forty separate entries. This was a bestseller and was the first cookbook to be published in America when it came out in Virginia in 1742. Yet none of its cake recipes were described as either sponge or pound, and most contained the familiar seeds, dried fruit (plum cake) or ginger. Even the 'ordinary cake to eat with butter' included yeast and spice – quite different from what we think of as a pound cake today, and again showing its close family ties with the fruited cakes from the last chapter.

By the middle of the eighteenth century, however, the new lighter, unfruited cakes were popular enough to be included in another best-selling cookbook, *The Art of Cookery*, which was published simply by 'A Lady' in 1747. The author was revealed posthumously two centuries later as Mrs Hannah Glasse, another writer who had gained her experience as a household servant to an aristocratic family. Her 'Pound Cake' illustrates the change in tastes and ingredients since Markham's time: it includes six egg whites and twelve yolks (which would have made it even richer), a pound of butter and a pound of sugar – but still the inevitable caraway seeds – and the unenviable hour's beating either by hand 'or a great wooden Spoon'. Even the 'good Pound Cake' which featured in the sensationally popular 1806 *A New System of Domestic Cookery* by English widow Maria Rundell (selling half a million copies on both sides of the Atlantic in twenty-five years and translated also into German) still contained traces of its cakey antecedents: it was flavoured with nutmeg, cinnamon, wine and caraway seeds, which are still classic flavourings in many north European cuisines. She did also include something called a 'Spunge Cake', however, with ingredient weights calibrated to the weight of ten eggs. Interestingly, the whites of these eggs were beaten separately from the yolks – which is a good way to introduce extra air, and suggests that this was a lighter cake.

It is in an American book that we finally meet a truly classic pound cake, however, albeit with a few unfamiliar twists. This is Amelia Simmons' *American Cookery*, first printed in 1796 and the first *American* cookbook to be published in the States. Simmons, who probably lived in New England, and whose frontispiece to the first edition of her book declared her to be 'an American orphan', was not able to write, and dictated her recipes to a scribe (a policy which she said resulted in many errors making their way into the first edition; a second followed in the same year). Her book was comprehensive, covering meats, fish, pasties, puffs, tarts, preserves – and 'all kinds of cakes, from the Imperial Plumb [sic] to Plain Cake'. Here is her recipe for pound cake:

> One pound sugar, one pound butter, one pound flour, one pound or ten eggs, rose water one gill [an American gill is half a cup; an Imperial one slightly more], spices to your taste; watch it well, it will bake in a slow oven in 15 minutes.

Several food historians and bloggers have recorded their experiments in making Simmons' cake, and found it to be dense compared to a modern one, but pleasant, with an unusual note from the rose water, which takes the place of our modern vanilla extract. Much else depends, of course on what your taste in spices is; those of the time ranged from the still familiar triad of nutmegs, cloves and allspice, to more piquant alternatives like cardamom. Vanilla, meanwhile, was for centuries second only to saffron among the rare spices, as it is so labour intensive to extract. It only thrives in a narrow band around the equator, and the technique of hand-pollination which was vital if it was to be grown outside its native regions in Mexico was only discovered around 1840. German chemists discovered how to produce a synthetic substitute in 1874 (still used today); all considerably too late for Amelia Simmons.

With Amelia Simmons' book we know that pound cake had definitely reached America by the end of the eighteenth century, where it has remained a staple ever since. There is even an annual Pound Cake Day in the American calendar (it falls on 4 March). In Britain, however, it went on to take a slightly different path, and a very distinctive name: the Victoria sandwich cake.

To those unacquainted with British culinary tradition, the Victoria sandwich probably means very little. However, for Brits, it is an emblem of national identity. It is, essentially, two light, round pound cakes filled with a layer of jam and usually, though controversially for purists, another of softly whipped cream. The lightness comes from chemical raising agents (which, as we will see, were invented in the late eighteenth century). It takes its name from Queen Victoria who was allegedly a famous fan, although she took only a simple layer of jam in hers. Its popularity goes further than its royal patron, however. It is a comfortingly airy, yet daintily pretty cake, with its stripe of red and creamy white, which has held its head up high through the ups and downs of cake fashion. In the words of British food writer and cook Nigel Slater, 'Put this sponge on a table with a yellowing, bone-handled knife alongside, and you have a picture of Britain as seen by our parents and grandparents.' It is no wonder that the Victoria sandwich has received a boost in popularity in our recent austerity-driven, nostalgic times; it's certainly the cake I turn to most frequently when baking for teatime guests precisely because of its simple but tasty beauty.

This beloved British cake makes one of its first recorded appearances in perhaps the most iconically British of cookbooks: 'Mrs' Isabella Beeton's *Book of Household Management*, which was first published in 1861 but was subsequently expanded out of all recognition by other contributors. So popular was the book that it was still being used by nearly half of British housewives in the 1930s. The closest Mrs Beeton came to a pound cake in her section on cakes was a 'Sponge Cake' which contained no fat. However, lurking under the chapter heading 'Creams, Jellies, Omelets, etc' appears a recipe for 'Victoria Sandwiches', requiring four eggs, their weight in pounded sugar (sugar at this time came in big blocks or 'loaves' which had to be broken up for home use), butter and flour, with a quarter 'saltspoonful' of salt, and some jam or marmalade. Here is her recipe:

Beat the butter to a cream; dredge in the flour and pounded sugar; stir these ingredients well together, and add the eggs, which should be previously thoroughly whisked. When the mixture has been well beaten for about 10 minutes, butter a Yorkshire-pudding tin, pour in the batter, and bake it in a moderate oven for 20 minutes. Let it cool, spread one half of the cake with a layer of nice preserve, place over it the other half of the cake, press the pieces slightly together, and then cut it into long finger-pieces; pile them in cross bars on a glass dish, and serve.

The ingredients in Mrs Beeton's recipe are immediately recognisable to a modern baker (right down to the 'nice preserve'), but the method is not. Today it is more usual to beat the butter with the sugar (the 'creaming' method), then add the beaten eggs, and finally, fold the flour in gently to avoid knocking out the air. This is neither here nor there, however, when we consider the curious fact that Mrs Beeton did not label her creation a cake at all. We can only assume that its cream and jam filling and elegant serving in 'finger-pieces' designated it more of a dessert. More pragmatically, it might have been where she found it in another cookbook; Mrs Beeton was a shameless plagiariser. Nonetheless, it is clear that by 1861, when her book was published, the pound cake was already being associated with its regal patroness.

One of the reasons that the Victoria sandwich is so beloved in Britain is that it is more than a cake: it is a symbol of nostalgic Britishness (one might even say *Englishness*, since, as we have already seen, the Irish, the Welsh and the Scots have their own national cakes). It is a mainstay of many iconic British social events: afternoon teas, village fêtes and that other traditional national institution, the Women's Institute, an organisation whose relationship with cakes was immortalised in memorable fashion in the film *Calendar Girls*. The film, not coincidentally, features a scene where the untraditional no-nonsense character played by Helen Mirren admits to having bought her prize-winning Victoria sandwich at Marks & Spencer (itself a British institution, of course). Her friends are horrified and amused in equal measure, and you don't need to know the finer details of either the Victoria sandwich or the Women's Institute to realise that this is just Not Done.

Agricultural and local fairs still have a strong emphasis on home produce, and in the UK a well-made Victoria sandwich is pretty and light enough to be a worthy entry. In fact, most fairs have a class especially devoted to them; our local agricultural fair in Warwickshire even has a category for Victoria sandwiches baked by male bakers. Pound cakes hold the same place in North America, especially when gussied up with citrus, the tang of sour cream or the sweetness of frosting. Adaptations like these make family pound cake recipes closely guarded and much beloved. Even the traditional Victoria sandwich can be embellished with coffee or lemon flavouring, and customised with different flavours of jam or lemon curd; such tinkering is even endorsed by the Women's Institute.

One of the other reasons that the Victoria sandwich has such established status in Britain is that it is an integral part of the traditional afternoon tea. This light snack of sandwiches, cake and a pot of tea was supposedly invented around 1840 by one of Queen Victoria's ladies of the bedchamber Anna Russell, the 7th Duchess of Bedford, as a cure for the 'sinking feeling' she experienced in the afternoon. As lunch had slowly migrated forwards to the middle of the day and dinner backwards into the evening, the leisured ladies of Victorian Britain had been left bereft of both sustenance and social engagement in the afternoons. The new meal filled both gaps, and it rapidly became an established part of the social round. In fact the Victoria sandwich allegedly got its royal credentials by being served at tea parties at the Queen's residence, Osborne House, on the Isle of Wight. The enlarged high-Victorian 1880 edition of Mrs Beeton's *Book of Household Management* described afternoon tea rather charmingly as 'a few elegant trifles' including 'cakes and knicknackery in the way of sweet eatables'. By this time it was an expected part of life in a well-managed household.

Sinking feelings aside, teatime is as much about having a pause for some chit-chat and a bit of a treat as about refuelling; in Nigel Slater's words again, 'afternoon tea may be the only meal we take that is purely and utterly for pleasure'. No wonder that it turns up so often in novels as a shorthand for a pause for leisure. A nutty variant on pound cake, 'Fuller's Walnut Cake', makes several appearances in Nancy Mitford's *Love in a Cold Climate*, always eliciting much delight, and the same cake took pride of place at the tea table during Charles Ryder's first week at Oxford University in *Brideshead Revisited*. It was made by Fuller's Cakes, an American company, who sold their baked goods and confectionery in shops across the UK in the early twentieth century, and featured a filling and coating of boiled white frosting. The top was decorated with its signature halved walnuts. Tea-drinking went on to become a popular habit across the social spectrum, and by the end of the nineteenth century a much wider cross-section of people had enough time and leisure to break their afternoon with a 'cuppa' and a slice of cake, either at home or in one of the new tea shops or cafeterias. Tea and cakes – like white sugar and white flour – had been democratised.

Let's pause for a moment, then, to think about the different processes involved in making this new cake. The key is the amount of air which is incorporated into a pound cake batter: this gives the cake a lot more 'rise' than a fruit cake. There are three ways to achieve this: beaten eggs, as seen in several of the early recipes for pound cakes, which introduce the honeycomb of air bubbles that give the cake its 'sponge'-like appearance; chemical raising agents which were beginning to be used in domestic kitchens at the end of the eighteenth century and which produce carbon dioxide via a reaction between an acid and an alkali in the batter; and, finally, the creaming together of the butter and the sugar, which is usually the first step in making a pound cake or Victoria sandwich, and which aerates the mixture, trapping the air inside. It is the expansion of this trapped air during baking which makes the cake rise. Butter also lends tenderness and richness to a light cake because it inhibits the formation of gluten, which is what gives bread its chewy texture. Finally, the butter keeps the cake moist, and allows the crust to colour nicely at the correct temperature for baking. This is why a *fatless* sponge (a true 'sponge cake' must be fatless) does not keep well: it lacks moistness from the butter. It also relies heavily on beaten egg to achieve its 'rise'.

The lightness of the pound cake also relies on the correct proportion of sugar to flour: too much sugar tenderises the proteins to the point where they can't hold the shape of the cake. The temperature of the oven does its bit too; if it is either too hot or too cool, the processes of expansion and setting will not occur in the right order, leading either to a heavy, sunken exterior, or to a too-brown surface and a 'volcano' top. All of these stages make the modern pound cake quite a different prospect from the fruit cake, which has fewer concerns about lightness: it is solid and dark from all the dried fruit and dark sugar, and is usually made by creaming and mixing rather than beating and aerating.

Another distinctive point about pound cakes is that they have always been more frequently baked in enclosed ovens with some degree of temperature control. We will see later on that by the late nineteenth century this was starting to mean a regulated dial; before that, a cake's success lay more with the baker's experience in knowing what the right temperature felt like or how long it took a wood-fired oven to cool to the appropriate temperature. When Amelia Simmons published her cookbook in 1796, Americans were still baking on hearths and over fires, and several of her recipes reflect this, but by the early nineteenth century domestic ranges were becoming more popular there too. When Simmons specified a 'slow' oven in her pound cake recipe she probably did not mean the sort of oven we are used to, but instead the heat from the fire surrounding an enclosed pot (which is also known as a 'Dutch oven'). The pot must have contained a much more intense heat than our modern ovens, since she said that the cake would be ready in only fifteen minutes.

We will return to all of these developments: oven technology, the greater availability of sugar, and the invention of chemical raising agents, shortly. But first, let us consider the most unchanging of the key ingredients for a pound cake: the butter.

Julia Child was voicing a popular sentiment when she said that butter makes everything taste better. Its richness and golden colour have always garnered it a lot of fans, even today when we know about its high levels of saturated fats. In fact, its popularity has had an upturn again since the 1990s when the health risks of trans fats in products like margarine were discovered (trans fats are made artificially when oil is put through a hardening, or hydrogenation, process). Butter has also benefited from the same desire to consume unrefined and 'natural' products, a trend that has also boosted the popularity of the Victoria sandwich cake. In 2014, the American Butter Institute reported that butter consumption had just reached a forty-year high and was standing at an average of 5.6 pounds per head per year (up from 4.1 pounds in 1997). The pleasurably rich taste of butter is not surprising when you consider that it is the most concentrated of all dairy products: it contains around 80 per cent fat in the US and up to 85 per cent in Europe (compared with about 30 per cent for cheese and 55 per cent for the richest clotted cream). All of this brings a huge 'feel-good factor' to everything it features in. One food writer has summed up the attachment felt by butter lovers as 'a loyalty so fierce and so unreasoning that it is called, by those opposed to it, the "butter mystique"'. This isn't only because of its taste – although that's important. It's also based on the whiff of green fields, clover and sunshine that comes from its golden colour and nurturing origins as mother's milk. No matter that the majority of modern butter is made in industrialised dairies or that making butter by hand is back-breaking work. In the words of anthropologist Claude Lévi-Strauss, butter is not only good to eat, it is 'good to think'.

If you look at a bowl of milk and a block of butter side by side it is not immediately obvious how one becomes the other, but leave the bowl of milk alone for a few days and it is quickly apparent that the liquid has leanings towards solidity. The first step to making butter in the pre-industrial world was to 'set' the milk in bowls until the cream rose to the surface and could be skimmed off. This made the richest and most sought-after butter, but the milk fat from whey or skimmed buttermilk could be used as a more economical alternative. The milk or cream would then be hand churned by pumping a paddle or 'dash' up and down in the liquid until grains of butter formed – a process which could require several hours of vigorous work and was affected by atmospheric conditions. What this process does is aerate the cream or milk and encase the air bubbles in fat. Gradually the fat and water are agitated into a different com-position, the water separates from the fat, and you are left with a creamy solid, and some watery buttermilk which can be drained off for drinking, feeding to animals or used for baking.

Needless to say, this is very hard but necessary work, and Laura Ingalls Wilder portrayed it vividly to generations of child readers in her autobiographical novel about her childhood in the American

Midwest in the 1870s, *Little House in the Big Woods*. In her family the churning took place every week on a Thursday (this was before the era of domestic refrigeration, after all). At the age of four, Laura was too small to take her turn at the big churn, but she enjoyed eating the carrot whose peelings went to colour the pale winter butter, and drinking the buttermilk left at the end. She watched her mother rinse the butter and salt it to preserve it better (since salted butter affects the taste of the end product, many eighteenth- and nineteenth-century cake recipes directed the baker to wash it thoroughly between their fingers to get the salt out again). Best of all for Laura was watching the butter being shaped into pats in Ma's strawberry-shaped mould. Different families often had their own distinctive mould to denote to buyers where the butter had been made. In Ma's case it was simply for prettiness.

In the eighteenth and nineteenth centuries, dairying was crucial for rural families like Laura's, who grew or made much of the food that they ate; in fact, it was an important focus for rural community life, too. Thomas Hardy showed us some of the folklore that grew up around English dairying in his novel *Tess of the D'Urbervilles*, which was set at the end of the nineteenth century. At one stage Hardy's heroine, Tess, takes a position as a milker at a large-scale dairy called Talbothays. One day, the butter just 'would not come' despite long churning by horse power. The superstitious dairymen and women were convinced that something unnatural was to blame, like a curse, or the presence of someone who was in love (a crucial point for the story, of course). Rather than examining the cream, the equipment or the weather, the dairyman prepared to call in a conjuror to dispel their bad luck, when, much to everyone's relief, the butter started to oblige.

Dairying (like baking) was traditionally part of women's work; the word 'dairy' is from the Middle English 'dey', which meant a female servant, and 'erie', the place where she worked. Talbothays was an exception because it was a large commercial business and so was directed by a man and employed male workers alongside the women. Skills in butter-making and other dairying tasks weren't confined to labourers' families either: landowners also kept cows, although they were less likely to do the dairying themselves. The author Jane Austen, whose father was a Church of England curate, wrote to her sister Cassandra in 1798 that 'we are very much disposed to like our new maid; she knows nothing of a dairy, to be sure, which, in our family, is rather against her, but she is to be taught it all'. Dairying did not even need a dairy, at a push: the American pioneers found that the rocking action of their horse-drawn wagons churned the butter naturally.

The Ingalls family may not have had the resources to set aside much of their hard-earned butter for treats like cakes, as the Austens did (Austen's books, of course, are one of the reasons we know so much about the teatime habits of the refined classes in Britain in the early nineteenth century), but better-off townspeople had acquired quite a taste for butter by the end of the eighteenth century. The butter mystique was taking hold: for the first time, more milk was being converted into butter than drunk in Britain, and other countries soon followed.

The sad thing is that, just as the well-off started to enjoy dishes liberally washed with butter, and light teatime cakes started to grace the tables of the rich and fashionable, they moved ever further from the reach of the poor. With the onset of industrialisation, more and more people moved into towns and, as agriculture became larger scale and more intensive, the poor were pushed into wage labour and away from their own small-scale cow-keeping. Even the middle-class homemaker was less likely to be making her own butter than before. When the British cookery author Eliza Smith published *The Compleat Housewife* in 1727, she included instructions for butter-making which started: 'as soon as you have milked, strain your Milk into a pot, and stir it often for half an hour . . .' Over the course of this century, it was increasingly unlikely that her readers would need instructions such as this, either because they no longer kept cows, or because they could simply go to a shop to purchase their butter. The poor found it increasingly hard to do either of these things.

But it was precisely as more people moved further away from the countryside that they became most attached to the pastoral ideal that butter conjures up. This separation from butter's origins was particularly pronounced in countries like Britain and the Netherlands which had historically high levels of urban dwellers, and (in the case of Britain) rapid and early industrialisation. In the north-eastern United States it was not until 1910 that a person became more likely to live in a town than the country; in the Southern states this was not true until the 1950s. Meanwhile, butter became more and more a foodstuff for the better off: by 1902 the highest social classes in England were consuming almost three times as much butter as the rest of the population. The urban poor had to make do with small amounts, or use alternatives like lard and dripping left from the meat joint. This changed in the 1870s, however, with the launch of an intriguing new product with a much lower price tag than butter. Its name? Oleomargarine.

Oleomargarine – or, as we know it today, margarine – was invented by the French chemist Hippolyte Mège-Mouriès in 1869, as the winning entry in a competition searching for a cheap alternative fat for the French army. Mège-Mouriès' invention used beef tallow to make a spread. The patent was soon sold to the Dutch company Jurgens (later part of Unilever) and the product became immediately popular, especially in Britain and Germany. Unsurprisingly, the dairy industry in those countries was unimpressed: not only did margarine challenge their hold on the market for fats, but it was also often passed off as the 'real thing' at a cheaper price. Margarine manufacturers in turn realised that they would do well to build on the best-loved characteristics of butter, and launched lines with names like 'Churno', 'Buttapat', and 'Creamo', which implied that their origins lay with a cow in an idyllic green field. In fact, margarine was originally called 'butterine' in the UK, which just underlines the point even more. In America the dairy lobby was strong enough to stamp its antipathy to margarine on to the market, and in many states the product was heavily taxed and even tinted pink to make absolutely sure that no one could mistake it for butter. The Canadians went further: margarine was banned altogether until 1948, except around the end of the First World War when butter was in short supply. A law forbidding the addition of yellow colouring to margarine (which made it look more like butter; margarine is white in its 'natural' state) was only lifted in Quebec in 2008.

Margarine was eventually to gain its own niche as a spread without the saturated fats of butter, and it has recently started to recover some popularity with the launch of trans-fat-free products. In wartime Britain margarine even came into its own specifically as a baking ingredient, although admittedly this was because many people preferred to save their meagre butter ration for eating. But it had a rocky road to acceptance. Its origins as a cheap alternative to butter hung over until after the Second World War; margarine was the only rationed product for which demand *fell* after wartime restrictions were lifted in Britain. Sales of butter, meanwhile, predictably soared.

When it comes to baking, opinion is still divided today on the acceptability of butter substitutes. American pound cake recipes rarely mention margarine as an alternative for butter unless it's a dairy-free spread to make a vegan version. Martha Stewart unequivocally backs the flavour of butter. In Britain and Australia, however, it has its fans. The modern British *Good Housekeeping* recipe for a Victoria sandwich cake specifies butter, as do the two best-known British domestic goddesses, Nigella Lawson and Delia Smith (of whom more in the next chapter). But those doughty guardians of traditional baking, the ladies of the Women's Institute, endorse either butter or margarine, or even a mix.

In North America a more acceptable alternative to butter for baking is oil, or vegetable shortening like the brand leader Crisco (named for its principle ingredient, crystallised cottonseed oil). Crisco first appeared on the market in 1911, and was marketed hard as a superior alternative to butter on every count imaginable: price, healthiness, versatility, taste and keeping qualities (much as margarine had been in Britain a few decades earlier). Since it was dairy-free it could even be sold as a kosher product and was endorsed as such by several rabbis: according to its manufacturers, one New York rabbi allegedly exclaimed on its launch that 'the Hebrew Race had been waiting 4,000 years for Crisco'! The product bulldozed its way into the market with special offers, advertisements and cookbooks to illustrate its versatility (naturally, this included recipes for pound cake). The Crisco pound cake was as simple as its more traditional predecessors, with the shortening matching the weight of the other ingredients. And it is to another of these ingredients that we turn next: sugar.

Sugar is all about comfort. The sweetness of sugar and the stodginess of carbohydrates are what make comfort foods so, well, comforting. Humans seem to be biologically driven to appreciate the taste of sweetness and quickly adopt it if it is not a native part of their diet. An experiment in the 1970s showed that even babies in the womb respond to injections of saccharine into the uterine fluid (this experiment has not been repeated: the ill effects of saccharine on foetal development were discovered soon afterwards). Many animals show the same inclination, for example, for sweet fruit, suggesting that sweetness has some intrinsic biological benefit above the feel-good factor, such as indicating that a foodstuff is edible, or that it is high in valuable energy.

Of course sugar is not the only sweetener used in cakes: maple syrup, honey and – as we saw in the last chapter – dried fruit all serve the same purpose. But sugar – especially white, refined sugar – is our strong favourite for domestic baking in the Western world, and it is the one that has the most revolutionary tale to tell in the progress from fruit cake to pound cake. It has been favoured partly because of its uniformity and reliability, but its whiteness also has those desirable markers of purity and wholesomeness that we met earlier on. In the developing world of sugar processing, the whiter sugars were the ones which had had the most refining, and were thus the most expensive. It is easy to imagine that the white, glittering crystals cut off the large loaf by the domestic cook – or, by the nineteenth century, sold pre-cut and pre-pounded in blue paper wrappers to show off their sparkle – were much more alluring than the yellowish tinge left by a lesser degree of refining. Today our darker sugars are usually artificially coloured with molasses, and 'unrefined' is a trait to be appreciated in foodie circles. Yet it is impossible to underestimate the revolution in tastes, markets, manufacturing and trade – not to mention human lives – which accompanied the increased availability of cheap white sugar in the nineteenth century. From being a luxury enjoyed only by the rich, sugar was to become a mainstay of the poverty diet: high in calories and sweetness, but low on nutrition.

Fully refined sugar is pure sucrose: a more complex molecule than its monosaccharide relations, glucose and fructose. It occurs naturally in both sugar cane and sugar beet, but has to be intensively processed to make it fit for consumption. Most of our sugar has historically come from cane, which is an ancient crop cultivated since at least 500 BC. It is so labour-intensive to farm that in the sixteenth century landowners started to make heavy use of slave labour from Africa and India to man their ever-growing plantations in places like the West Indies, Madeira and the American states of the Deep South (that triangular trade again). In 1550 there were five sugar plantations in Brazil; by 1623 there were 350. The work was arduous and unremitting, and the slaves suffered from diseases and horribly high levels of premature death. The plantations also brought huge wealth: in the nineteenth century sugar represented over 90 per cent of exports from places like Barbados and Haiti, although the workers saw little of it even after slavery was abolished and they became contracted labourers.

The process of harvesting cane and extracting the sugar before the onset of industrial processes makes domestic butter-making look like a walk in a field of idyllically grazing cows. First the tough and tall canes needed to be cut down, then the juice inside them had to be extracted by mashing and distilling. The next step was to heat and clarify this juice by boiling it, which concentrated the sugar syrup. Finally, the sugar itself was crystallised out, leaving behind molasses which was drained off out of the bottom of the large cone-shaped moulds (back to the sugar loaves we met earlier). It was not until the advent of mechanisation in the seventeenth century, using first animal or water power, and later steam, that productivity rose enough to bring a drop in prices. In the early nineteenth century, only half of the raw sugar which entered American refineries emerged as the finished product, with another quarter turning into molasses (and the rest of too poor quality for sale). Nowadays, the whole process is mechanised using equipment like centrifuges which separate out a much more uniform and whiter sugar. The milling and refining processes are also very efficient these days in terms of waste by-products: molasses has its own market as a foodstuff rather than being simply drained away, while the cast-off parts of the cane can be used for fertiliser and fuel.

By the time that domestic cooks were starting to experiment with baking pound cakes, sugar had diversified to take on many of the forms which are still known to us today. The British baker of the late eighteenth century might have had brown Demerara sugar in her pantry (named for its place of origin, an administrative district in British Guiana). She could purchase double- or even triple-refined sugar, more uniform granulated sugar, and by the last decades of the nineteenth century she could even get sugar cubes, though more likely for putting in her tea than in her cake. By the end of the eighteenth century, her sugar purchases might even be infused with politics, as many British families boycotted the produce from slave plantations in support of the abolition of the slave trade. Slavery was abolished in Madeira in 1777, and across the French empire in 1794 (although this was rescinded by Napoleon in 1802). In 1804 Haiti became independent and ended slavery, while Spain outlawed it in 1811 (although, conveniently, not in Cuba, which was one of the main sugar-producing areas). Britain followed suit, a little belatedly and thanks to the efforts of MP William Wilberforce, in 1833. The first draft of the America Declaration of Independence in 1776, meanwhile, called for an end to the traffic in human slaves; but the clause was lost to negotiations between the representatives from the northern and southern (slave-owning) colonies. Slavery was finally abolished in the United States in 1865, when the Thirteenth Amendment to the Constitution made it illegal.

Not all sugar came from cane, however; at the start of the nineteenth century Napoleon Bonaparte encouraged the development of a domestic sugar crop to reduce France's reliance on British imports. And so entered the sugar beet, an unlikely cousin to the graceful and willowy cane, resembling instead a sort of turnip, but which yielded exactly the same sort of sucrose that we put in our cakes (and countless other products) today. Production flourished in Germany, and sugar became for a while one of Germany's key exports. Beet production is still focused in Europe, but the United States has now joined the list of the top producers. Nonetheless, beet sugar only accounts for one-fifth of all the sugar we produce today, not that you'd know from the taste which one you were eating.

Together, sugar cane, and later sugar beet, took Western diets by storm. In the words of sugar historian Sidney Mintz: 'a rarity in 1650, a luxury in 1750, sugar had been transformed into a virtual necessity by 1850'. In medieval times it was so expensive that it was often kept under lock and key with the rarest of spices. At a shilling or two per pound (between £30 and £50, or US$50–$85 in today's money), it is unsurprising that average consumption under the Tudors was only a pound per person per *year* (less than a small modern bag). It was so desirable that it was used to make those centrepieces for the table, known as 'subtleties' – a way of showing that the hosts were so wealthy they could afford to display their sparkling riches rather than eat them. Elizabeth Raffald, who had a particular interest in confectionery, included a whole section on making table decorations from spun sugar in her 1769 cookbook *The Experienced English Housekeeper*.

By the eighteenth century, sugar had become cheap enough to be considered a regular foodstuff and was starting to be more generally available. It quickly became a vital condiment for tea, which was found to be bitter and benefited from sweetening (in fact the English needed little encouragement here: they had a long and merry tradition of drinking sweetened wines and meads). Jane Austen wrote to her sister Cassandra in 1813 of the latter's anticipated homecoming, 'the comfort of getting back into your own room will be great! – & then, the Tea and Sugar!' But the rapidly dropping price of sugar in the early eighteenth century meant that almost everyone's diet was becoming sweeter. It had already fallen by a half in the seventeenth century and dropped by another third between 1700 and 1750. One historian estimates that around 24 pounds was available per head per year in

Britain in around 1775, or about a teaspoon per day (in America, in contrast, consumption was between 3 and 5 pounds per person per year in the middle of the eighteenth century; now it's close to half a pound a *day*). The lower consumption in America was partly due to heavy taxes on sugar and molasses – a measure which had the unexpected outcome of pushing people away from (molasses-based) rum and towards whiskey. This whole series of changes was nothing short of a revolution: of tastes, of buying power, of supply and of manufacture, based on a worldwide system of trade and empire.

The problem was that sugar was *too* attractive and, as the price came down, the poor started to use it at the cost of other foodstuffs. A diet of little except sugary tea and bread with margarine became the norm for countless families, especially women and children. This situation only worsened in the nineteenth century, as industrialisation and immigration produced large pockets of poverty in the expanding towns of the Western world. In fact, in many ways, sugar enhanced this trend by making other foodstuffs more palatable, and turning a hot drink into something approaching a meal. Britons were consuming an average of 49 pounds per head per year in the 1870s; by the start of the twentieth century this had risen to 79 pounds – considerably more than the average person would encounter over their entire lifetime in the medieval period, and now spread much more evenly across the social scale. Today it is 1.25 pounds per person per week (a little over 560 grams), or 65 pounds (29 kg) over a year.

The trouble with the democratisation of sugar was that, unlike the parallel rise in butter consumption, it made available a foodstuff which has no great nutritional value. Sugar gives energy in large quantities but it does not provide any of the more useful major nutritional building blocks like protein. Since excess energy (i.e., calories) is easily stored as fat, this has brought it increasingly negative attention, as has its role in tooth decay. At the same time, however, sucrose (and its even more denigrated modern cousin, high fructose corn syrup) has been introduced into more and more of the things we eat and drink. This is because it not only makes things taste better to our modern palates, but also acts as a preservative and a flavour enhancer, so lengthening the shelf life of processed goods.

We are now so used to the taste of sweetness that we don't always notice it, but we do notice it when it is gone. The generation of Europeans who experienced rationing in the Second World War missed out on a ready supply of sugar, making do with a small weekly allocation topped up with treats like carrot fudge and carrot 'jam' (this was also recommended as a cake filling). No wonder that the American GIs were so popular among children in Allied Europe, with their easy access to chocolate bars and chewing gum. When sweets rationing ended in the UK in 1953, there was such a run on stocks that restrictions had to be reintroduced while they were built back up again. And it was not only children who were rushing for the sweet-shop. A government report on the ill-fated attempt at derationing in 1949 noted, in habitually dry style: 'It seems clear that the public are regarding sweets rather as a food than a luxury, and women particularly are purchasing sweets in preference to cigarettes and ice cream.'

All of this meant that sugar was making an increasingly significant contribution to the food intake of the Western population. Sugar made up around 2 per cent of total calories in the British diet at the beginning of the nineteenth century, but 14 per cent by the start of the twentieth. It is now about 18 per cent, although US Department of Agriculture data showed a rise in the United States to almost a quarter of the average American's diet in 2008. The WHO recommends 5 to 10 per cent. We have already seen that this rise in consumption was not a good thing as far as nutrition was concerned, nor did it necessarily signify that the population was getting wealthier. What it does show is that people were becoming increasingly wedded to the taste of sweetness. By the 1860s, the increased availability and popularity of jams, jellies, biscuits and desserts – as well as cakes – show how sweetness had become embedded in the Western diet. Author John Steinbeck saw this at first hand: he spent the summer of 1920 working at the largest sugar beet refinery in the world, earning $100 a month, and later used the experience in his novels about working men. Sugar was also now serving some of the same functions of display and status for the poor that it had originally done for the rich – in fact, the well-off weren't using it in this way any more since sugar was no longer an elite foodstuff. For those newly able to consume something they thought of as a luxury, however, this was transformative. It was only in the twentieth century that dentists started to realise that this was at the cost of their teeth.

The effects of empire, industry and changing tastes brought the key ingredients for a pound cake into the reach of home bakers (plus a heightened desire to eat them). The transition to the light and spongy cake we recognise today was made complete with the help of science and technology: namely, the temperature-controlled domestic oven and the discovery of chemical raising agents which gave added 'rise' to the batter without all that tedious whisking. Amelia Simmons, whom we met earlier, is one of the first known writers to recommend adding 'pearl ash' to a baking recipe – now known as potassium carbonate, it was originally used in the making of soap and for bleaching cloth. Pearl ash was an effective raising agent but it produced its leavening gas by reacting with the acids in the batter, and this had a tendency to leave a soapy flavour in the cake. To counter this, bakers turned next to bicarbonate of soda (or baking soda), also an alkali, which produces carbon dioxide via a reaction with an acid ingredient such as tartaric acid or lemon juice, but which leaves a less pronounced flavour of its own. Finally, around 1850, baking powder arrived, which contains both acid and alkali and reacts when moistened (hence the need to put baked goods containing baking powder straight into the oven after mixing). It rapidly made its mark: Eliza Acton recommended 'carbonate of soda' as a raising agent in her *Modern Cookery for Private Families* of 1845, advising that a small portion be 'thrown in just before the [cake] mixture is put in the oven'. Such a small amount, she said, would not leave a discernible taste. These developments meant that a cake batter was likely to rise well, and with considerably less effort from the baker.

The final step to a successful pound cake was a reliable oven with a temperature gauge which took away the educated guesswork of times gone by. In fact, we could even go so far as to say that an enclosed oven is vital to the definition of baking: the relevant entry in the modern *Encyclopaedia of Food and Culture* pinpoints the drying process within an enclosed oven as the key part of the procedure. As we've seen, in medieval and early modern Europe ovens tended to be beehive-shaped structures fired with wood. Experienced bakers could gauge the internal temperature of the oven by hand, but the sort of variable control necessary for a well-risen and browned sponge cake did not arrive until the eighteenth century, by which time, of course, cakes were also being baked in metal or wooden hoops placed on a metal sheet, giving them a more regular shape and a less pronounced crust on the sides.

Perhaps even more importantly for the domestic associations of cake, developments in science, technology and manufacturing were bringing reliable stoves within the range of the domestic user. A cast-iron coal-fired kitchen range was patented by Briton Thomas Robinson in 1780, and gradually the accuracy of the temperature control and the constancy of the heat were improved; the heat from a small fire could be adjusted by a system of flues and metal plates, for example. These were expensive, though: we have already seen that Amelia Simmons did not expect her American readers to have their own ovens at the end of the eighteenth century, and this remained true for poorer families into the early twentieth century. The first patent for a gas oven was taken out in 1826 by another Briton, James Sharp, and although it took a while to become common in homes (partly because of suspicions about gas), this was the most common source of fuel for domestic stoves into the 1920s. Even where there was an oven or range, the cost of fuel would often prohibit its use on a daily basis, and any cakes that were eaten would be baked in old traditional ways, or bought from a shop. We will see when we consider domestic goddesses how all of this mapped on to women's roles in the home.

After two centuries of huge social, economic and cultural change, home bakers had the equipment and wherewithal to make something we would recognise as a pound cake. It had taken industrialisation, the rise of urban centres, world trade and an upsurge in technological development to make it possible, and it shows us the changes in people's homes, diets and tastes. Who would think now, as they tuck into a slice of this simple cake, that they were actually partaking of a slice of history?

One of the most striking things about this story is the way that the pound cake has become a symbol of national identity in many different places. The Victoria sandwich is an emblem of elegant but class-conscious Britishness, and found its niche as a centrepiece of the leisured tea party. In Germany, *sandkuchen* (named after its sandy texture) and *eischwerkuchen* (named after the mode of baking: weigh the 'ei' or eggs and match the weight in the other ingredients) take their part in another sociable pause – but this time for coffee, as we will see in Chapter 8. In the Caribbean, whence the *quatre quarts* was taken by the French, local ingredients like rum and mashed banana are added for moisture. However, it is the Americans, with their ready access to sugar cane, and accelerated move into industry and commerce, who have really made it their own. Nowadays pound cake is regarded as unmistakeably American, where it has been brought up to date with sour cream, cream cheese, green tea, pumpkin and all manner of other varieties. And while the Victoria sandwich is always round, a pound cake is either loaf-shaped or baked in a special ring-shaped Bundt tin – which shows its immigrant associations with another German cake we will meet again: the *kugelhopf*.

One of the reasons that the pound cake is so enduringly popular is its simplicity. It is easy to make, using ingredients any regular baker is likely to have in their pantry, and its flavour is pleasant and satisfying without having the cloying qualities of chocolate or the tricky cutlery challenges of French pâtisserie. More than this, it has grown to be a symbol of nostalgia for an earlier time in our history, when women baked their own cakes and used fresh and unadulterated ingredients. It is no surprise that it is one of the most frequently baked cakes in our modern society, and the recipe most commonly turned to by a new baker. It could scarcely be further from the next item that we will meet: the almost impossible to bake angel food cake.

4

DOMESTIC GODDESSES

There is scarcely a more ridiculous or daunting cake for the home baker than the angel food cake. It is the direct opposite of the solid, buttery pound cake: the angel food is all light and foam, contains no fat, and uses the whites of up to a dozen eggs, well whipped to introduce as much as air as possible into the batter. It was an American invention of the 1870s and 1880s, and it gives us a real insight into the way that homemakers of that era spent their time. This was, after all, before electric mixers and cake mixes came along, so anyone serving up a home-made angel food cake needed a fairly substantial amount of spare time, resources in the way of eggs, and elbow power – that, or staff to do it for her. It was not a good choice to bake if the purse strings were short: with so many egg whites required the cook must either be able to afford to waste a lot of yolks, or have plans for other rich cooking, like sauces or custards. In this chapter we will consider what this cake can tell us about gender roles, women's work and the creation of the domestic goddess.

The angel food cake is a very demanding one; it has a rider which would put some of our top pop stars to shame. It needs to be baked in a tall round tin with a hollow tube in the middle so that the resulting cake comes out shaped like a large, preposterous doughnut (the tube disperses the heat evenly through the batter). The pan must not be a non-stick one so that the mixture can get a grip on the sides as it rises, and has small 'feet' attached to its rim so that the cooling cake can be supported in an upside-down position away from the work surface, so precarious is all that air whipped into the egg whites. Everything must be done gently to avoid knocking out the lightness, and the flour is best sieved multiple times just for a little further aeration. Its name, it is thought, comes from the angel food cake's sublime airiness, and it is a peculiarly North American specialty (President Rutherford B. Hayes (in office from 1877 to 1881) used to enjoy his wife Lucy's famous home-made angel cake for dessert). The Pennsylvania 'Dutch' (of German, or *Deutsch* descent) bake them as wedding cakes so that the couple is blessed by angels, and African-Americans bring them out at funerals in commemoration of the soul that has gone to heaven. To see how they were originally made, let's take the earliest recipe given on the food website foodtimeline.org, from *The Boston Cooking School Cookbook* of 1884:

One cup of flour, measured after one sifting, and then mixed with one teaspoonful of cream of tartar and sifted four times. Beat the whites of eleven eggs, with a wire beater or perforated spoon, until stiff and flaky. Add one cup and a half of the fine granulated sugar, and beat again; add one teaspoonful of vanilla or almond, then mix in the flour quickly and lightly. Line the bottom and funnel of a cake pan with paper not greased, pour in the mixture, and bake about forty minutes. When done, loosen the cake around the edge, and turn out at once.

The baker of an angel food cake in times past probably thus had free time – for all that palaver of beating, watching and cooling, and a comfortable income. She was also likely to have an eye to display and hospitality. A cake like this is, after all, all about appearance and demonstrating one's skills. The angel food cake therefore really sums up the key attributes associated with femininity around the time that it started to appear, particularly in America, but to an extent in the UK too. Middle-class women were expected to preside over a calm, well-ordered and aesthetically pleasing home. They were assumed to have a certain level of education and skill, but predominatly of the sort to equip them to be homemakers. They were also just starting to have access to the consumer goods which made making a cake like the angel food possible; it is no coincidence that the recipe was established soon after the invention of the manual rotary egg whisk and the tube pan. And it's worth noting that they might also have been aware of the lower fat content of a cake that contained no egg yolks and no butter or oil, to fit with the ideal of feminine beauty at the time.

The problem was, though, that just at the time that women were expected to be the proverbial 'angel in the home', they were least likely – because of urbanisation, migration and shrinking family sizes – to possess the domestic skills their mothers and grandmothers and generations before them had learned by observing and doing. In short: they were expected to be a domestic goddess, but increasingly they needed the tuition of others to teach them how to achieve this. In this chapter we will uncover some of the most influential guides who sprang up to help them. These women (for they were mainly women) – authors, cooks, later radio and then television personalities – in turn, comforted, led and instructed women in the ways of the kitchen and the home. But while some women gained confidence and a sense of joy in cooking by following their prescriptions, others felt anxiety and a fear of failure. If the contestants on the bake-off programmes watch their cakes anxiously through the glass on the oven door, how much more anxious must the new housewife making an angel food cake have felt as she prepared to entertain guests? She couldn't even rely on the temperature control of her oven. The rise of the domestic goddesses thus goes direct to the shaping of modern womanhood.

The phrase domestic goddess is, for most Brits, unmistakeably associated with cookery author Nigella Lawson, whose hugely popular baking book (first published in 2000) is called *How to be a Domestic Goddess* and subtitled *Baking and the Art of Comfort Cooking*. It won Nigella the Author of the Year award at the British Book Awards in 2001 and the book has countless fans (it is my own 'go to' baking bible). However, its title and the underlying message that women (and the title, of course, is highly suggestive of a female audience) should want to spend their time in the kitchen, and to frame their sense of self-worth through providing treats, attracted a lot of negative attention. Nigella herself is adamant that this is a misreading of her book and its message. She states in the preface that the book is not about rules but about evoking a sense of comfort in cooking, and that she is talking about 'not being a domestic goddess exactly, but feeling like one'. True, she also admits that this is partly about a dream of glamorous womanhood, but states that that dream is at least partly an ironic one. Baking, she says, is about unwinding, feeling good and making people happy – and yes, impressing them too. In many other interviews, Nigella has stressed that she is a home cook, not a chef, and that she makes food that is messy, inviting and good to eat. But the title of her book continues to divide people, with some embracing the tongue-in-cheek union of femininity, baking and happiness, and others reluctant to engage in anything which places women back in the kitchen, cooking to please others.

We will return to this controversy, but it's worth noting that actually Nigella was not the first to coin the phrase domestic goddess; she was not even the first to popularise it in mainstream culture. That distinction goes to the American comedienne Roseanne Barr who quipped in her early stand-up routines that she hated being called a housewife and wanted instead to be known as a domestic goddess (Barr's official website carries the byline 'The Original Domestic Goddess'). It became something of a defining statement for her later television persona as the working mother 'Roseanne', for she made it funny precisely because she did not look or sound like the image 'domestic goddess' conjures up – and she knew it. She was both an outspoken real-life feminist, and the head of a fictional unruly but loving family, by turns thwarted by their desires and liberated by a willingness to put herself first. But, like Nigella, Roseanne attracts negative attention, although for quite different reasons; in her case because aspects of her persona both on screen and in real life seemed too far from the domestic ideal (her outspokenness and her size among others). Ironically, of course, Nigella's detractors seem to find her flirtatious persona on screen and in print, as well as her self-proclaimed enjoyment of food, equally at odds with the female ideal despite the fact that she *does* look like a 'goddess' and presents an image of domestic order and cheerfulness. Even in the late twentieth and early twenty-first centuries, certain stereotypes continue to circulate as to the appropriate behaviour of women, especially with regard to femininity and the home.

But in fact the phrase domestic goddess predates Roseanne too, and in a very different context, although Barr was referencing this usage in her ironic gag. It appeared in print in 1974 in Helen Andelin's guide to achieving a happy marriage, *Fascinating Womanhood*. In one chapter Andelin describes domestic goddesses as good homemakers, but more than that, they are women who elevate their domestic role to sacred heights. They must go beyond the simple call of duty to create a warm, comfortable and beautiful house for their husbands and children, finding fulfilment in even the most mundane tasks.

Andelin's book has attracted huge numbers of followers; her method is still taught today and resonates with many modern women. Feminists, on the other hand, tend unsurprisingly to decry its message as promoting submissiveness to a patriarchal family structure. This is certainly what Roseanne was doing by inverting the phrase 'domestic goddess': her gag was funny because of her self-proclaimed *failure* to meet that ideal. And although Nigella clearly *does* fit the mould to a much greater degree – in her appearance, her domestic skills, and her television shows which portray friends and family enjoying informal time together – she was also using the phrase to point out that actually women could choose what they wanted to be. They could bake a cake as an expression of their femininity or their love for others, or they could bake simply for the pleasure of it. And while for Nigella, and presumably her readers, baking is a pleasurable act, she is elsewhere at pains to stress that shortcuts and shop-bought are equally acceptable alternatives.

It must already be apparent that the term domestic goddess is loaded with meaning, although perhaps the key problem is that those meanings are rather vague and all-encompassing. The phrase clearly relates to the home, but it's about more than just being good at household tasks (for Andelin it's about going 'the second mile' to create a perfect home). In modern mythology a domestic goddess achieves calm, beauty and accomplishment in the house, but in a seemingly effortless way. Her home is clean and well ordered, her larder is full of wholesome home-made food, and she presents a beautiful and manicured outward appearance. But the image is ridiculed as much as it is aspired to; in fact, it is probably its complete unattainability in the modern world which helps to define it in today's more irreverent age. Allied search terms on the wiki-based 'Urban Dictionary' at the time of writing are 'princess', 'amazing wife' and 'baking', which really says it all. Those who use the term to describe themselves are usually doing so with their tongue firmly in their cheek.

Yet there is an interesting historical aspect to all of this. When we speak of being a domestic goddess today, we are often referring to household tasks which could be classed as 'old fashioned', such as baking, darning or knitting, which are newly resurgent today, but are not part of the core of household tasks needed to keep a modern home running. This is where the sense of unease on the part of feminists comes in: there was a reason why countless women campaigned to be able to leave time-consuming household tasks like these behind, after all. There is also a class question to worry about: clearly one needs a certain amount of money and leisure to aspire, even tongue-in-cheek, to domestic goddess status. If we set this question aside for now though, it seems that the key difference for modern women (and yes, some men too) is that if they bake, darn and knit, it's because they want to, rather than because they have to. But just like generations of their forebears, they often lack the intrinsic know-how gained from growing up in extended families of women for whom this knowledge was ingrained. This is why the domestic goddess is such a high-profile figure today, just as she was for our eighteenth-century predecessors.

Nigella and her equally familiar counterparts, Delia Smith and Martha Stewart, are very far from being our first domestic goddesses. The very first were, of course, the mothers and grandmothers who showed young girls how to run a household by example, handing on manuscript books of family recipes and remedies. (First Lady Martha Washington's manuscript book – the one featuring the recipe for Christmas gingerbread – was just such a one, given to her in 1749 but apparently brought from England by earlier generations.) But the woman most commonly credited with being the first domestic goddess in terms of being a purveyor of a complete image of accomplished housewifery, is 'Mrs' Isabella Beeton, who along with her *Book of*

Household Management (first published in 1861) we met in an earlier chapter. Mrs Beeton's name still conjures up an image of a sturdy, smiling matron, whose wisdom was distilled from years of experience over a warm kitchen range and placed into one easy to reference (albeit increasingly doorstop-sized) manual. The image could scarcely be further from the truth. Isabella Beeton was actually a young woman, sometime writer and highly *inexperienced* cook who wrote the book at the suggestion of her husband, the publisher Samuel Beeton. She had previously written a cookery column and had some editorial experience on one of her husband's publications, the *Englishwoman's Domestic Magazine*; she had also had instruction in pastry work and cake-making from a local baker after leaving school, but she was by no means an authority on domestic matters. In fact, her first published recipe for 'A Good Sponge Cake' had to be followed up with an apologetic correction as she had left out the flour. The recipes in her book were mainly lifted from other published sources, often unattributed, and almost certainly not, as she claimed, tested. Those that were, were not necessarily a success. Isabella's half-sister Lucy remembered being given a cake to try while the book was being researched, which unfortunately had a close resemblance to a biscuit. Her book was, however, immediately sensationally popular. Mrs Beeton's own story was much less happy, sadly; she did not see any of the later editions come into print, and died following childbirth at the age of only twenty-eight.

One of the reasons that Mrs Beeton's book became so popular was because it was so authoritative. Unlike later books it did assume a certain amount of knowledge on the part of the reader (the baker of her Victoria sandwich is instructed simply to use a 'moderate' oven, for example, and several of her recipes for jam state that it should be cooked 'until it is done'), and it was aimed as much at women running a household of servants as those doing the cooking themselves.

Her stated 'target audience' was a household with an income of £1,000 per year and a staff of at least five, but she did also give alternatives for those living on less comfortable incomes, and subsequently published the recipes on their own (without the information on household management), for a readership of cooks. Nonetheless, her book (cleverly marketed in instalments in advance of publication) did contain many reassuring rules and tips. The chapter on cakes, for example, started with a section called 'A Few Hints Respecting the Making and Baking of Cake' which ran through a set of simple rules, from breaking the eggs one by one into a separate cup so that each could be inspected and rejected if necessary, to whisking eggs very thoroughly so that they gave sufficient 'rise' to the cake.

Clever marketing continued to imply a matronly authorship even after the editorship had passed on following Isabella's death to Samuel and an assistant – later to be his second wife. Food historian Nicola Humble thinks that part of the appeal was the clarity of language, and also the magisterial breadth of coverage in the book (from cakes to animal husbandry) which also appealed to readers' intellectual curiosity. Certainly Isabella lacked the grounding in domestic service which many of the other well-known female cookery authors were at pains to stress in this period. However she was absolutely representative of British cookery writers of the time in her gender: the vast majority of cookbooks were written not by professional male chefs, like most of those produced in France at the same time, but by respectable working-class women.

The first notable antecedent to Mrs Beeton (and to whom she owed a considerable amount) was Mrs Hannah Glasse, whose *The Art of Cookery Made Plain and Easy* was published in 1747, went through seventeen editions up to 1803, and was still in print in 1843 (several of her recipes appear in Martha Washington's family recipe book). In it she said that she had 'attempted a Branch of Cookery which

Nobody has yet thought worth their while to write upon'; that is, simple and clear recipes. The book was aimed at more modest households than Mrs Beeton wrote for, and went into a similar level of detail: the pound cake was to be baked in a 'quick oven', although she made a few suggestions for the mode of mixing: by hand or with a 'great wooden spoon' (Mrs Beeton, in her turn, suggested the addition of a glass of wine 'but it is scarcely necessary'). Mrs Glasse had gained her experience as a member of the domestic staff of the Earl of Donegall, although she was running (and supporting) her own household by the time she wrote her book. Like Jane Austen a few decades later, she published simply under the title of 'a lady', and her name did not actually appear on the book until after her death. Not that Mrs Glasse was such a paragon of authenticity either; it is estimated that she lifted over a third of her 972 recipes from other sources, particularly from a book by another female author, Mrs Hannah Woolley, called *The Lady's Companion*. She did initiate one novelty of format though: the detailed index which allowed a reader to navigate easily to the sections she needed.

However, more influential in terms of baking was Elizabeth Raffald, whose *Experienced English Housekeeper* appeared in 1769 as the market for cookbooks was really taking off, and whom we met in the previous chapter. As the title suggests, this work was aimed at the superior servant class, and like Glasse, Raffald stressed her pedigree in service to justify her knowledge. Raffald, again like Glasse, was the mother of a large family with a husband whose ability to earn an income was variable at best, and had earned her stripes at Arley Hall in Cheshire, where she rose to be the housekeeper before marrying the head gardener and setting up her own confectionery shop in Manchester. She was keen to stress that examples of her own work – including her speciality cheesecakes, christening and wedding cakes – could be viewed and purchased from her shop. Her

book went through thirteen editions and was widely plagiarised;
Mrs Beeton was, perhaps unsurprisingly, particularly reliant on it for
her chapter on cakes and confectionery. In fact, Beeton's introduction
to her cake-making section bore striking similarities to Raffald's
'Observations upon Cakes'. Raffald herself, meanwhile, insisted that
she was above such pirating.

Elizabeth Raffald was writing at a time when the new technology of
enclosed ovens was still in its infancy; the directions in some of her
recipes to keep the entrance of the oven open suggests that she was
still using a wood-fired oven rather than one maintaining a constant
heat. The tone of her book was humble; aware that there were many
other cookbooks on the market, the preface written 'to the reader'
urged the public 'not to censure my work before they have made trial
of some one receipt, which I am persuaded if carefully followed will
answer their expectations.' Each section began with a paragraph of
'Observations', setting out what the reader needed to know. The one
on cakes was authoritative and was clear on what the consequences of
not following her rules would be: if you left beaten eggs sitting, for
example, 'they will go back again and your cakes will not be light'.
Seed cakes, rice cakes and plum cakes should all be baked in wooden
pans, for tin ones led to burnt crusts and a poor rise (because the heat
cannot penetrate into the batter). However she also allowed for a
measure of baker instinct, for example on the matter of ovens, saying
that 'though care hath been taken to weigh and measure every article
belonging to every kind of cake, yet the management and the oven
must be left to the maker's care'.

The last notable influence on Mrs Beeton – and by extension on
cookery writing for women in the late eighteenth and nineteenth
centuries generally – was Eliza Acton. Like Beeton, she was not
especially well qualified to write a cookbook in the professional
sense; in fact her earlier writing had been poetry, but her publisher

suggested that a cookbook might be more lucrative. Posterity shows that he was correct. Her *Modern Cookery for Private Families* appeared in 1845 and led the market until the appearance of Beeton's book in 1861. As her title indicates, the book was written for families rather than the staff of large households (it was dedicated to 'the young housekeepers of England'), and like all of the key reference works mentioned so far, intended to give instructions which were clear and concise, and which prioritised simplicity and economy. It was Acton who thought of the innovation of offering a brief summary of the recipe first and the ingredients and cooking times at the end (a cook would read through the method first, so it was more useful to have this information placed at the start) – a novelty later attributed to Mrs Beeton. Acton also stated that all of her recipes could be 'perfectly depended on', and she had tested most of them herself in her own kitchen (one hopes with greater success than Mrs Beeton).

Eliza Acton was the source of many of Beeton's fish and meat recipes; less so for the sections on baking, which had already been well furnished by Raffald and the author of another domestic encyclo-paedia called Maria Rundell, whose *A New System of Domestic Cookery* appeared in 1806 to considerable acclaim. However it is Acton who is particularly championed by several of our more recent domestic goddesses, who feel that she has been unfairly overshadowed by Mrs Beeton. Food writer Elizabeth David praised her engaging style and the details which made her methods seem more trustworthy. For example, in her directions for making a sponge cake, Acton told her reader that:

The excellence of the whole depends much on the manner in which the eggs are whisked; this should be done as lightly as possible, but it is a mistake to suppose that they cannot be too long beaten, as after they are brought to a state of perfect

firmness they are injured by a continuation of the whisking and
will at times curdle, and render a cake heavy from this cause.

Not only were directions like this clear and direct, Acton also
employed the technique, now familiar in many modern cookbooks, of
including the reader in her confidences and experiences in gaining
her knowledge (on creaming butter for cakes, for example, she
counselled that 'we find that they are quite as light when it is cut small
and gently melted'). Acton died in 1861, just two years before the
appearance of the *Book of Household Management* which was finally to
eclipse her work, although *Modern Cookery for Private Families* was still
in print until 1914.

The sorts of straightforward instructions by female writers like
Acton, Raffald and, yes, Beeton, were increasingly common in British
recipe books of the eighteenth and nineteenth century. Although the
recipes were not as comprehensive in terms of method or baking times
as modern ones (nor did they always separate out ingredients from
method, or specify the size of tins), they did address the fact that
home cooks might not always 'just know' the basics. The second half
of the nineteenth century was the zenith of the secluded domestic,
private – and economically unproductive – middle-class female sphere.
This meant that women were in greater need of instruction to replace
the sort of learning-by-observing done in larger families. It was also
simply more possible to be specific about baking and cooking methods
by this time, as the surge in production and technology brought about
by the industrial revolution had produced a wealth of new goods for
the home; including clocks for timing, more efficient and smaller
ovens, and a greater range of kitchen equipment. All of these developments made cooking and baking at home a more manageable and
reliable prospect.

The British publishing industry reacted quickly to accommodate the new market for this sort of instruction: 300 new books on food and cookery were published over the century between 1700 and 1800, at a price that most middle-class households could afford – three to four shillings (the full-bound version of Mrs Beeton's first edition cost seven shillings and sixpence). Many, including the *Book of Household Management* were published in serial form at sixpence a month, and copies traded hands on the second-hand market too. Although they covered a range of topics, almost all of these books contained chapters on cakes, indicating both the demand for baked goods and the need for instruction on them. Eliza Acton reflected reluctantly on this demand when she wrote that she had decided to include some cakes in her *Modern Cookery for Private Families* despite her own opinion that they are 'sweet poisons' taking away space from more useful recipes, because she did not want to 'cause dissatisfaction to any of our kind readers'. However she could not resist pointing out 'that more illness is caused by habitual indulgence in the richer and heavier kinds of cakes than will easily be credited by persons who have given no attention to the subject.' Fortunately, not all cakes were written off so disparagingly: simple buns and biscuits, yeast and sponge cakes and meringues were deemed the 'least objectionable' on account of their lightness and delicacy. Almond and plum pound cakes and brioches came in for the worst notice, because they were so rich.

But what of North America, one of the modern heartlands of home baking? The States has always been a rich market for cookbooks, and baking books in particular. We'll talk more about this in a later chapter, but suffice to note for now that the imported baking traditions of European settlers, plus the traditions of making things from scratch on isolated homesteads and farms, seem to have set up an eagerness for new recipes and baking novelties. In addition to this, domestic help and extended family was in short supply in the early decades of settlement, at least in the northern half of the country, while the westward pioneers had to rely entirely on their own skills. Books telling them how to cater for their families and households were therefore particularly valued.

It took a while for a tradition of distinctively American cookbooks to emerge though. At first, American housewives had to rely on imports of British books, the first notable success being Eliza Smith's 1727 *The Compleat Housewife* (although legend has it that an earlier book, Gervase Markham's *English Huswife* was taken out to America on the *Mayflower*, and it was undoubtedly useful if it was, as it contained advice on all matters to do with running a household, from dairying, to brewing, to making household remedies, as well as cooking). Smith's work was printed with adaptations for American tastes and food markets in Williamsburg, Virginia, in 1742.

America did not get its own native-born cookbook until the enigmatic orphan Amelia Simmons whose 1796 *American Cookery* we met in the last chapter. Her aim to write specifically for Americans was well conceived, as they were accustomed to quite different ingredients and tastes than those in Europe, and often found European recipes to be overly complicated. *American Cookery* was a small book; even the extended second edition which appeared the same year contained only 47 pages of approximately 120 recipes of which 26 were for cakes of different types ('from the Imperial Plumb to Plain Cake', as the title page proclaimed). Unlike many of her British counterparts, Simmons stressed that she lacked authority in terms of education, but her book sang of practicality and usefulness (moreover, at two shillings and threepence it was comfortably affordable by people – as she stated – of 'all Grades of Life', and especially those who, like her, lacked family). That's not to say that all her recipes were original; they certainly weren't, but it was the first time that dishes using ingredients like cornmeal and pumpkin, and recipes for distinctively American baked goods like the griddled cornmeal johnnycakes and slapjacks appeared in print. She also used the term molasses rather than the British treacle for her gingerbread recipes.

More significantly for our purposes, Simmons was also the first cookbook author to publicise a technique which was to transform the experience of making cakes: the use of the leavening agent pearl ash (potassium carbonate, used for soap-making and cloth-bleaching, and therefore readily found in many households). Pearl ash featured in her recipes for gingerbread and cookies; in fact this was also the first time that the word 'cooky' rather than 'little cake' was applied to these treats in an American cookbook, derived from the Dutch *koekje*. It's not hard to imagine the impact that the publicising of pearl ash would have had for home cooks: an hour's hard egg-beating could be substituted with a dash of powder (the angel food cake's reliance on beaten egg whites alone is one of the several ways that it is so demanding to make). A report of the use of pearl ash in a London newspaper in 1799 apparently provoked a storm of interest from female readers who wanted to know how it could be used in making cakes. Interestingly, Simmons also prescribed another leavener in her recipe for 'Plain Cake': 'emptins', which was another very American term, meaning the yeasty sediment left over from brewing, and often used for making bread. Cake-making had still not entirely abandoned its connections with bread.

Simmons' book was extremely popular, but the mantle of leading American cookery writer was by the 1820s being taken up by another woman: Eliza Leslie, whose was to produce some of the most popular cookery and etiquette manuals of the nineteenth century. Miss Leslie lived for much of her young adult life in her mother's boarding house and, in the 1820s, possibly as a way of making a greater contribution to its running, she attended Mrs Goodfellow's cooking school in her home town of Philadelphia. In 1828 she published a collection of recipes from her time there, entitled *75 Receipts for Pastry, Cakes and Sweetmeats*, and this was followed up with many books on household management, etiquette and cookery. Her 1837 book *Directions for Cookery, in its Various Branches*, was one of the most popular books of its day.

Like many of the British writers we met earlier, Leslie's style was matter of fact, warm and designed to lead the reader through a recipe. She did not assume that people had access to what we now see as basic equipment: her book started, for example, with an overview of weights and measures, which she stated was necessary 'as all families are not provided with scales and weights'. She also stressed the originality and reliability of her recipes, and said that she had aimed to write 'in a style so plain and minute, as to be perfectly intelligible to servants and persons of the most moderate capacity'. Like Acton, she was an innovator in the form of her recipes too, with all the ingredients and their quantities this time listed at the start, 'a plan which will greatly facilitate the business of procuring and preparing the requisite articles'. And finally, in an even more overt style than Simmons, she asserted her distinctively American outlook, noting that English and French books could be hard to follow, partly due to their lack of clarity, but also because of differences in equipment, fuel and fireplaces there compared to those found in the States. 'The receipts in this little book are, in every sense of the word, American', she said, and included those for federal cake, Connecticut cake and election cake.

Leslie was confident that good – and economical – results in baking could be achieved easily by following her recipes. However, like Acton, she was also prepared to admit that changes could be made by the home baker, as long as she understood the fundamental rules. If she needed to save money, for example, she could omit spices, brandies, rosewater and essences, as long as she stuck with the prescribed proportions of the key ingredients: flour, eggs, sugar and butter. Her language was inviting and she directed bakers to different tins for different types of cakes, depending on ingredients or aesthetics. Large cakes should be baked in tins with straight sides, for instance, for that way 'they cut into handsomer slices' and were also easier to ice. Gingerbreads and pound cakes should go into the oven in earthen pans as they burn easily, while 'spunge' and almond cakes should be baked in very thin pans – presumably to allow the heat to penetrate the batter more readily. There was, however, no room in her recipes for chemical leaveners, which she declared brought an unpleasant taste to the finished cake.

Finally, Leslie gave clear and recognisable signs of 'done-ness': when a twig or wooden skewer thrust into the cake comes out clean; also it will have shrunk away from the sides and 'cease making a noise'. (The twig, along with the instruction to remove the coals if the cake is being baked in a Dutch oven, or covered pot, is a salutary reminder that not all cooks had access to specialised equipment and stoves at this time.) Perhaps most endearingly of all to a novice baker, however, she admitted that things still sometimes went wrong: 'If the cakes should get burnt, scrape them with a knife or grater, as soon as they are cool.' Thirty cake recipes followed, ranging from pound cake, through several French-inspired items like macaroons and French almond cake, to crullers (deep-fried twists of dough of Dutch or German origin), English jumbles and gingerbreads, and cupcakes (to which we will return in the final chapter). Her books certainly garnered her a significant group of followers; she ended her days as something of a Philadelphia tourist attraction, living in portly retirement at the United States Hotel.

Eliza Leslie's work was authoritative, but it was also familiar and chatty, which contrasts with the increasingly professional and detached approach which was to follow. If one of the features of a domestic goddess is to be a companion in the kitchen, then perhaps Leslie and Acton are the closest that we have come so far, with their more informal and inviting language, easy-to-understand descriptions, and frank admissions that things can go wrong. This style of writing didn't last long, as it was soon overtaken by a group of women writers interested in the science of kitchen work, and who were keen to promote the benefits of rules based on nutrition as well as common sense. They were also addressing a class of women even less likely to have servants than their British counterparts, thanks to the more democratic way of life in the States and the burgeoning of work opportunities for young women. American bakers were also encountering a whole host of brand-new ingredients in the New World, from pineapples to coconuts, both of which were soon appropriated as cake ingredients.

By the middle of the nineteenth century, ideas about homemaking had become firmly tied to a distinctively American vision in which domesticity, femininity and motherhood were closely linked to the creation of healthy citizens. Some of these ideas came to the fore in Britain as well, but there, notions of domesticity had strong class overtones and naturally lacked the association with the forging of a new republic. This American vision, which has been referred to as a cult of womanhood, defies easy categorisation in our modern way of thinking. It placed a very high value on domestic skills, but almost exclusively within the traditional female sphere; this was no early feminist movement if we can think in those terms. However, for writers and education activists like Catherine Beecher (sister to Harriet Beecher Stowe, of *Uncle Tom's Cabin*), running a well-functioning, hygienic, serene and, yes, scientific, household, represented an achievement beyond any other. For by learning these domestic skills (which in her book included many branches of science and nutrition which were not traditionally taught to girls at that time), women would be able to influence the development of their families, and thus cast the American nation on the path to Christian morality and prosperity. Men brought up in this domestic environment would instinctively do the right thing by their wives and children – the reason why women themselves did not need to participate in the public sphere of politics and the like.

The eldest of thirteen children left motherless at a young age – she was only sixteen when she took over the running of the household in 1816, and her sister Harriet only five – Catherine Beecher worked tirelessly to set up a system of better schooling for girls, living off the proceeds of her popular household manuals (of which her 1841 *A Treatise on Domestic Economy for the Use of Young Ladies at Home and at School* was a bestseller). In 1846 she published an accompanying volume of recipes, under the title *Miss Beecher's Domestic Receipt Book*, and the two were incorporated twenty years later into one revised work co-written with Harriet, entitled *The American Woman's Home*.

The *Domestic Receipt Book* aimed to do many of the same things as Leslie had done, but with greater scope. The book was also absolutely and distinctively American in its coverage. It included many regional American dishes such as Pennsylvania flannel cakes (griddle cakes which could be made with rye flour, although Beecher noted that this often made them stick to the pan), Boston cream cake, pilgrim cakes (cooked under coals and ashes in the oven), as well as many recipes which featured corn rather than wheat flour. Crullers were present again, as was an early antecedent of another beloved American baking tradition, the layer cake, in the form of a jelly cake, sandwiched together with jelly or marmalade. But what marked Beecher's work out as different was the underlying stress on nutrition and science.

Like Leslie, and by implication Amelia Simmons also, Beecher found that recipes from imported English cookbooks were overly rich, poorly explained and too involved to be attractive for the average American housewife. Her recipes, in contrast, were clear and concise, and while they lacked the chatty tone of Leslie's work, they did present the reader with the scientific reasons for working one way or another. This was, however, softened by the recognition that cooks would often be acting within the bounds of economy and personal judgement, and that common sense was frequently as necessary as scientific rules. The ubiquitous 'general directions' on cake-making included some instructions which clearly emanated from Beecher's interest in science and hygiene: tie your hair back, she said, and wear a long-sleeved apron. Use a spoon to mix the cake, not your hand. Her instructions were no-nonsense and called for high standards, just as her beliefs about the high purpose of female domesticity would have us expect:

> If you are a systematic and thrifty housekeeper, you will have your sugar pounded, all your spices ready prepared in boxes, or bottles, your saleratus [another early type of raising agent, which produced potassium bicarbonate when combined with an acid] sifted, your currants washed and dried, your ginger sifted, and your weights, measures, and utensils all in their place and in order.

The organised baker would also spend some time the first time she made a recipe weighing her ingredients and then measuring them into a small cup, so that next time she could save time by referring to her measurements (a suggestion which preceded the institution of calibrated measures by later domestic scientist Fannie Farmer, by fifty years).

Mixed in with these prescriptions, however, were many more personal suggestions which may have made her book easier to digest. Rather than Leslie's twig, Beecher suggested testing for done-ness with an easy-to-find household object: a broom splinter. She also offered a common-sense way to judge whether the oven had reached the required temperature, and one which women had probably been using for generations: 'A quick oven is so hot that you can count moderately only twenty; and a slow one allows you to count thirty, while you hold your hand in it.' It might have been reassuring for the struggling home baker to read that if things went wrong, it was probably because of the oven temperature. On the other hand, the instructions for making a sponge gingerbread direct the cook to add enough flour to make the batter as thick as pound cake, which is assuming a certain amount of knowledge on the consistency of specific cakes. I was intrigued enough to give it a go, but personal judgement about the flour actually turned out to be the least of my problems. I immediately fell foul of the fact that the ingredients are not listed in the order in which they are used, as in a modern recipe, and I had to turn to my modern domestic goddesses for guidance on baking temperature and time. The end result was, it must be said, well worth it.

In other areas too, Beecher's readers were permitted to follow their own tastes: her recipe for icing for a plain cake uses a quarter of a pound of sifted sugar to two egg whites, for example, but she also noted that other cooks use only one. Some bakers says that the 'Child's Cake' improves with a quarter of an hour's standing ('Try and see', she invites); and the Boston cream cake requires between six and twelve eggs 'as you can afford', with any extra liquid from the use of the higher number buttressed up with flour. This latter instruction, interestingly, is a rare invitation for a baking recipe to break away from a 'formula' and still achieve success. We can only speculate on whether these touches made her book seem more approachable, or whether her readers, raised on the need for formulae rather than instinct, preferred to be told exactly what to do.

Catherine Beecher herself had rather an ascetic attitude to rich food and said that tempting items should only be eaten at mealtimes. The inclusion of rich cakes in her book is therefore surprising, and we may assume that it was partly from reader demand, although she did recognise that people ate for pleasure as well as sustenance. This austere outlook did not last long. By the 1870s cookbooks were beginning to promote the fun aspect of baking, especially as sugar got cheaper and cheaper. A slew of community and fundraising cookbooks shared individual housewives' favourite recipes, like the 1877 *Buckeye Cookery and Practical Housekeeping*, which originated in Ohio (the buckeye is its state tree) but was soon published countrywide with a new edition each year under the title *The Dixie Cookbook*. One edition made the wistful but prophetic comment that 'All systematic housekeepers will hail the day when some enterprising Yankee or Buckeye girl shall invent a stove or range with a thermometer attached to the oven so that the heat may be regulated accurately and intelligently.'

These books show us that little cakes and cookies were starting to be seen as items to be baked with children, while cakes generally grew in popularity as desserts and teatime treats. The number of cookbooks devoted entirely to baking sweet items exploded in number, suggesting that women were spending more and more time on what one author has called 'recreational cooking' or indulging a desire for sweetness. Back in Britain the end of rationing after the First World War brought a new light-hearted and chatty voice to many cookbooks as they guided home bakers back to a life of relative abundance and sweetness. It was at this point that American recipes like angel food cake first started to appear in Britain, where a new range of women's magazines like *Good Housekeeping* (launched in America in 1885 but not until 1922 in Britain) tried to speak directly to homemakers.

By this point, women were also more likely to have a range of labour-saving amenities and machines in their kitchen: electricity, running water, hot water on tap, fridges (hardly any American households owned one in 1918; by 1940 just under half did), and at last, ovens with calibrated dials. The latter which, as the authors of

Buckeye Cookery had predicted, were to have such a big impact on home baking, really took off from the 1930s in America, although not for another decade or so in the UK. Whether these innovations really had the impact ascribed to them is questionable. Survey figures show not only that an ever growing number of women were balancing home work with paid employment (African-American women had always been more likely to work than their white counterparts), but that household tasks were actually taking longer by the 1950s and 1960s than they had in the 1920s. With more items to buy, the more there was to clean; and the demands of keeping a tasteful and immaculate house had not gone away; in fact the emotional trappings associated with motherhood had if anything increased with falling family sizes. The new modern ovens were not quite as self-regulating as the manufacturers liked to suggest either: a cook still needed to balance the instructions with the demands of her pans, her ingredients and the type of cake she was baking. The broom splinters were not to be thrown away just yet.

Nonetheless, the women guiding other women to domestic success were increasingly likely to be sharing a sense of fun and enjoyment by the 1930s, and the name most intimately connected with 'joyfulness' in the kitchen is Irma Rombauer, author of the eternally popular American work, *The Joy of Cooking*. Rombauer was born to a German-American family in St Louis, Missouri, in 1877. Her parents were educated and cultured, and she grew up as a clever and engaging child who spoke only German at home. Her cultural roots can be seen in the baking sections of *The Joy of Cooking*, and she was later to recall early memories of the German bakeries in St Louis, where she ate coffee cake and little sponge cakes.

Irma was not brought up to a profession; her family was comfortably enough off that her early married life was a whirl of voluntary and social engagements. She did pause in 1915 to take a cookery class, however, which later proved to be the springboard for her book. Her two children remembered her as a busy woman who loved to entertain, but not one who was accomplished in the kitchen – except, it must be said, in the field of cake decorating. How on earth, then, did she come to write one of the best loved cookbooks of the twentieth century? The answer is simple: expediency. Her husband committed suicide in 1930, leaving her financially precarious and with little purpose to her days.

For some reason, Irma, now aged fifty-three and with two grown children, decided that the answer was to write a cookbook. She began with the recipes she had learned on her course years previously, and added to them with recipes enthusiastically sought from friends and acquaintances. Three thousand copies of the book were published in 1931 at her own expense under the title *The Joy of Cooking: A Compilation of Reliable Recipes, with a Casual Culinary Chat*. It was quietly popular, at least locally where Irma's own charm and drive no doubt did much to get it noticed. Eventually, however, thanks to an introduction at a dinner party, Irma secured a contract from the publisher Bobbs-Merrill. Thus began one of the most acrimonious relationships in publishing history, with every new edition of the book accompanied by fights over costs, corrections and copyright – which Irma had, unfortunately, signed away to the publisher. Luckily this did not affect sales: 10,000 copies were printed and 6,838 were sold in the first six months, helped by an aggressive marketing drive from the publisher, and a 'money back' guarantee.

One of the key reasons for the success of *The Joy of Cooking* is what we would now recognise as one of the core attributes of the media-savvy domestic goddess: the strength of Irma's own voice, engaged in 'casual culinary chat' as the original title put it. Put simply, it made her readers feel as though she were a friend as well as an instructor (Elizabeth David made the same point about Eliza Acton). Irma also had no particular axe to grind in culinary terms: she did not see herself as a teacher, and her tastes were eclectic and not bound by any particular philosophy. A recipe based on a tin of condensed soup was as good as one made from scratch as far as she was concerned (and sometimes better). Nor was she always very well informed: her nutritional information was patchy and many of her cake recipes called for bread flour – although she was up to date with the inclusion of precise oven temperatures rather than the usual descriptions of 'medium' or 'hot'. The people at Bobbs-Merrill tried to get rid of her chatty head notes, which often digressed from the recipes into little anecdotes and recollections, but Irma was adamant that they remain, and her instinct that they made the book stand out was a good one. Her readers felt that they knew the woman behind the book in a way they did not with the other 'cooking bibles' of the time.

By the time the first Bobbs-Merrill edition was published in 1936, Irma had come up with a novel way of presenting her recipes which helped the home cook to make sense of the directions. This has become known as the 'action' method, whereby the ingredients and quantities appeared in a list at the start of the recipe, but were then repeated within the text, indented and in bold type. The cook thus read the recipe in a single flow, her eye caught by each new ingredient as it was needed. She further increased the appeal of her book by adapting to changing tastes and technology in the kitchen. The 1943 edition included time-saving and rationing-friendly recipes; the one of 1946 covered the new quick method cakes which could be made in one bowl (they were created by General Mills although Irma neglected to credit them until 1951; the 1946 edition was rather a rushed job, much to Irma's displeasure). By the 1950s, Irma was increasingly incapacitated by a series of strokes, and her daughter Marion became more and more involved with the book, eventually becoming a co-author. Her own interests were reflected in the growing presence of health-food recipes and the inclusion of more information on nutrition. Yet for many affectionate readers, it was Irma's own voice which was key. Irma died in 1962, with her place in cultural and culinary history assured. Her book was the only cookbook to feature in a list of the 150 most influential books of the century put together by the New York Public Library in 1995. In 1996 Irma's biographer estimated that total hardback sales since 1931 had reached 9.3 million.

The Joy of Cooking was intended to cover all types of cooking; in fact it became increasingly comprehensive with every new edition. However, the section on cakes has always been among the most popular, probably because here Irma was clearly speaking from the heart. Baking and cake decorating were her own favourite kitchen tasks, and many of the recipes were based on her own German heritage. They were also, to put it simply, among the most 'joyful' parts of the book. The 'Rombauer Special' makes a star appearance, for example (a chocolate cake topped with fluffy white icing and a coating of dark chocolate), as well as a sour cream apple soufflé cake which came from Irma's grandmother and travelled over to America from Germany, a Christmas stollen, two *kugelhopfs* and several yeasted and fruited *kuchen* (to which we will return in another chapter). In fact, in total, baked goods represented more than a third of the original 1931 edition, among them an angel food cake, which Irma noted was the aspiration of every novice. Her 'culinary chat' abounds in this chapter, from the anecdote about Queen Mary making a sponge cake for her husband King George V (the resulting bake is 'somewhat uninteresting' but 'highly digestible'), to the fact that the ex-King of Spain was a dunker of his coffee cake. Her style exudes confidence; even the angel food cake, she said, was simply a matter of having the right technique: fine sugar, fresh cream of tartar (the latest in the chemical raising agents), chilled eggs for separating, but room temperature for whipping, and an oven at high heat when the cake was placed in it,

with the temperature decreased thereafter. She offered two base recipes
for angel food cake, one 'light', the other 'so light it seems to melt
away.' But by this time, a wire cake tester could be called on – or in a
pinch, a straw.

The Joy of Cooking remained an icon of American cookery until the
end of the twentieth century, thanks both to Irma's congenial style
and its adaptability to new tastes. She was never a pioneer of a
new sort of cooking, but we can regard her as perhaps the first
modern domestic goddess in the way that she promoted cooking for
enjoyment. Her personality as an amateur but enthusiastic home
cook was present through the book (a feature which was carefully
preserved even through the early editions of Marion's co-authorship,
just as the fiction of Mrs Beeton's editorship was maintained after
her death) in a way which was simply not true in many of the contemporary kitchen 'bibles'. She also reached out to women at home all
day in their increasingly shiny, purpose built and modern – but
potentially lonely kitchens. Those women were increasingly in need of
a friend to teach them the ropes and Irma was one. One of the other
most popular candidates, however, did not actually exist. Her name
was Betty Crocker.

The Betty Crocker website calls her 'The First Lady of Food'.
Food historian Laura Shapiro describes her as 'the most successful
culinary authority ever invented'. She has a face (actually several faces,
as her portrait has been updated multiple times over the decades
to reflect what women wanted from her; the most recent version is
based on a composite of seventy-five women who embodied her
company's characteristics: an enjoyment of cooking and baking; a
commitment to friends and family; resourcefulness and creativity in
everyday tasks; and community engagement), a signature, hundreds
of cookbooks, a radio voice and (briefly and not very successfully)
a television persona. She offered advice to thousands of American

cooks and a much-appreciated safety net in her cake mixes. Yet Betty
Crocker never drew breath.

She was invented in 1921 by General Mills, the owners of Gold
Medal flour, as a persona to answer baking queries from customers.
She was not the first fictional figurehead for a baking company: Aunt
Jemima lent her kindly face to pancake mixes from the 1890s; Ann
Pillsbury of the rival flour company to Gold Medal was also made up.
Women were thought to respond better to a product (especially one
used in such an essentially family-oriented activity as baking) if it was
fronted by a woman who looked as though she used it herself. Betty
Crocker was actually a little different on that front, as she was portrayed
as a professional woman rather than a housewife. When she appeared
on television it was often as the expert who oversaw the test kitchen,
rather than the one donning an apron. This may have been because
General Mills made much of the extensive testing process that went
into their products and recipes. Recipes were tried out in the test
kitchen and then sent out to housewives for trial in their own homes,
sometimes with a company official on hand to observe how they did
it. This fed into directions like the one still reproduced in American
recipes today, to spoon flour into a cup and level it off with the sweep
of a knife, rather than to pack it in (the latter will result in too much
flour being added to the recipe and thus risk a poor outcome –
anathema to a company which marketed their recipes and products as
foolproof). Novice cooks could attend the Betty Crocker School of the
Air, listen to Betty Crocker on the radio, and collect her recipes from
magazines. The first *Betty Crocker Picture Cook Book* (affectionately
known as the Big Red Cookbook) was published in 1950 and became
a bestseller alongside Irma Rombauer's *Joy of Cooking*. By the early
1940s her name was known to nine out of ten American homemakers,
and according to General Mills' website, she was by 1945 second only
to Eleanor Roosevelt as the best-known woman in America.

Although Betty herself was the professional face of the company, the books put out under her name had much of the chatty and personal style that had by now proved to be so popular. It was now common to state that recipes had been tried and tested, but Betty Crocker could make the unique appeal that her own trustworthy voice was backed up by a scientific test kitchen and a horde of test bakers. Reliability was guaranteed; as the preface to the first edition of the Big Red Cookbook stated: 'Only those that passed the home testing with a top score for perfect results and eating enjoyment were included.' The stars awarded to certain recipes by members of the staff lent a further personal touch. Tips followed, including pictures on the all-important process of precise measurement, a lexicon of special terms, an overview of useful kitchen items (including an array of cake pans: square, round, oblong, tube), information on meal-planning, and a section on making an attractive table, which shows how much homemaking was still bound up with creating an image of blissful domesticity. The baker could even follow the blueprint to become a 'good ar-cake-techt' by securing good materials, checking the 'framework' (the flour), and having the right tools.

The 'Big Red Books' (for there were many editions) covered all types of cooking, but the Betty Crocker name was always particularly associated with baking because of her origins with a flour company, and the ubiquitous cake mixes, to which we will return. Certainly the first edition of the cookbook managed to find an admirable number of niches for cake to occupy: the cinnamon rolls which made the 'quick morning wake-up' sweeter; 'special coffee cake' which could form part of a 'charming lunch'; the 'festive coffee cakes' which brightened up a 'leisure breakfast or brunch'; the 'homey coffee cake' which acted as a 'meal finisher'; and the fancy breads which rounded off a late afternoon or evening snack. The notes were not only chatty, they directly engaged the reader: 'May we introduce you to breads with a story?' begins the section on quick breads (which, as it goes on to explain) descended from King Alfred's failed efforts. And why were they quick? Because they were made with the latest fast-action leaveners: baking powder or baking soda mixed with acidic sour milk. Most of the cake recipes were given in two forms: one using the old traditional creaming method, the other the new 'Double-Quick Method' for women short on time.

Ease and reliability in the kitchen were watchwords of mid-twentieth-century marketing. Technology and the experiences of wartime demands on food meant that food manufacturers were creating ever more 'convenience' products, from frozen 'fish sticks' to cake mixes which required only the addition of a cup or so of water. It was therefore in their interests to create the impression that this is what women wanted. The reality, as historian Laura Shapiro has shown, was more complicated than that. Most women still enjoyed cooking from scratch, and convenience foods were taken up only slowly and usually alongside raw ingredients for home cooking. While marketing copy promoted an image of women who were harried, inexperienced and overstretched in the kitchen (and no doubt some were, although full-time homemaking had risen again with the end of the war), this did not translate into a ready market for convenience goods. This was the context in which the almost-instant cake mixes entered the fray – and, they hoped, the heart of America's kitchens.

The problem was that baking represented more than just the kitchen – even more than cooking did, or the other household tasks supposedly being made easier by new technology. Baking was a marker of women's pride in their families and their ability to make them happy, especially in America, where cakes represented domesticity, love for the family, and the sort of easy ability to entertain that we associate with the term domestic goddess today. Cake mixes thus had a difficult path to acceptance, and it was a long time coming.

Aunt Jemima's pancake mix had been launched in 1889, requiring only the addition of water or milk, plus any extra sweetness or richness the baker desired in the form of sugar and butter. The market did not really hot up until the 1930s, however, when Duff brought out a gingerbread mix, and their lead was soon followed. Things stepped up another gear when the two flour giants, General Mills and Pillsbury entered the fray, with, yes, a Betty Crocker Gingercake, and a pair of white and chocolate cakes respectively. Pillsbury conquered the angel food cake in 1951, and soon the market was flooded with different companies and lines of cakes all offering the possibility of premixed perfection in a box.

The mixes had a fairly brief heyday in the 1940s and 1950s but they never replaced baking from scratch in the way that the manufacturers had imagined. There is a popular theory that one reason for their failure to catch on was that customers felt too estranged from the process of mixing and measuring to engage with it (the mixes actually saved very little time). However, this is not correct. The early packages did indeed require the addition of nothing other than liquid, but General Mills decided to alter the composition of their mix so that bakers also had to add an egg (to recreate, it has been argued, that engagement and sense of making something fresh). But Pillsbury did not, and yet the two companies remained equally in control of the market – suggesting that estrangement was not such an issue after all. In fact, the egg issue was, Laura Shapiro says, more to do with the poor taste of the powdered egg in the mixes, and nothing at all to do with making women feel involved in the act of baking.

Gradually, cake mixes did carve out a niche for themselves and, interestingly, it was in two different ways. The appeal for some was the convenience and reliability; many bakers kept one in the cupboard 'just in case' even if they also baked from scratch. For those wanting to capture the perfect airy layer cake or angel food cake but unsure of their abilities to do so, the mix was the perfect answer. In fact, some American schools started to use them from the early 1950s because they would produce reliable results (naturally, the lessons were sponsored by the cake mix companies). Baking books increasingly featured recipes made from scratch and those based on mixes alongside each other (Betty Crocker's Big Red Book was unsurprisingly among them, setting out side by side how many ingredients and utensils were needed for a cake mix cake (three and six) versus one made from scratch (eight and fifteen). However, the real 'eureka moment' for the manufacturers came with the realisation that the mix could be marketed simply as the start of a process of creating a beautiful cake. Now the cake mix baker was no longer lazy, untutored, or to take this train of thought to its logical conclusion, failing to love and nurture her family; she was, instead, investing time, love and skill in creating something stunningly beautiful. This change of tack is still vital for sales of cake mixes today, and it's been fully embraced by their manufacturers. Duncan Hines' mix for cake pops (see Chapter 9) directs the baker to first use the mix to bake a cake, then crumble it, use the accompanying pack of frosting to bind the crumbs, and then shape them into balls before coating in nuts or chocolate. One wonders if it would be much more effort to make the cake from scratch too, but for many bakers, this is the least appealing part of the process compared to the challenge of the presentation (taste is not neglected, but is taken care of by the 'no-fail' promise of the mix).

Today, cake mixes are hugely popular for this very reason. In 2012 Betty Crocker launched a *Betty Crocker Ultimate Cake Mix Cookbook*, while Anne Byrn, the 'Cake Mix Doctor' has a whole line of books (and mixes) devoted to 'doctoring' boxed mixes to produce wonderful results. It should be added, however, that cake mixes are not a universally popular product. They are well loved by many American bakers, where Betty Crocker still dominates the market (her most popular offering currently being the 'Supermoist'). In Australia, too, where cake decorating is also a high art, boxed mixes have a secure place in the kitchen. The bible for baking mothers, the *Australian Women's Weekly Children's Birthday Cake* books recommend using mixes for the cake itself, with the real focus being the decoration (although they do also give recipes at the back if the baker wants to make her own). In the UK, however, they are reserved principally for baking with children; that's certainly where my own experience of them began, and very empowering they are too for a young baker. A 2013 review of cake mixes in the *Guardian* newspaper felt it necessary to start with the strapline: 'Don't turn up your nose at ready-made cake mixes – they're ideal for emergencies when the store cupboard's bare.' Hardly a ringing endorsement. Even the Cake Mix Doctor herself states that she turned to mixes as a busy mother of two small children, but feels the need to add that she was 'not ashamed'. Moreover, she draws the line at canned frosting: this is an area where a baker cannot 'fool' by cheating. Even lovers of cake mixes (of whom there are many) seem to have an ambiguous perspective on the fine line between honest toil and cheating. What is absolutely clear though, is that using a cake mix need not take away the label of domestic goddess; in fact it can increase the possibility of attaining it.

The cake mix manufacturers only got it partly right when they launched their products in the 1930s, then. Many women clearly did still have a love of baking from scratch, and the value that this had for them is demonstrated nowhere more clearly than in the huge popularity of the first great baking competition: the Pillsbury Bake-Off, the opportunity *par excellence* to show off the skills learned through years of practice.

The bake-off is a very American institution. Until its modern counterpart, *The Great British Bake Off* hit UK screens in 2010, competitive baking in Britain was confined to village shows and county fairs. But, while county and agricultural fairs exist in the States too, the Pillsbury Bake-Off was something new. It was launched in 1949 by the Pillsbury flour company under the title the Grand National Recipe and Baking Contest. The only requirement was that entries must use at least half a cup of Pillsbury's best flour; other than that it was an open field (no cake mixes were allowed until 1966 when a special award was made for the winning recipe which featured a mix). The women (and a handful of men) of America rose to the challenge with a vast array of cakes, cookies, pies, tarts and breads: 200 were chosen for testing, and the inventors of the 100 best were invited to the Waldorf Astoria for the competition. The first winner (who took away the princely sum of $50,000) was Mrs Theodora Smafield with her 'No-Knead Water-Rising Twists', which were cinnamon and nut-coated twists of enriched sweet dough. Third prize, however, went to Mrs Richard W. Sprague's 'Aunt Carrie's Bonbon Cake' – a chocolate layer cake with a praline filling and a fudgy frosting. The top prize in both 1950 and 1951 went to a cake (respectively, a nutty 'Orange Kiss-Me Cake' by Mrs Lily Wuebel of Redwood City, California – I gave that one a try and very moist and citrusy it is too – and a 'Starlight Double-Delight Cake' by Mrs Helen Weston of La Jolla, California, the latter containing frosting as an ingredient for the cake as well as a topping). In 1953 the appropriately named 'My Inspiration Cake' – a layer cake containing pecans and chocolate – won for Mrs Lois Kanago of Webster, South Dakota. The only male winner to date, Mr Kurt Wait of Redwood City, California, baked his way to victory with a Macadamia Fudge Torte in 1996.

Laura Shapiro speculates that one of the reasons for the unlikely success of the bake-off at a time when women were supposedly losing interest and skills in the kitchen, is that it gave them validation, reward and publicity for their work. For the women entering the Pillsbury Bake-Off the time and effort required to make a showstopper cake were clearly both worthwhile and rewarding. In reality one suspects that baking always had a bit of a competitive edge, even for those not motivated to put themselves through a national contest. At a time when most women worked in the home, baking something sweet and beautiful purely for a social occasion rather than sustenance, was always something to be proud of. This is the reason that cakes were – still are – such an essential part of the trappings of domestic goddessery. By the 1960s though, those equations were all starting to break down: more women were working outside the home; more were starting to admit that they were fed up with the round of domestic chores and felt unfulfilled by tasks like baking. And for women like this, looking for inspiration to go their own way, there was a whole new range of role models. The domestic goddess was falling, to be replaced by women who forged their own paths.

Part of this change in outlook meant a complete rejection of housework as a way of measuring female worth. For feminists, taking pleasure in baking an attractive cake for other people was pretty much everything they sought to oppose. We will return to this line of thought in the last chapter. For now, we are concerned with another way of thinking which emerged at the same time: this involved working out how to meld cooking and other household tasks together with a strong female identity. The culinary role models for this new generation of women who wanted to cook, but not to be defined by it; to feel competent but enjoy it, were clever, confident and erudite: women like Julia Child in the States and Jane Grigson and Elizabeth David in Britain.

None of these women were professional chefs (though Child had attended a professional-level cookery course at the Cordon Bleu school in Paris); all of them promoted knowledge and enjoyment in the kitchen and at the table – for they all saw food as a shared activity and maker of memories. Nor were any of them writing (or speaking, in the case of Julia Child, who also had a successful television show, *The French Chef* which aired in 1963) specifically to women in the way that the earlier authors were. Child said that she was talking to anyone interested in food; though *not* specifically to ordinary housewives since they had so much information produced for them already. Grigson and David, who both wrote food articles for the British broadsheets, spoke for the educated and interested public (David's early columns for the *Sunday Times* were initially printed in the women's section of the magazine but she felt constrained by the expectation that her food writing had to be accompanied by recipes).

Julia Child is perhaps the least likely domestic goddess figure of all those we have considered here (and was probably one of the least likely to be interested in accepting the title too). She was very tall, with an unusually deep voice, and she was extremely clumsy, at least on camera. Her televised miscalculations and cover-ups were legion, but by joking about them and passing them off as fixable, she was responsible for showing the public that food and entertaining need not be perfect. Cake did not actually play a very large part in her famous book of 1961 *Mastering the Art of French Cooking* (co-authored with Simone Beck and Louisette Bertholle); the breadth of coverage meant that there was room for only five exemplars. Nonetheless, the instructions for the butter sponge cake (*biscuit au beurre*), the *gâteau à l'orange* and *à l'orange et aux amands*, the *reine de Saba* (Queen of Sheba) and *le marquis* (a chocolate sponge cake) are extensive and peppered with general rules for success in cake-making; one of the 'fundamentals' covered in the book was how to fold beaten egg whites into a cake mixture to retain their volume. Julia Child was also very unusual for making her mark in the field of *French* cookery, arguably the most male-dominated cuisine in the world. Her dishes were often complex, but there was no hint that this was because the cook should aspire to impress with showiness and refinement. Instead, this was simply the food that she felt tasted good, and she wanted to share that knowledge with anyone who cared to tune in or read her book. In this respect she had much in common with Irma Rombauer, albeit with more coherence to her tastes, and considerably more training and skill behind her. She recognised that know-how was key (that and good ingredients). An inspirational figure to feminists and women cooks alike, Child can perhaps only be described as a domestic goddess with one's tongue firmly in one's cheek. But then isn't that how Nigella Lawson meant us to read the title of her baking bible, too?

Other women writers of the early post-war period were similarly rejecting the dainty femininity of earlier decades, which included exquisitely neatly presented cakes and other dishes. In 1963, the same year that Childs' television show aired, Betty Friedan captured the attention of bored housewives everywhere with the publication of her book *The Feminine Mystique*, which put a name to the malaise that many women felt went with full-time homemaking. What British cookery writers Jane Grigson and Elizabeth David did was something a little different: they quietly combined cookery writing with erudition, furthering a tradition which saw food history and shared culture as equally, if not more important, than sharing the 'how to'. Both championed the colour, flavour and simplicity of Continental foods, and were interested in reclaiming those qualities from the British culinary past (David, born in 1913, wrote a magisterial volume on *English Bread and Yeast Cookery*, which included many of the English specialities we met in the first two chapters). Both were well educated, well travelled and cultured women, who wrote warmly and invitingly about their food journeys. Both of the books which touch most closely on cakes – *English Bread and Yeast Cookery*, and *English Food* respectively, contained recipes, but they are also full of history, personal recommendations and travel tales. Food (and baking) was for both of these women a matter of deep pleasure and memory-making irrespective of gender. Interestingly, both championed earlier cookery writers like Acton, Glasse and Raffald, who predated the fussiness of the Victorians, and who represented what they saw as a genuinely British form of cooking.

Cakes and baking form a part of this sense of personal and culinary heritage. While writing about gingerbread in *British Cookery*, for example, Grigson shares a lovely imagined picture of the poet laureate, William Wordsworth, tramping with his sister Dorothy across the countryside to Grasmere, to satisfy a sudden craving (sadly unmet – the shop stocked only the wrong kind), alongside her own Aunty Bell's recipe for parkin, some notes on the origins of the name ginger-bread, and a few words on the traditional grain crops of the north of England. In a phrase which could as easily come from Nigella herself she describes the texture of a good parkin: 'nubbly with oatmeal, the taste dark with treacle'. Personal touches abound: maids of honour are 'well worth making if you are not within reach of London' where the best ones could be purchased, and readers are counselled to follow their own preferences on the size of the cake tin to use, along with a brief note as to her own choice. In her recollections of children's birthday cakes, family recipes and trips to Betty's Tea Rooms in Harrogate, one can sense the warmth and enjoyment not only in baking, but in sharing food experiences.

This really brings us back full circle, for what is Nigella doing but precisely this? She has said that she wrote *How to Be a Domestic Goddess* partly to commemorate her food memories of her mother and sister, both of whom died young. She may most embody the traits associated with domestic goddessery today – largely because of the title of her book, of course, which reflects her interest in a very traditionally female sort of cooking – but also because of her image of juggling things to have it all, her groomed appearance and the distinctiveness (and intelligence) of her voice both in print and on screen. But I hope that this chapter has suggested that there is more to the domestic goddess than this. If we think of these women as people who have helped their disciples to take control of their domestic tasks; to feel befriended rather than isolated in the kitchen; and eventually, encouraged a sense of joy in cooking and baking which is starting to transcend gender altogether, we may find a more fruitful and satisfying way of squaring household tasks, baking and female identity. And that is something we will address head on in the final chapter.

What, finally, of the angel food cake with which we started? An emblem of domestic accomplishment, leisure time, delicacy and snowy-white purity, it is now easier to make than it was when it appeared on the baking scene in the 1870s. Food technologists in the 1930s realised that it was easier to achieve the desired light and glossy texture if the egg whites were whipped only to the soft peak stage (which must have been something of a relief for those whipping with the perforated spoon mentioned in our sample recipe), and also if some of the sugar was introduced with the flour. The angel food cake soon donned a range of party frocks, from cherry to butterscotch flavours and fillings: Irma Rombauer offered spices, nut, butterscotch and chocolate examples; Betty Crocker's Big Red Book added peppermint, cherry and a gold-silver variant ('for those special anniversaries') which broke all the rules and contained egg yolk in the yellow portion. In the 1940s it became fashionable to make a channel through the middle of the cake which was filled with a hidden 'surprise' of flavoured cream. Today it is easier still to bake one, with pre-separated egg whites available from the supermarket, high-power electric mixers to take on the task of whipping, and specialist pans available in shops and on websites. Easier yet, we have boxed mixes to which the cook only needs to add water. Baking is now more democratic and gender-blind than it has ever been before. But perhaps most importantly, we now have access to a huge bank of friendly voices, skilled in photography but also prepared to admit their mistakes and laugh about their failed efforts: the food bloggers who document their every foray into the world of baking. But it hasn't always been that way. For centuries, people have adapted their recipes and their practices to accommodate what they had to hand. And that is where we will turn next.

5

THE CARDBOARD
WEDDING CAKE

In 1942, Nancy Biglin, aged nine, was a bridesmaid at her brother's wedding in Hull, north-east England. The Second World War had been underway for two long years already, and people in Europe were resigned to the monotony and uncertainty of their national diets. Imagine Nancy's excitement, then, at the prospect of tasting the traditional white-frosted cake standing on the table, ready for cutting. And imagine her disappointment when, photographs taken, the beautiful icing was revealed to be a cardboard façade, concealing only a small fruit cake. 'I think I just sort of looked at it and I think I could have burst into tears,' she told an interviewer for the Imperial War Museum London's Sound Archive half a century later, 'I was never so disappointed in all my life.'

This wartime trick perfectly sums up the theme of this chapter: bake with what you've got; or, perhaps, Make Do and Bake. It also reveals how important cake continued to be even in straitened times when we might suppose that such a frippery would be laid aside.

Making do is a pretty sober affair when you have little choice: in periods of economic depression, for instance, or wartime, when ingredients were in short supply. Recipes for eggless, butterless or sugarless cakes (occasionally all three) abounded during the Second World War, especially in Europe, where food restrictions were far more extreme and long-lasting than in the States: food rationing did not finally end until 1954 in the UK. Here, all of the major ingredients for cake baking were rationed, and bought cakes were often in short supply. The weekly ration per person was around six ounces per week of butter and margarine combined (the proportion of each varied according to supplies), eight ounces of sugar, and one fresh egg per week. You were in luck if you kept your own chickens (as many more people did in wartime); otherwise you were left to the vagaries of dried eggs, which were shipped across in large quantities from America. They were a very useful product but reactions were varied, some reporting that they had an unpleasant taste, and others that scrambled reconstituted dried eggs bounced when dropped. The availability of cakes actually became more problematic after the war, when an even more stringent system of rationing for bread and other flour products had to be introduced because of shortages.

We might think that in a situation of such tight restriction and threat to life on a daily basis, cake would not be high on anyone's list of priorities. Yet actually it seems that it had a significant impact on morale, especially as the war years wore on. When the polling agency Gallup asked people about their difficulties in getting unrationed foods in November 1941, 9 per cent of those who said they had had problems mentioned cakes and biscuits, close behind the most commonly mentioned foodstuffs of cereals (14 per cent) and fish (11 per cent). Even the authorities, led by the popular Minister for Food, Lord Woolton (remembered forever for the patriotic but uninspiring vegetable pie which was named after him), recognised that it was important to acknowledge and support the ongoing desire for small comforts. His Ministry of Food regularly published pamphlets and broadcast programmes on baking with rations, and even increased the sugar ration for the young at Christmas. He realised how crucial it was to keep some butter in the fats allowance simply because people were so attached to it – especially in comparison with the much-maligned margarine. It was an astute decision: it has been suggested that in periods of stress, these little hints of normality are all the more important.

We are fortunate to have a lot of diaries which recorded details of daily life in Britain from the wartime period, thanks largely to the efforts of the social investigators, Mass Observation. This was an organisation set up by a pair of anthropologists who were keen to understand modern society by creating an 'anthropology of ourselves'. They did this by asking people about a whole range of topics from fashion and drinking in pubs, to attitudes to the monarchy. They also had a big panel of diary-writers, who regularly sent in their entries on their day-to-day lives. One of the best known and most prolific of these writers was Nella Last (known to Mass Observation as 'Housewife, 49' after her occupation and age) who lived in the northern port town of Barrow-in-Furness. She was a keen baker who missed her pre-war pastime and all the happy memories of family life that it brought, and she recorded these feelings in her diaries. Both of her sons were away in the forces and she and her husband made a rather uncomfortable truncated family unit. On Good Friday 1941, Nella wrote about a picnic that the two of them had gone on, taking two slices of cake which she had made the previous summer when ingredients were in greater abundance. Cutting this cake seemed to present her with a mix of feelings. She had made two, one for Christmas, and one for her husband and younger son's December birthdays, but she had put off cutting into this one until Easter. Eating it represented an almost unbearable pleasure because it would take with it all its memories of having family around her, and the ingredients to express her love for them. She wrote in her diary that she expected it to be the last good cake she would have for years at least. She did not record whether this poor cake lived up to the hopes and desires invested in it, but her diary entry is a perfect representation of the way that baking a cake can be an expression of love and nurture – and the sadness that the loss of it can bring. Through the war Nella continued to save ingredients to bake when her sons visited, as a special treat both for them and for her. She was not alone in associating cake with family, love and comfort; cakes and other nostalgic or sweet foods were among the most commonly requested items in food parcels sent to the troops in the war.

Part of this nostalgia was undoubtedly also linked to happier pre-war celebrations of occasions like birthdays. Several of the other Mass Observation diary-keepers recorded the difficulties they had in trying to preserve some of these occasions. Pam Ashford, who was an office worker in Glasgow, could only furnish the cakes for her office leaving tea by visiting six different bakers and appropriating another that her mother had secured for the family. She was astonished to find that cakes were much more abundant in the English border town of Berwick-upon-Tweed when she went there on holiday in 1942. Nella Last found the same when she went to Blackpool in the same year – both of course coastal towns but lacking in the ports and strategic industry which made Glasgow and Barrow prime targets for aerial bombardment. Meanwhile, a Lyons tea shop menu from 1940 still included a range of cakes, buns and scones, the latter even available with butter, unlike the sandwiches and toast which now came with margarine.

The uncertainty over cake availability led to a lot of resentment, especially since many women felt that what was on offer wasn't worth queuing for. A Mass Observation report in 1942 found that the most common food 'grumble' from the people surveyed was about cake, reported by almost a quarter of women, and overtaking the chief 1941 grumble about cheese. Another survey found that 12 per cent of those questioned had used a cake mix in the last week, and 18 per cent did so occasionally. In contrast, 67 per cent had bought a cake in the last week and even more bought biscuits or small cakes – but mainly because they could not do as much home baking as they had used to. By the next year the numbers were even higher. Similarly, three-quarters of those who said they didn't have enough cooking fat wanted it for baking.

Newspapers, magazines, food manufacturers and official bodies like the Ministry for Food all did their best to keep the desire to bake alive under rationing. For some manufacturers this was actually all they had to offer as their products were temporarily off the shelves because of shortages. Margarine was sold under one government label with no brand names, so companies like Stork had to use 'advertorials' to keep the name in people's minds, and Be-Ro Flour, Stork and Borwick's Baking Powder all published cookbooks and leaflets to help the harried housewife. Borwick's also continued to sponsor cake-making competitions. The Ministry of Food went all out with their own recipe leaflets, talks, demonstrations (including many by the much-loved food economist Marguerite Patten) and radio broadcasts to give people new ideas for cooking and baking. Several of their leaflets focused on party or Christmas baking, acknowledging that people still wanted sweetness and celebration in their lives. As one leaflet put it, in typically bright tones, 'After all, our precious rations and allowances do us just as much good when they're in party dress as when they are served in more everyday fashion.'

Cookbook authors became quite innovative in 'making do' with scant and substitute ingredients in their cake recipes, but while often trying to produce cakes that looked and tasted as much like their pre-war versions as possible. Josephine Terry's 1944 cookbook *Food Without Fuss* contained a recipe for cake icing using saccharine, milk powder, water and sugar, which she said looked and tasted so much like the real thing that it might fool guests into thinking the baker had dabbled in the black market! She also devised a way to present a 'fancy tea without fuss' by dividing, cutting and icing one simple cake (bought or home-made) to make three different fancier-looking ones. Other recipes used stale cake or biscuits, like Terry's French chocolate cake, which was a thick chocolate blancmange spread over a base of leftover biscuit or cake crumbs, and topped with the same; or her wartime trifle, again using stale tea buns and tea fancies. Another proposed economy was to plan out a 'baking day' so that many dishes could be made in the same hot oven – just as they had been in the old days of the communal beehive ovens. Cookbook author Constance Spry, on the other hand, threw all caution to the wind in her 1942 *Come into the Garden, Cook*, and recommended that bakers should simply save up their rations and splurge them on a good old traditional cake. A more romantic, but probably less satisfying, wartime cake was the one recalled by cookbook author Barbara Maher: a 'flower cake' which was a bowl of soil with garden flowers arranged prettily in it.

It was evidently a real challenge to keep up the usual cake habits in wartime, yet people did not abandon luxuries like cakes; instead they seem to have craved them all the more as they were such potent symbols of normality, family and friends, and of having a little time and leisure to treat oneself. In April 1943 the tea bar in the Fulham branch of Woolworth's was reported to be the only counter not making a loss, as customers continued to come in for a cup of tea and a slice of cake.

Wartime and economic depression were at least relatively short-lived, however. In other scenarios shortages were more fundamental; because of a lack of technology or ingredients. The migrants on the westward pioneer trails in America from the 1840s to the 1890s had to rely on fireside cooking, fat saved from slaughtering hogs, wild honey and fruit for their baked goods. Just as with the wartime example, we might suppose that baking was not high on the list of priorities for the westward settlers, especially given that they had to carry all their provisions with them. Nonetheless, the same desire for sweetness seems to have prevailed. Most baking was done when the wagon train halted to wait for the spring grass to grow. Then cakes appeared in greater numbers, still most likely those without eggs, and using molasses rather than sugar. One child pioneer of the 1850s recalled a birthday cake made from flour collected from the dust at the bottom of the cornmeal sacks, wild honey and a wild turkey egg. Home-made baking soda, sour milk and a small bit of butter made up the rest of the batter, which was cooked in the old-fashioned way in a skillet over an open fire, with coals banked up around it. Once again, we see the extraordinary resourcefulness of people determined to maintain the most beloved of cake traditions.

The ability to survive long journeys was a prerequisite for baking ingredients in early twentieth-century Australia too. In this still newly settled land, the urban centres were far removed from the farms where agricultural goods were produced. A huge rail network quickly sprang up to carry goods to their markets: by 1870 a thousand miles of railway had opened in eastern Australia, and by 1890 it was eleven thousand miles. However, any ways to make fresh produce like milk keep for longer were welcome, else farmers would be left with an unusable surplus. The answer was canning, and the Australian fondness for condensed milk was born.

The process had been invented in wartime France in 1795. The army needed cheap and tasty food which was easy to transport, and so a competition was launched for a solution (this was a tried and tested practice in late eighteenth- and nineteenth-century France; similar competitions produced margarine and a domestic sugar beet industry). The winner was a confectioner and cook called Nicolas Appert, who realised that early experiments with sealing air-evacuated bottles and heating them could be made more reliable by the addition of sugar. His bottling method was taken on by the army and it soon spread to England (Appert himself had agreed not to file a patent, but the prompt patent application from another inventor in England may have been a way around this). In Britain, glass bottles were soon replaced with metal canisters, and although the method was still expensive, canned rations were carried by soldiers at Waterloo, in the Crimea and during the American Civil War, where both sides carried canned rations of meat, stews and even oysters. By the mid-nineteenth century British sailors carried canned meat onboard ship.

Canned foods were available on the American frontier trails, but they were scarce because of the cost of canning; until the process was improved in 1849 each can had to be made by hand, the food inserted through a small hole in the top, liquid poured in and the hole soldered save for a small pinhole. The whole can then had to be boiled until steam escaped from the pinhole, which was in turn then soldered shut. In 1851, the process was exhibited at the Great Exhibition in London, and the price began to fall. Meanwhile an American named Gail Borden, a jack of white-collar trades from surveying to real estate, had started to ponder how canning could be applied to milk after seeing cows on a voyage to London become too seasick to milk. There was actually already a British patent registered by the time that Borden had perfected his method in 1852, but his was by far the more successful. At the time, the process of sterilisation was not fully understood – only that sugar improved it (it inhibits bacteria). By the 1880s the heating stage had been improved enough that sugar was no longer necessary, and canned evaporated (unsweetened) milk joined the market in 1890. Back in Australia, the first milk condensers were installed in Melbourne in 1882, and Nestlé established its first plant

– the largest in the world – at Toogoolawah in southern Queensland in 1908.

The principal benefit of canning for the troops was that it meant they could rely on the quality of their rations. It also, of course, made them much easier to transport, with minimal risk of breakage or damage. However, dessert lovers everywhere soon made the discovery that (carefully!) heating a tin of condensed milk produced caramel, and with much less effort than the traditional method of melting sugar and milk. It is no coincidence that Australians (and New Zealanders) love their caramel, chocolate and coconut slices, their grubs, bumblebees and caramel kisses, to be found in every bakery, but easy to make at home too, or that condensed milk found a huge market in the hot countries of Central and South America, where *tres leches* cakes and *dulce de leche* were already popular.

Although Borden promoted the health benefits of his condensed milk for all and sundry, and especially for growing children, the story of his product is not a uniformly happy one. Budget brands cut corners and used skimmed milk, which made a product with much lower levels of fats and vitamins. Since many mothers had unfortunately taken to heart the message that condensed milk was safe, pure and scientific, this had terrible results for the health of babies fed on the product. In Australia condensed milk formed part of charity handouts in the Depression, alongside other manufactured foodstuffs like golden syrup and bread, which also speak to a diet poor in nutrients.

Our final example of baking with what conditions throw at you is a little different. We're not talking here about isolation, lack of ingredients or new foodstuffs, but something more fundamental: altitude. I remember being completely nonplussed when I saw the modification for baking at altitude on the side of a cake mix my brother-in-law had brought back from Colorado. This is simply not a problem most

Brits will ever encounter. But in parts of the States like the Rocky Mountains, it is a real issue. Just as bakers outside the Southern states will have difficulties capturing the light consistency that is achieved with Southern soft flours, so too will bakers in Denver or Boulder (or Calgary or Johannesburg) struggle to perfect a recipe written for sea-level dwellers.

The problem is that air pressure is lower at high altitudes and this affects the temperature reached in the middle of the cake when baking, and in turn, the structure achieved by the interaction between flour and eggs. It also makes the moisture escape more quickly, producing dry cakes. After what was no doubt a series of flops in the early days, bakers in Boulder and the like discovered what they needed to do to correct for the unique conditions they were baking in (raise the temperature, increase the liquids to allow for the greater moisture loss, and lower the quantity of sugar and raising agent), and while recipes were passed on from friends to families, or sourced from local community cookbooks, everything was fine. But as soon as mass-market books started to appear, there were problems. In 1950, *The Betty Crocker Picture Cookbook* included a short section on baking at altitude and a formula for the adjustments that must be made per 1,500 feet of height above 3,500. Certain cakes needed extra care, including the notorious angel food, and all sponge cakes, for which the egg whites should be beaten only to a soft peak so that they still had capacity to expand in baking.

More pressing for Mrs Crocker and her helpers was the impact of altitude on cake mixes. Their primary selling point, after all, was reliability, and a standard mix would simply not achieve the best results at high altitudes. Their answer became famous and must surely go down as one of the most innovative responses to a problem in the history of baking: they built a 'flying kitchen'. Naturally, issues of cost and practicality meant that Pillsbury's flying kitchen never actually left the ground; it was a pressurised high-altitude simulator from the Second World War with a stove fitted in it and a viewing window through which the observers could watch and monitor the cake being made. After sixty-four 'flights' in the late 1940s, special instructions calling for more liquid to be added were inserted into all cake mixes distributed in areas at altitude, and they still are today.

Necessity really is the mother of invention when it comes to cakes. The domestic goddesses might tell us we need a set of rules to bake a cake, but the examples we've met here show us how far a bit of ingenuity can go if those rules can't be met. The efforts that bakers go to maintain their treats and celebrations also reminds us that a cake is often as much about the occasion as about the taste. When times are really tough, sweetness and comfort go a long way in preserving some sense of normality. In the next chapter we will meet this idea in new form: when cakes became international travellers, accompanying their bakers on diasporas across the world.

6

THE CAKE THAT TRAVELLED THE WORLD

In May 1673 French explorers started to make their way up the Mississippi River. It was not their first foray into North American territory as French-speaking Canadians will testify, but it marked the start of French influence around the Mississippi and Gulf Coast states. At the height of their influence the French owned a huge tract of land covering 828,000 square miles through the centre of the continent, stretching from Canada to the Gulf Coast and the Mississippi Valley in the south. With them the French brought language, culture and food, including one cake which has remained firmly associated with the Louisiana region and New Orleans in particular. It is now known as the king cake (or as the French called it, the *gâteau des rois*) and it is a cornerstone of the world-famous New Orleans celebrations of Mardi Gras. This cake is just one of the most famous of many globetrotting cakes.

In this chapter we will trace some of these 'foodways' of distinctive local and national cakes, and follow them as they journeyed. We will also meet the ingenious marketing drives to get new and unlikely ingredients adopted into the home baking industry (I won't spoil the surprise, but suffice to say that some were fizzy, and others came from cans you wouldn't necessarily find in the baking aisle).

But let's start at the beginning. The most straightforward reason for the invention of distinctive local cakes is necessity: baking with what you've got in its simplest form. When markets were local, recipe books scarce or non-existent, and methods of baking dependent on fuel sources and regional oven technology, a baker had no choice but to use what was produced on his or her doorstep. So, pecans are popular cake ingredients in the American South and filberts (a diminutive hazelnut) are not much met outside Oregon. Lingonberries are found in Norwegian and Swedish baking, because they are abundant local crops – and also in eastern Canada which sits on the same latitude line. Cranberries, blueberries, strawberries and plums were all wild and native to America and feature prominently in many American baked goods from cakes and muffins to pies. Mexican cakes often contain chilli or pineapple, and Jamaican ones ginger, while Chinese moon cakes are sweetened with the local specialty red bean or lotus seed paste instead of sugar, and Middle Eastern and Eastern European cakes make more use of honey. The Canadians and New Englanders, meanwhile, use syrup from the local maple trees to make their baked goods sweet, and many British and American recipes for heritage bakes like gingerbreads still employ molasses or treacle. In fact, molasses was such an important source of income within the British Empire that the British government passed a Molasses Act in 1733 to protect imports from within the Empire. They got more than they bargained for, as it was one of the triggers for the American Revolution. Fats differ too: butter is preferred in northern Europe and oil in the south because of the difference in emphasis on dairying and crop-growing (newcomers to Australia in the eighteenth and nineteenth centuries stubbornly stuck to their butter even in red-hot temperatures).

Sweetness and fats were not the only cake components governed by local tastes and availability; the same was true for flour, a cake's basic structural building block. We are used now to baking almost exclusively with wheat flour as it is such a dominant crop in the Western world. Not so in past centuries, even in Britain: we've already established that oatmeal and barley meal were common crops in the north-west, for instance, and were used for cakes as well as bread (domestic goddess Mrs Beeton would almost certainly have been familiar with barley bread, and perhaps cake too, from her childhood visits to her grandfather in Cumberland). We have also noted that the first American woman to publish a cookbook, Amelia Simmons, included cornflour (maize) in many of her recipes, because of very different harvests in the New World than in the Old. Cornmeal is popular for baking in Spain too, which reflects their shared history with New World colonies. Even wheat flours are not created equal: the crop grown in the Southern states of America is a distinctive 'soft' winter variety which makes tender cakes and pies; Canadian flour, meanwhile, is much 'stronger' with a higher protein (gluten) content, and more like a British bread flour. Cakes made from these flours may turn out quite differently from one another, which was another reason that different parts of these vast land masses developed their own specialities (and also why a Southern domestic goddess might not be able to impart her knowledge successfully to a Canadian one). Modern American cake recipes are much more likely to specify 'cake flour' than British ones, where this speciality is relatively unheard of: Pillsbury started to manufacture it in 1932. Another alternative stemmed from necessity and a peasant subsistence diet − chestnut flour; chestnuts grow wild and are free for scavenging in parts of North America (they were a feature of Native American cooking, but chestnut flour and bread were also eaten in the eastern parts of the States into the nineteenth century), and also in parts of southern

France and Italy where chestnuts are still more popular and abundant than in other areas of Europe. The dense Italian dessert cake, *castagnaccio*, is one classic example (flours made from nuts contain no gluten and so are not disposed to rise like wheat flour). In the Far East, rice is used for baking, either cooked and moulded, or pounded into flour, as in the chewy balls known in Japan as *mochi*. And let's not get started on the differences between measuring techniques and oven temperatures, a lesson a Canadian friend of mine learned the hard way when trying to reproduce a recipe I had sent her (she forgot that Brits refer to oven temperatures in degrees centigrade, not Fahrenheit; that cake was never going to cook through).

A lot of what we're talking about here – distinctive ways of cooking and eating – can be described as 'foodways'. This is a term which means more than just the food itself; it also describes the way that people felt about and reacted to food items and occasions. Cake is an excellent way to think more about these concepts, as it speaks of many of the ties that bind families and communities together: celebration, pleasure, love and shared heritage. As Hasia Diner has written in her book on foodways in America, bonds like these draw those who share food customs together, especially when they move to a new land. In fact, she says they can actually maintain links and shared tastes with places of origin for descendants who have never been there, and perhaps have never tasted the original foods they now recreate.

So, some of what concerns us is the simple transfer of foodstuffs, know-how and technology from one place to another. The spread of cereal growing is a good example, with actual grass seeds taken on early voyages to the New World (and others brought back to the Old). Sugar is another, spreading outwards from where it originally grew in New Guinea, via Asia, India and the Arab lands before making its way to Europe, whence it was taken to the New World for further, lucrative – but for the thousands of slave workers, misery-filled – cultivation. But the other factor – and the one which is arguably more interesting if we're thinking about what cake means to people – is the one captured by the more complex meaning of foodways: the sense that foods followed people, and were prized by them as reminders of home and shared cultures. This is fundamentally based on patterns of colonisation and migration, but it also speaks of the reasons that people move: poverty, persecution, the promise of new opportunities, and not least importantly, access to food.

It is hard to think of a more extreme example of an ethnic 'melting pot' than the United States. From its origins in Native American culture, America was settled by groups of people from a host of different European nations: British, Spanish, French, Dutch, Danish, Swedish and Portuguese to name just but the earliest (notably, all white, and mostly Protestant). Gradually the European settlers moved into new areas, finding fertile land and hard work but also rich reward. Their families and compatriots followed them, creating communities with shared foodways, language and culture. Around thirty million Europeans went to America between the 1820s and the 1920s in successive waves: the Irish fleeing the Great Famine in the 1840s (and a second wave in the two decades on either side of the turn of the twentieth century: over a million Irish went to America in these years, many of them women); Eastern Europeans from the 1870s, many of them Jews fleeing persecution in Russia, Poland and Romania; Italians around the same time as the second wave of Irish; and, of course, the many African-American slaves who had first come to the States decades earlier. Many came intending to stay permanently; others planned to return (others, of course, had had no choice), but all carried their sense of identity as Irish, Jewish or Russian with them, and recreated it via their foods. We will see some of the ways that they had to adapt their recipes to accommodate different ingredients shortly; and others that they chose to adopt from convenience or changing tastes, but for almost all, cakes were as important as reminders of family and communal celebration as their other vegetable, meat or bread recipes were for subsistence. And all met food in an abundance that they could never have imagined at home.

Many of the new citizens of what became the United States came from traditions steeped in home baking. The Dutch brought a taste for fried doughnut-like cakes (called *oliebollen*) as well as waffles and pancakes with them when traders settled New Netherland in the early seventeenth century. Manhattan was taken over by the British in 1664, but remained a stronghold of Dutch language and culture. The ascetic Puritanism of the New Englanders didn't stop their baking traditions, but it meant that their cakes and pies were simple affairs and usually part of a meal rather than a separate treat – Catherine Beecher would have approved. Their fruit cakes, while not a big feature of American baking now, left their legacy in bakes like the Hartford election cake, which was a large, yeasted and fruited offering made for the electoral representatives who flocked to the Connecticut town of Hartford for the ballot count in the eighteenth century. Amelia Simmons included the earliest known published recipe for 'Election Cake' in the second edition of her book *American Cookery* of 1796. The very British Sally Lunn which we met in Chapter 2 also travelled successfully to the States, retaining her brioche-like character, and appeared in many American cookbooks into the nineteenth century.

It is German immigrants whom modern Americans have most to thank for many of their most beloved baking traditions, however. 'German' settlers in America (they came from a variety of lands: 'Germany' did not exist until 1871) were a significant presence; they were the largest non-British group of settlers, and over the whole nineteenth century more than a tenth of Americans spoke German. The key areas of German settlement were around Pennsylvania, soon spreading into the Appalachian area and on into Ohio and Indiana. South Dakota has even adopted *kuchen* as its official state dessert. The word *kuchen* simply means 'cake', but in South Dakota it generally denotes a baked sweet dough base (originally raised with yeast), with a fruity custard-like filling and, sometimes, a sugary 'streusel' topping too.

Between them, these groups, although economically and culturally diverse, brought a whole range of baked goods, from fried dough funnel cakes (inventories of personal goods from the seventeenth show that even quite poor German households owned specialist equipment for making cakes like these called *strauben*, which were piped into hot oil), types of doughnuts, *lebkuchen*, *kugelhopfs* and *kuchen*. Babka, beloved of New York Jewish families, shares character-istics with both of these last two types of cake: it is a yeasted dough which is twisted and folded to fit in its pan. The name means 'grand-mother' in several Eastern European languages and the cake's pleats are supposed to evoke a grandmother's skirts – the place where so many children learn about making and tasting cakes. The cake has now become so thoroughly American that it stars in a *Seinfeld* sketch where it is the basis for an argument between Jerry Seinfeld and his friend Elaine over the best dinner party gift (the argument lasts so long that all of the chocolate-filled babkas have gone, and they have to resort to a second-rate cinnamon one). One of the earliest books on Pennsylvania cookery, a work of fiction-cum-recipe-book, *Mary at the Farm and Book of Recipes Compiled During her Visit Among the 'Pennsylvania Germans'*, published in 1901, devoted a whole chapter to cakes. German speakers brought specialist skills too; pastry dishes like strudel and potica required the fine dough to be stretched out so thinly that the pattern on the tablecloth was visible through it, before being covered in a nut or spiced fruit filling, and rolled up for baking. (Potica is a national dish in Slovenia, Serbia and Croatia and is popular in many of the areas immigrants settled in the States.) German cakes quickly became an enduring and defining part of life in these regions.

Perhaps more importantly, the Dutch and the Germans, like the English and the Scandinavians, brought a tradition for social occasions featuring cake – usually breakfast, or a mid-morning or mid-afternoon break. These habits formed an intrinsic part of this particular foodway, offering a space for leisure and chat, accompanied by a taste of sweetness. This is almost certainly one reason why there is still such a strong tradition of German-type cakes in the United States. The German style of *kaffee und kuchen* was part of Irma Rombauer's family heritage and explains the heavy presence of German cakes in *The Joy of Cooking*. By the time that the first *Betty Crocker Picture Cook Book* was published in 1950, these cakes were mainstream enough to feature heavily (many of them in the 'Breads' chapter because they were based on a yeast dough): streusel coffee cake, *apfel kuchen, kaesa kuchen*; and Hungarian coffee cake, Swedish tea ring and Swedish coffee braid to name but a few.

The Germans, British and Dutch weren't the only ones to bestow a lively legacy on the cake scene in America. One of the most exuberantly colourful and joyful cakes you will find in the States is the green-gold- and purple-topped, and fruit- or preserve-filled Mardi Gras king cake, relation of the British Twelfth Night cake, which we met in Chapter 2; or to give it its original name – and clue as to its origins – the *rosca de reyes* or *gâteau des rois*. King cakes are an essential accompaniment to the pre-Lenten Mardi Gras festivals which take place in many parts of America, but with particular energy in New Orleans, and other towns around the Mississippi and Gulf Coast area. This is real Creole country: an area where Spanish and French influences mix with Mexican, West Indian and Italian, all infused with an underlying tradition of Catholicism from their founding fathers.

The influence of the French and Spanish in America is enormous, both directly in terms of numbers of migrants and indirectly in terms of the trade links they set up between their colonies in the Caribbean, South and Central America, and the American states. Those states which border Mexico to the south are particularly rich in Spanish-influenced culinary traditions, both savoury and sweet, while Florida and New Mexico originated as Spanish colonies. We've already heard about the huge French influence through the centre of the continent – a supremacy they held until the end of the Seven Years War in 1763 when their lands reverted to Spain (and those in Canada to Britain). They came back to France after the fall of Napoleon, whereupon they were almost immediately sold to the Americans under the 50-million-franc 'Louisiana Purchase', which doubled the land mass of the country (the total amount paid, including the cancellation of debts, would be more than $230 million in today's money). There was an ex-American ambassador to France in the White House at the time, complete with his own French chef: Thomas Jefferson. This shifting of cultural influences, plus the influx of African-American slaves and people fleeing the Haitian slave revolt in 1791 made up the unique ethnic mix of the region.

But let's come back to the king cake. It is another bake with yeasted, brioche-like origins, served in a crown shape, much like several of the other European specialities like *kugelhopf* and the French savarin which we will meet later on. Perhaps for this reason king cakes tend to be bought rather than home-baked. It is named for the three kings who visited the infant Jesus on the twelfth night after his birth (Epiphany); the event which marks the start of the Mardi Gras festivities. One of the key features the king cake has in common with the Twelfth Night cake is the hidden trinket – originally a bean, now more often a plastic baby to denote the infant Jesus – which confers good luck on the finder, and the obligation to bring the cake next year! One of the New Orleans companies of merry-makers, the Twelfth Night Revelers, have for years staged a Cake March and dance, presided over by a huge mock cake. This cake contains a series of drawers, each in turn containing slices of real cake, which are given out to the single ladies. The one with the golden bean inside it is nominated the queen of the festivity (suspicious minds say that this is not an entirely random procedure). The bright colours on the top of the real cakes are those adopted by the Mardi Gras festivities and are all associated with the Catholic Church. More generally, of course, the sort of feasting and excess seen – albeit on a grand scale – at the Mardi Gras festivities are symbolic of the dawning of the austere period of Lent and echo the misrule and inversion which we saw goes back to Roman celebrations of Saturnalia. Epiphany is as important a celebration as Christmas in Spain and Mexico, and the time when children receive their presents. Today, there are many famous Mardi Gras festivals around the world, from the huge processions in Rio de Janeiro to the LGBT parades in Sydney.

Spanish and Mexican influences, meanwhile, abound around the border states from Texas to California. Sponge cakes (originally brought from Spain) are often chocolate and flavoured with cinnamon, chilli and vanilla. Mexican and Mexican-American families still make and buy sweetened *pan de muerto*, or 'bread of the dead' to commemorate their lost loved ones. These are shaped loaves of sweetened dough, topped with a sweet glaze and decorated with bones, skulls and other symbols of death and remembrance. Like many of the other soul cakes we met in Chapter 2, these are meant for celebrations rather than mourning, and are traditionally eaten on All Souls' Day, a commemoration brought to Mexico by the Spanish, and enmeshed with elements of an ancient Aztec summer festival to celebrate the passage of the dead to a new life. In an increasingly familiar pattern, some of the breads of the dead now contain a lucky trinket; in this case, a plastic skeleton.

Another baking tradition common across the Spanish-influenced lands of Southern and Central America (and taken thence to parts of the States) is the use of milky caramels as a topping or ingredient for cakes. One of the most famous is the *tres leches* cake, which is a sponge topped with a syrup made from three milks: condensed milk, evaporated milk and whole milk. This particular cake was apparently invented by those savvy manufacturers of condensed milk towards the end of the nineteenth century but the tradition of baking with caramel syrups (or *dulce de leche* in Spanish and *doce de leite* in Portuguese), goes back much further. Several stories pinpoint its origins with the early nineteenth-century maid to a military general – either Argentinian or French depending on the narrator – who overhears what she thinks is an attempt on her boss's life and so rushes to tell his men, leaving her milky drink warming unattended. In all the stories there is a happy ending: the supposed threat turns out to be a peace treaty negotiation, and the drink has thickened and burnt to the point of becoming *dulce de leche*. In fact, the syrup is very similar to French *confiture de lait*, which we know was being made in the fourteenth century. It is made by slowly heating sugar and milk (or nowadays, by heating a tin of condensed milk in a pan – with attendant risks of explosion) and thus differs from caramel, which is melted sugar alone. *Tres leches* cakes often appear at the important *quinceañera* coming of age celebrations for a girl's fifteenth birthday in much of Latin America. *Dulce de leche* is also sticky enough to be used as a filling in rolled cakes, or as a filling in layer cakes. Eggy custards are another common filling for cakes and tarts in Spain, Portugal and their ex-colonies, possibly to use up egg yolks once the whites had been employed in clarifying sherry.

So far we've been talking about foodways which took many now beloved and familiar cakes around the globe. We have seen that they still mean a great deal to the descendants of those original migrants and settlers because they form part of a shared heritage and denote celebration and family bonds. Let's turn now to a few examples of cakes which the melting pot of America has made its own, and see again what they say about people's identities.

We've already seen that all of the early food habits of the American colonists were brought from elsewhere, although they were soon adapted to local produce, and sometimes also to the influences of Native American habits and know-how. The occasions for cake-eating were also imported: namely the impressive English-style afternoon teas catered by rich plantation owners; the breaks for *kaffee* and *kuchen* brought by wealthier German speakers; and the sweet desserts and celebration parties which were a feature of almost all immigrant groups. So it is, perhaps, unsurprising that it took quite a long time for anything coherently and distinctively American to emerge.

There has been fierce debate over the question of whether there is truly an American cuisine, or whether it is built entirely on the back of earlier traditions. When it comes to cake, we can certainly identify a range of attributes which slowly started to emerge as distinctive. It's also worth noting in passing that the Brits also have something of an identity crisis about their national cuisine despite their much longer history; but again, *cake* actually proves to be one of the most distinctive features of the national diet, perhaps because it arose from a combination of specific historical trends (access to food types whether domestically or from imperial sources), and the development of sociability and customs (teatime; the class divide; the willingness to follow domestic instruction and new trends). In all of these regards American bakers had what turned out to be quite different tastes and priorities from those elsewhere: first, they loved to bake – the best beloved of American cakes were all originally home-made, unlike the professional creations of French pâtisseries which we will visit in Chapter 8. This was related to the fact that in the early decades of mass immigration there were relatively few professional bakers (and many of those who came were of German origin). At the same time, many people lived in fairly isolated rural areas where there was little access to bought goods, but where butter and eggs were fairly freely available: at the end of the eighteenth century only about 200,000 of the country's four million inhabitants were *not* farm-dwellers. Fuel, meanwhile, was cheap, in contrast to parts of England, where firing up the stove was an expensive business. Second, American bakers loved colour and novelty, perhaps allied to the optimism and wealth experienced by the top half of society in the late nineteenth century's 'Gilded Age'. Third, although they were not afraid to embrace complex baking projects (think of the angel food cake), American bakers were generally quicker to take on the new chemical raising agents (and the instant cake mix) than their European counterparts, where the tradition of yeast-raised cakes persisted for much longer. In America, in contrast, the light, moist layer cake was queen.

Certainly, American bakers did not remain wedded to their British heritage of rich fruit cakes for long. They soon lost most of their fruit and brown sugar, in favour of the rich whiteness of pound or Savoy cake (a lighter, butterless sponge with a smaller proportion of flour to sugar and egg). Appearances started to matter, and especially cakes which made an impression on the buffet table: even the ascetic Catherine Beecher included recipes for the popular pair of silver and gold cakes (one made with egg whites and one with yolks), often cut to show their insides and presented alternately down the table. Layer cakes were also making an appearance by the 1830s and 40s, consisting of two or three (or sometimes many more) cakes stacked on top of each other, and with a bright slick of jam showing in between each one. Meanwhile pearl ash had caught on as an effort-free leavening agent, although one had to be cautious with the amounts to avoid the soapy taste in cakes which weren't heavily spiced. We've already seen that the publication of several recipes containing pearl ash in Amelia Simmons' *American Cookery* caused a storm among British bakers who had not previously heard of it. Still, it seems that American women were much earlier and more willing adopters than the Europeans, who regarded chemical leaveners as undesirable adulterants. They ushered in an era of simple formula cakes which were lighter on ingredients, and by extension, on the purse, like the 1, 2, 3, 4 cake which was popular by the end of the Civil War (consisting of one cup of butter, two of sugar, three of flour, and four eggs). Americans still refer to this cake as a 'yellow cake'. Convenience and reliability became bywords, further enabled by the spread of enclosed ovens.

This was the era when American cakes became really impressive, the era of the angel food cake in particular, which shouts so loudly of wealth and leisure. If we're thinking about baking with what you have on hand, then the angel cake denotes abundance, and also reliable technology: the oven, and the specialist cookware to support the cake's many needs. The stylish tea tables of the Gilded Age would invariably feature an angel food, alongside many other tinted, frosted and layered offerings, as appealing to the eye as to the palate. The disdain for Old World 'decadence' had been replaced by a desire for highfalutin' French entertaining, and cake was an integral part of the party scene. And while the authoritative *Encyclopedia of Food and Drink in America* tells us that the era of the layer cake ended with the Gilded Age, they have retained an unmistakeable niche in the American cake canon. The first Betty Crocker Big Red Book of 1950 stated that no cake is so glamorous as 'the typically American concoction of richly tender layers, crowned with luscious, creamy icing.' In fact, 'meals are more satisfying, special occasions more festive, with one of these delicious cake creations.' However, as the new century approached, a new baking ingredient appeared which was to transform cake tastes for ever. This, of course, was chocolate.

It is a sign of how entrenched certain foodways were that chocolate had not been incorporated into cake batters before the middle of the nineteenth century, although it had been well known as a drink for over a hundred years (and considerably longer in Latin America where it formed an important part of Mayan and Aztec culture). Its appeal was not in doubt: Linnaeus had placed it in a genus he had named *Theobroma* which translates as 'food of the gods', and the Aztecs used it as a divine offering. The beans and know-how to toast and grind them were brought back to the Old World by the Spanish explorers and we know that it was being tentatively experimented with at the Spanish court by the middle of the sixteenth century. From there it was taken to the Spanish colonies in California, Florida and Louisiana. By the later seventeenth century Europeans were adding chocolate to many different dishes, both sweet and savoury; the Marquis de Sade instructed his wife to send him chocolate 'pastilles' biscuits and cakes in prison (he was most particular about both the type of cake and the icing).

The late addition of chocolate to cakes was probably partly because of its cost and also because of its still quite bitter taste. In 1828 a Dutch chemist called Casparus van Houten worked out how separate out the cocoa butter from cocoa powder, which could then be made milder in flavour by an alkalising process (this type of milder and darker cocoa powder is still known as 'Dutch cocoa' in America). This also made the cocoa easier to dissolve in water, another reason perhaps why it featured in a greater variety of drinks and then puddings and pies before it made its way into cake. In fact, the earliest 'chocolate cakes' which date from the first half of the nineteenth century, were really sponge or yellow cakes with a chocolate icing (interestingly, the Marquis de Sade *did* specify that his cakes have chocolate inside them, but the fact that he had to give such precise instructions and had been previously disappointed suggests that it was not yet a trend). Things were completely different by 1894, when the famous Hershey company started making chocolates which were affordable to the masses. They soon brought in a line of baking chocolate, and Americans took chocolate cakes to their hearts. Imagination was the mother of invention in the case of this still most beloved of cake species, and chocolate cakes grew ever richer, denser and fudgier. Red velvet and devil's food cakes both emerged around the turn of the twentieth century – the former featuring cocoa powder in the mix, the latter a rich chocolate topping. The modern vogue for brownies also has a long pedigree: there are recipes dating back at least to the early twentieth century. The ultra-decadent Mississippi mud cake, on the other hand, was a johnny-come-lately of the 1960s.

The baking traditions that produced a distinctively American cake scene were thus made up of a composite of sometimes quite contradictory trends, like the readiness for highly intensive labour alongside the desire for speed and convenience (it is surely no coincidence that America produced the Bundt cake, which is a quick version of the yeasted German/Austrian/Alsacian *kugelhopf*, creating a whole new type of non-stick bakeware as it did so); or the fondness for colour and height alongside a deep attraction to cakes that are so rich and chocolatey that they fall in on themselves in the oven. These are certainly common trends in the story of American baking, but it was not a homogenous tale. We have already seen hints of the local variety in American cakes – possibly more pronounced than anywhere else save for the huge range of small local cakes and fairings we saw in medieval and early modern Britain. But in certain places cake traditions converge to tell a particularly interesting story. The Deep South is one such place.

Collectively, the people of the Southern states of the USA (loosely, those of the pre-Civil War Confederacy) have a very sweet tooth. Fully half of many Southern cookbooks are devoted to sweet things, especially cakes, and they are often towering confections of colour and mallowy delight. Southern bakers are historically innovators of the highest order, partly because of their love of entertaining, partly because their cakes require considerable skill, and partly, and perhaps most uniquely, because they bake in a tradition of cultural crossover, albeit one with a long and tense history: that of relations between Anglo-Americans and African-Americans.

The historic reliance on slave labour is quite possibly the reason that many of the distinctive Southern cakes are so labour intensive: in the Deep South the layer cake is truly queen of all the cakes. The social system was built on the English plantation model, so afternoon tea and teatime entertaining were soon an established part of Anglo-American society, catered for by African-American cooks, slaves and indentured servants. The angel food cake is thought to have originated in the South; it certainly appeared in cookbooks of that region before any other, and it is also a popular cake for African-American funerals. It has many light, white brethren: the white mountain cake and the enigmatically named Lady Baltimore, for instance, the latter hailing from Charleston in South Carolina and featuring a nutty and fruity filling and a white topping. It is often baked for weddings. Like Sally Lunn, nobody knows who it was named after, or whether the cake was created before or after the publication of Owen Wister's 1906 novel of the same name (which also featured an eponymous cake). Enterprising bakers have spawned a whole family of relations for her though: the Lord Baltimore is the traditional gold (yolk-rich) partner to his lady's silver, while the *Betty Crocker Cookbook* featured 'Baby Baltimore Cakes' too, with the yellow tint of their father and the fruity, nutty filling of their mother. The South has produced several other cakes named for local notables: the layered orange and lemon Robert E. Lee cake (named for the Confederate Civil War general, although probably in his honour rather than created for him, since recipes appear only after his death in 1870). It is still made in his honour in Virginia. Also the Lane cake, created by Emma Rylander Lane of Alabama, featuring an egg-white sponge in four layers, filled with a buttery, egg-yolk-rich, whiskey-spiked filling, and topped with a boiled white icing. It had been a prize-winner at the county fair in Columbus, Georgia, and featured in the novel *To Kill a Mockingbird*, where all the whiskey in it made the little girl Scout 'tight'. Both are time-consuming works of art, whose names evoke the pride in the history and traditions of the region.

The long growing season and fertile soil of the area produce a huge variety of luscious fruits as well as sugar, sorghum and soft winter flour, and they all find their way into the local bakes, as do other more exotic goods imported into the region's ports. One classic example is the hummingbird cake, which sings with sweetness, bananas and pineapples (it allegedly made eaters 'hum' with happiness, although others say it is named for the nectar-loving national bird of Jamaica, which may have inspired it). Tinned condensed milk is another popular cake ingredient as the region is not one of cow-keepers, hence the love of caramel cakes which appear in print from the 1870s, as well as the famous Florida Key lime pie.

Many of these cakes have lasted for generations and now have universal appeal. But their origins as treats of the (white) wealthy class, often baked by black slaves or servants, should give us food for thought. That said, while it would be wrong to skate over the economic and social conditions of the enslaved and poor black population, it is worth noting that it was often they who held the knowledge on how to create these sweetened calling cards for society ladies, working from recipes given to them by women who had probably never made them themselves. The highest-profile black cook of the antebellum era was a man named Hercules, who was slave cook for George Washington (and baked renowned currant cakes). We know that African-American cooks often brought aspects of their own cooking knowledge to plantation kitchens, and carried new tastes back into their homes. Cake was not a major feature in the diets of antebellum black workers and it was a treat to be savoured when it was, but it was occasionally baked in easy-to-find receptacles like tin cans, which were buried in the fire's ashes. These cakes often featured the flavours that formed part of the bakers' own foodways, like ginger and molasses. Other cake-shaped staples were cooked on improvised materials, like hoe cakes which were baked either literally on the blade of a hoe or something shaped like one. These are of course much more akin to the earliest version of cakes than the confections being eaten in the plantation Big Houses. Plantation owners and employers did, however, occasionally provide desserts for their workers which included cakes, pies and tarts.

With the ending of slavery many African-Americans went into food service, and a few women started to write their own cookbooks, keen to share their knowledge and create an awareness of their foodways and cultural identity. Two became particularly influential: Mrs Abby Fisher's *What Mrs Fisher knows about Old Southern Cooking* which was published in 1881 (Fisher herself was an ex-slave from South Carolina), and Marion Cabell Tyree, who collected together recipes from 250 ladies from Virginia and neighbouring states and published them as *Housekeeping in Old Virginia* in 1877. The cake section in Tyree's book is voluminous and speaks to the popularity of many of the cakes mentioned already (there must have been a reason why she recommended every baker keep a 'close cake-box' in which to store their baked and cooled cakes). She even suggested that bakers purchase two separate egg beaters, one for egg yolks and one for egg whites. The reason for this soon becomes clear on perusing the selection of cakes on offer: white, white mountain, snow mountain, white mountain ash, silver, delicate and lady cakes all feature large numbers of egg whites, with the requisite accompanying gold cakes. There are also many fruited and citrus cakes, two recipes for Robert E. Lee cakes, a number of marbled and jelly cakes and several chocolate cakes – one including grated chocolate in the batter, the others only in the icing or filling. Clearly this was a society which loved its cakes and which had ingredients to spare. We may think of the early English recipes for 'great cakes' which required twenty eggs, but they made large cakes. In the era in which Tyree was writing it seems it was nothing to include upwards of ten in a family layer cake.

But we should not ignore the fact that the relationship between black cooks and white slave-owners or employers helped to perpetuate an image of black women, in particular, which is very troubling to modern sensibilities. On the one hand, brands like Aunt Jemima, which manufactured the first ready-to-mix pancake batter in 1880, created an image of black women who held expertise and a comfortingly reassuring presence in the kitchen. Right up until the 1980s, packaging on the Aunt Jemima products displayed a very similar image to the original one, of a large woman wearing a headscarf and holding a bowl, pancake flipper, or other baking accessory. On the other hand, feminist scholars and those interested in race have suggested that 'Aunt Jemima' (another domestic goddess who never actually existed, although several different women played her part at different points in time and lent their faces to the advertising) is branded – even fetishised – as a black domestic to a market of servantless white women. Even the name Aunt Jemima came from a song originally sung by field slaves. Since the 1970s the branding has changed, the manufacturers evidently becoming more aware of possible connotations like these. Aunt Jemima is still a black woman, but the associations with slavery or lower status have been removed; her physique has been slimmed down to remove her from the stereotype of the black slave-cook, and she is now branded simply as a African-American working woman of mature years. We may feel uncomfortable thinking about these things when we sit down to an afternoon slice of cake, but it is worth doing so. Cake may be a simple pleasure now, but it does offer a genuine slice through history – and it is not simply a white, Anglo-Saxon one, nor always a happy one.

In the decades after the end of slavery and as African-American families began to gain a little more in the way of purchasing power, cakes became as important a part of entertaining and the female negotiation of pride and competition as they were in white circles. The author Maya Angelou described her grandmother's pride in her caramel cake which was such an acknowledged favourite that none of the other women in her circle dared attempt it. Kathryn Stockett's novel *The Help*, which is set in Jackson, Mississippi in the 1960s, also depicts many scenes where cakes – invariably baked by the African-American maids, like the central character Minny, who is renowned for her caramel cake – are points of pride at sociable gatherings. (Minny also uses her speciality chocolate pie to deliver a particularly memorable lesson to one of the white ladies.)

Baking a cake became big business with the onset of industrialisation, and women were the target market. Towns were burgeoning, railways were linking the country with ever greater speed, prices of foodstuffs were falling, women were staying at home, and advertising was really taking off. In both Britain and America food manufacturers realised that they needed to up their game to stand out from the competition, and started to invest heavily in brand advertising, packaging, give-aways and promotions. The manufacturers of baking powder, flour, condensed milk and chocolate all produced cookbooks, and pro-motional recipes appeared on their packaging alongside innumerable giveaways and gimmicks. The fruit growers Ocean Spray managed to use promotions like these to popularise cranberry muffins; pineapple upside-down cake got a boost from a 1925 contest for pineapple recipes organised by the Hawaiian Pineapple Company (later known as Dole's after its founder). A baker named, appropriately enough, Harry Baker (actually, an insurance salesman by profession), launched a revolutionary new cake which featured salad oil, touted by its promoters as the only genuinely new cake for a hundred years. He kept his recipe secret for years before selling it to General Mills in 1947, not coincidentally the time when post-war bakers were eager for innovation. Baker's bake was called chiffon cake and it was both moist and easy to make as the ingredients were almost all piled in together into one bowl. General Mills released the recipe in 1948 in an article in *Better Homes and Gardens* magazine, and then in a recipe booklet called *Betty Crocker Chiffon Cake Recipes and Secrets*, all, naturally, featuring its own brand of Softasilk Cake Flour. The *Betty Crocker Cookbook* summed up the charms of the chiffon cake in the words, 'Light as angel food, rich as butter cake'. I tried it: they were right.

The other really important baking innovation of the twentieth century was launched by Procter & Gamble in 1911 and was another truly North American ingredient: the butter substitute vegetable shortening Crisco. It was cheaper than butter, kept well, lent extra tenderness to baked goods, and was marketed as the product America's housewives hadn't known they had been missing. They believed it and converted in droves. The marketing of Crisco was exceptionally well conceived and contrasts completely with the reception received by margarine on both sides of the Atlantic. Despite widespread exposure and some acceptance during the Second World War, margarine did not manage to shake off its image as something unnatural and synthetic until the discovery of the ill effects of saturated fats in butter in the 1980s. Somehow, Procter & Gamble managed to bypass this, despite the fact that their product was also made via the process of hydrogenation, or the forcing of hydrogen into a liquid fat. In doing so they succeeded in marketing Crisco as a hygienic and safely manufactured product in a way that margarine makers had tried to but failed. It helped that a well-known domestic economist, Marion Harris Neil, editor of the *Ladies' Home Journal* was enlisted to write *The Story of Crisco* (1913). It also helped that, as we have seen, several high-profile rabbis endorsed its utility for Jewish bakers as it was not only kosher, but also 'parev' (it did not contain dairy or meat produce and so could be used in the production of either dairy or meat dishes). However the key factor for success seems to have been a total saturation of the market in leaflets, offers, products and recipes. Crisco was taken to Americans' hearts and has never looked back (a butter-flavoured version is now available too). American recipes for cakes and cookies are still far more likely to include shortening than British ones, and for many, shortening is still synonymous with Crisco.

The lifting of wartime restrictions on food led to a raft of other innovations in baking. Cola drinks started to make an appearance in cakes, starting in the South (Coca-Cola and Dr Pepper are both based in the South: Georgia and Texas respectively). Perhaps even more surprising was the key ingredient in the 'mystery cake' which started to appear in recipes from the 1920s. Possibly the manufacturers felt that calling their new offering 'tomato soup cake' was a step too far, but that's what it contained and it proved to be very popular. The original was a spiced layer cake containing allspice, cinnamon and cloves as well as the can of soup, sandwiched and iced with a cream cheese frosting. American housewives were quite familiar with condensed soup as an ingredient in savoury dishes, so they were more receptive to its inclusion in baked goods than they might otherwise have been. Campbell's Soup was another savvy marketer: their recipe book sold more than a million copies in the 1950s, taking sales of its soups to a million cans per day.

*

Today, many of the cakes which started off as distinctively local or national affairs have become thoroughly international, largely thanks to the internet, food bloggers and the growing interest in food history which they facilitate. International coffee shop chains think nothing of placing a red velvet cake next to a Victoria sandwich, or a rose-infused sponge next to a coconut one. Layer cakes are the indulgence de rigueur wherever Western-style cakes are served, and no longer a speciality of the Southern states. Second-generation bakers are always more likely to embrace the foods of their new land than their migrant parents, resulting in further modifications and fusions. Yet some heirloom cakes do live on in isolation, either because they are too labour-intensive to travel well, because they rely on local ingredients, or because they simply happen not to have piqued the interest of an influential foodie. The Appalachian stack cake remains unique to its region; ditto the Smith Island cake, and come to that, the Twinkie and the mini Battenberg tend not to travel outside speciality import shops for expats. For home-baked creations are not the only favourites which travellers take with them in their memories of home. In the next chapter we will meet some of the more manufactured goodies which can sweeten a cake lover's day

7

A CAKE JUST
FOR YOU

A search for birthday cakes on the online pinboard site Pinterest brings up so many results that the site generates an automatic list of sub-categories. These range from the straightforward common searches you might expect (men, women, kids, easy, chocolate, twenty-first); through to the imaginative (car, awesome, DIY, vintage); the on-trend (*Minions*, *Frozen*, Lego); and on to the mind-bogglingly specialist: a cake for your dog, anyone? I clicked on it just to make sure and can verify that it does consist mainly of cakes *for* your canine, with a smattering of dog-shaped human offerings and the odd rogue cake for a cat. The fact is that almost every occasion and every interest has a cake to serve it now. Whatever you do, whatever you achieve, and whoever you are, there is a cake that will try to make you feel good about yourself. In the next chapter we will examine cakes which are good for looking at as well as eating. But for now, we will confine ourselves to the occasions when a cake is all about you: birthdays, commemorations, guilty snack-time pleasures. We have already met a lot of special commemorative cakes on our journey, starting with the mythical cakes which are forever associated with King Alfred, through Queen Victoria's sandwich, the Lady Baltimore and the condensed

milk *tres leches* cakes that are baked across Latin America to mark a
girl's coming of age, or *quinceañera*. Now we will draw them together
into an honour roll of cakes that are all about one special person. Let
us start with that Pinterest inspiration: the birthday cake.

Birthday cakes are really only partly about the birthday person. They
are also about the cake provider. For every child (or grown-up) who
gets the special candlelit treatment, there is someone who made or
bought that cake as an expression of love – and, let's be frank, sometimes also an expression of that competitive edge that goes with so
many aspects of motherhood. But the principal joy of the cake is
marking someone out as special for a day. The cake itself, the burning
candles (traditionally one for each year of the birthday person's life),
the formal procession to deliver the cake to the head of the table,
and the chorus of 'Happy birthday to you!' all serve to heighten the
sense of occasion and the rite of passage. Finally, the cake is cut and
distributed to the guests in a form of junior largesse. The commonalities
with the more formal and 'adult' wedding cake are striking.

Birthday cakes only really became popular in the eighteenth
century as part of the same watershed expansion in ingredients and
equipment that we have seen several times already. Occasion cakes
could now be a special treat for the masses rather than just the elite.
It's also worth noting, however, that the recording of ages wasn't
always very accurate prior to this, and many people outside the higher
social echelons did not know either exactly how old they were or the
precise date of their birth. This changed definitively in Britain with
the 1836 Births and Deaths Registration Act which for the first time
mandated that a record be made of a person's *birth* as opposed to a
church register of their baptism (which could be several months
or even years later – or not at all if the family was not Church of
England). Candles have been used to decorate sweet offerings since

ancient times, though – we saw in Chapters 1 and 2 that smoke and fire both had great significance in pagan and Roman traditions, and the Greeks used candles to make sweet offerings glow like the moon. In fact it is thought that the round shape of the birthday cake stems from celebrations to mark the birthday of Artemis, Greek goddess of the moon.

The early Christians did not commemorate birthdays; for them the birth of a child was a dangerous time as it marked the arrival of a new soul who was tainted with original sin. Gradually, however, the celebration of Christ's birthday became more popular (hence the emergence of Christmas as a time of celebration), and this started to be transferred to birthdays more generally. The traditions of candles and cakes did not unite in popular tradition until the Middle Ages, however, when the German *kinderfest* emerged. This was a day of celebration for the birthday child, but also one of caution as evil spirits were supposed to be particularly predatory on that day. A candle known as the *lebenslicht*, or 'light of life' was therefore left burning all day to protect the child, and it was only after the evening meal had been eaten that it could be extinguished and the cake cut and consumed. This special candle soon became the 'one for luck' or 'one to grow on' which some families still include in addition to those marking out the child's age. The smoke from the candles as they were blown out was supposed to carry the birthday child's wishes up to heaven. These traditions were passed around Europe and on to German-settled parts of America, where they took hold as an increasingly integral part of birthday celebrations.

Birthday cakes took on two further attributes over the nineteenth century. The first was their specialisation as fancier layer cakes, like the ones becoming generally fashionable in America, but with added decorations marking them out as something special. The second was their adoption as part of the growing consumer culture surrounding children – literally a business of childhood. Historians of childhood have offered a number of reasons behind this trend, including the shrinking of family sizes which offered parents the opportunity to spend more money on each child, and the lowering of infant and child mortality which may have induced them to invest more emotionally in them too (though this is a rather dated and tricky argument which scholars no longer find very convincing). As middle-class families grew more affluent and consumer-oriented, so businesses rushed to provide them with ways of spending their money, from cribs and perambulators to toys, clothing and the wares to go with birthdays, christenings, confirmations and bar/bat mitzvahs. The cake, like the banners, balloons, special outfits and new toys, were all a new and growing aspect of the rituals marking the important events of childhood. The intimate portrayals of loving family occasions in Queen Victoria's family (including family Christmases with all the children present in informal, tumbling joy) only served to strengthen this change in spending habits and make them more fashionable. By the later nineteenth century, professional bakers were starting to customise birthday cakes with personalised messages, and it is no coincidence that the famous 'Happy Birthday to You!' song (a twist on an 1893 Kentucky school welcome song 'Good Morning to All' written by sisters Patty and Mildred Hill) had started to become popular by the 1920s and 30s. In theory the song has been under copyright since 1935, but in 2015 a judge in California ruled that this covered only one specific piano arrangement, leaving countless children free to enjoy the song unencumbered. By the turn of the century birthdays, and especially children's birthdays, were big business.

Birthday cakes are still now particularly associated with children, especially the more lavishly decorated and colourful ones. There are shelves of books (and reams of Pinterest boards) available to help you make a cake in the shape of a princess, a favourite animal, a football or a character from the latest children's blockbuster, and many a mother has stayed up into the night, cursing as she forms sugar paste animals, tries to make candies stick on to a doll's cake skirt, or layers on the papier mâché to make a child-sized Mexican piñata. I have been there myself (including the cursing), slavishly trying to copy the picture of a train cake in my *Australian Women's Weekly Children's Birthday Cake Book* for my son's first birthday – complete with carriages bearing popcorn. I will shortly be returning to the field for his third birthday, this time with the boy himself supervising and exercising quality control. Baking a birthday cake is one of the most anxiety-inducing tasks a home baker can try because on their success hinges the happiness of the loved one (let's face it, taste is secondary when it comes to young children's birthdays). Professional bakers do a storming trade in themed and gorgeously decorated birthday cakes, personalised with names, messages and family jokes. My musical youngest sister's twenty-first birthday was marked by a piano-shaped cake, complete with a musician wearing the very same dress the birthday girl wore to her party (that part required a bit of subterfuge and planning on the part of her mother). My tenth birthday featured a cake shaped like a hockey stick, not because I was good at sport, but the reverse: I was such a skinny child that the need to find me a lightweight hockey stick for school had become a family joke. These stories are one of the key reasons that birthday cakes are special: they make memories in which the birthday person is quite literally, the star of their own party. The original 1980s edition of the same *Australian Women's Weekly* book that I pored over has its own Facebook page where thirty-something-year-olds reminisce fondly about their child-hood birthday parties (the duck-shaped cake with the popcorn coating is as warmly remembered as the scary-looking clown and the jelly-filled swimming pool). The Australian news site news.com.au winningly called it 'the best book ever written in this country' in

March 2015, and comedian Josh Earle has completed an entire stand-up comedy tour based on it.

We don't start to see recipes specifically for birthday cakes until the late nineteenth century, but cookbook authors had been including special cakes for children for several decades longer. These were distinguished in one of two ways: either they were appropriate for children because they were plain and thus wholesome, or they were decorated in a way to make them appealing to the young. Mrs Beeton's famous 1861 *Book of Household Management* gave several cake recipes of the first type: a 'nice plain cake for children', and 'a common cake, suitable for sending to children at school' (the latter containing clarified dripping, fresh yeast, dried fruit and spice; presumably one of the attractions being that it would keep well). Fellow British cookery writer Esther Hewlett Copley had made the rather charming distinction between 'a good family cake' (another dough-based mixture) and 'a nice family cake' in her 1834 *The Good Housekeeper's Guide*, both containing dried fruit. Both *Good Housekeeping* and the magazine of the Women's Institute, *Home and Country*, included articles on putting together a school tuck box in the 1920s, in which cake was an integral component: 'really substantial cakes are *sine qua non* of the tuck-box' said one author. These cakes were plain and hearty, partly because they lasted a long time, but also reflecting ideas about children's diets, which generally also leaned towards the plain and hearty rather than the sweet and indulgent.

However, it is the more joyful varieties which come closer to the modern birthday cake. Mrs Porter's *New Southern Cookery Book* of 1871 included a recipe entitled 'Little Folks' Joys', presumably small cakes given that they are 'joys' in the plural, and containing sour cream, baking soda and 'flavor to taste'. They were, according to the directions, 'nicest eaten fresh and warm'. American Eliza Leslie's *75 Receipts for Pastry, Cakes and Sweetmeats* (1828) made no mention of birthday baking, but Catherine Beecher earmarked several recipes for children: like Mrs Beeton, a 'Good Child's Cake' and a 'Child's Feather Cake', both based on dough, although only the former was specified as a 'raised dough'. She also included recipes for a 'Little Girl's Pie' which was a crusted apple and molasses affair, a 'Little Boy's Pie' which was essentially a rice pudding, and a 'Birthday Pudding', which was made up of bread and butter soaked in milk, and layered with fruit. By 1911 the new revised edition of Fannie Farmer's authoritative *The Boston Cooking School Cook Book* still only included one recipe called a birthday cake – this time an orangey fruit and nut butter cake with the rather surprising inclusion of sherry – but this was soon to change.

By the 1920s the language of celebration and childhood was evolving: in 1928, the British version of *Good Housekeeping* published an article on 'cakes for the party', which were styled as 'perhaps the most important item of all at the party, particularly in the eyes of the small folk'. And by the post-war era the end of rationing and the retreat to middle-class suburbia had brought a burst of colour to the kitchen, and recipes for cakes in all sorts of special shapes, either baked in moulds or cut and assembled from large square cakes. Amateur cake decorating was really taking off too, and a slew of new decorating products were entering the mass market. Their services no longer required for war work, mothers and wives had more time to spend on baking and indulging the birthday requests of their little ones (we will return to whether this was an altogether good thing for the women involved in the final chapter).

By the time that Irma Rombauer was putting together *The Joy of Cooking* in 1930, these sorts of cakes were much more common. Shaped moulds were accessible enough that she could specify a cake made in the shape of a lamb in the first edition of *The Joy of Cooking*. She suggested completing the picture by covering the cake in white icing and grated coconut, and tying a blue ribbon with a small bell around the lamb's neck. It was not specifically envisaged as a birthday cake, but she did say that it was a favourite with children. In one of her classic frank but drily witty asides she counselled the baker not to worry if the lamb's head came off when removing it from the tin: 'it probably will'. The damage could be mended with the judicious use of toothpicks. This sort of fanciful cake sculpture was not at all new, though: British food historian Dorothy Hartley recorded 'hedgehog cakes' which were baked in an oval shape, soaked in sherry and decorated with spines made from split almonds. She did not give a date but said they were based on sponge cake, which would suggest a late eighteenth-century provenance (there are certainly recipes extant from the mid-nineteenth century). Society chef Alexis Soyer, whom we will meet in the next chapter, went a step further, creating *trompe l'oeil* dishes like 'Haunch of lamb *glacé en surprise*'; the surprise being the fact that the cut of meat was actually an ornately decorated cake, right down to the currant jelly and wine gravy. However, baking shaped and decorated cakes for children's birthday parties was undoubtedly a part of the changing experience of childhood for the leisured classes in the post-war era, and it soon became more widespread still. One study of 200 families with young children in the north of England in the 1980s showed that 93 per cent of the children had had a cake for their birthday, across all the social classes.

Birthday cake traditions abound worldwide, but there are very different customs dictating the traditional shape, decoration and occasion. According to cake historian and baker Krystina Castella, birthday cakes, or *lagkage*, in Denmark are layered affairs, filled with jam or custard and decorated with piped whipped cream, fruit, and small Danish flags. In Austria, butterfly cakes are common for birthdays, while in China, longevity peach buns (steamed yeasted dumplings filled with lotus seed or bean paste) mark the special occasion. Russian children receive a fruit pie with their name on it, and Egyptian birthday cakes feature fruits and flowers on top to symbolise life and new growth. Many countries also have traditional cakes to mark the birth of a baby, the sweetness of the cake evoking the sweet hopes for the child's future. In China, steamed *ang ku kueh* cakes are red and shaped like a tortoise shell – tortoises being long-lived, and the colour red denoting courage and success. They are eaten at a child's first month birthday, and at birthdays of the elderly to ensure long life. In Korea, sweet rice and bean cakes are made for the child's 100-day birthday and placed around the house to bring happiness and good fortune. And in many Western countries we have variants on the christening cake, which is traditionally a layer saved from the parents' wedding cake, and the much newer and endlessly customisable baby shower cake. The latter are sometimes even used to reveal the baby's sex to the gathered friends and family: the first slice reveals either a pink or a blue interior.

Birthday cakes are a particularly ritualistic form of food which often symbolise family relationships. Since cake is not a vital foodstuff or one that confers rank on a day-to-day basis, it has traditionally been an acceptable way to raise a child's status for their own special day. All of this means that cake often has a special set of meanings for children, who are usually naturally predisposed to like sweet, calorie-dense foods, and the treat-like occasions when cake is served. If we think more about it we can see why: these tend to be informal occasions where the usual rules of mealtimes don't quite apply, and where it is not unusual for children to have more leeway and status than in other food encounters. Cakes appear often in children's books, and they usually symbolise happiness, informality and familiarity, where children are often in charge. When Lucy Pevensie enters the strange world of Narnia through the back of an old wardrobe she is reassured by the tea she is given by Mr Tumnus the fawn which includes sugar-topped cake (although those familiar with the story will know that the tea is actually a stalling device to keep her in Narnia while Mr Tumnus contacts the White Witch). The animal characters in *The Wind in the Willows* are never far from their next tea or picnic, and when the dwarves turn up unexpectedly at Bilbo Baggins' house at the start of *The Hobbit* they all cheerfully demand cakes. Bilbo had, luckily, made two himself that afternoon. The lively English schoolboy star of Richmal Crompton's *Just William* series, which were first published in the 1920s, is an inordinate lover of cake, which usually gets him into trouble. William ruins one family teatime by inadvertently bringing a burglar along (he eats half the cake), and a tea party held for his older siblings by eating most of the spread before the guests arrive. After another misadventure during which William and his friend Ginger are treated to tea elsewhere, but which results in the stoppage of William's pocket money, solace is found in the memory that '[t]hey were jolly good cakes, wasn't they?'

Cake isn't always what is expected of it in children's books though, and this is often a way to illustrate a world tipped upside down. The child reader knows what cake *should* be, so the unexpected is a signal of inversion, comedy, or something going wrong. The cake that Alice finds at the bottom of the rabbit hole in Wonderland has the words 'Eat Me' studded on it in currants, but it has a most unusual effect in making her grow very tall. The Mad Hatter's tea party, on the other hand, is a riot of confusion – perhaps why the only food mentioned is bread and butter. The adolescent Anne of Green Gables does her best to impress the new vicar's wife with a cake she has made herself – but disastrously adds anodyne liniment instead of vanilla, and Miss Trunchbull, the mean headmistress in Roald Dahl's *Matilda* finds a particularly cruel punishment for a greedy child by making him eat an entire chocolate cake in front of the school (her punishment backfires as he heroically completes his task). These scenes all make sense to children because they understand that cake is meant to be a pleasure and a treat, and they are familiar with the types of occasion when it appears. Even a small child will know that eating a cake in the tub like the Cat in the Hat is out of order, and it's the child characters who tell the Cat so.

Being a birthday guest of honour will get you special attention – a boon for attention lovers and a nightmare for the shy – and a snap for the family album. But it brings much more for the children of the rich and famous. The British press worked themselves into a state of high excitement over third-in-line-to-the-crown Prince George's first two birthday parties in 2014 and 2015, but since the royal family is usually rather private about such matters, they could only speculate on the arrangements (though with a party planning business in the family on his mother's side it seems likely that the cake was an important feature; his Uncle James supplies cupcakes by post, after all). According to her erstwhile personal chef, Queen Elizabeth II has requested the same chocolate cake for her birthday every year for the last eighty years, meaning that it has been a favourite since she was nine years old. (It is an egg-yolk rich affair with a cream and chocolate ganache filling, since you ask.) The Queen's mother, meanwhile, first charmed her husband-to-be (later King George VI, then known simply as Bertie) at a children's birthday party where she gave him the glacé cherry from the top of her cake. Her fondness for cake continued into later life; it was apparently her nickname, and her own favourite was a flourless chocolate number.

Today the tabloid newspapers are full of the latest celebrity birthday cake, usually outrageously over the top creations full of references to the celebrity's signature style, latest film or best-known pastimes. One wonders how often they have actually chosen their cake as opposed to being presented with it by sponsors and fans. Prince Charles apparently received six cakes for his sixty-fifth birthday from well-wishers. And although Henry VIII may have left no record of his favourite cakes, one was baked to celebrate the 500th birthday of one of his royal palaces, Hampton Court, in 2015: a three-foot high, five-tier creation (one for each century) featuring images depicting the history of the palace and created by cake specialists Choccywoccydoodah.

Residents of the White House, meanwhile, have made a big, and very public, splash with their birthday cakes. Probably the most memorable presidential birthday was JFK's forty-fifth in 1962, which was the one made famous by Marilyn Monroe's sultry rendition of 'Happy Birthday, Mr President'. If it weren't for that more people might remember the cake, which was a huge, tiered affair with an edible depiction of the presidential seal on the side (the seal recently went on auction with a guide price of $5,000). More than 15,000 people attended JFK's party that year as it doubled as a fundraiser for the Democratic Party; it raised enough money to wipe out the party committee's debts. In 1961 JFK had been presented with a birthday cake of equally gargantuan scale, modelled in the shape of the White House.

JFK was not the first president to use a birthday as a fundraising occasion. Franklin D. Roosevelt had a 'Birthday Ball' every year to raise money for the Georgia Warm Spring rehabilitation spa where he had had therapeutic treatment for the after-effects of polio (they were later expanded into the famous fundraising 'March of Dimes'). His favourite birthday cake was an old-fashioned fruit cake, while his wife favoured angel food. Bill Clinton's fiftieth party in 1996 featured a giant cake shaped like the American flag with the name of each state iced on to it, and raised $10 million for the Democratic Party. Mamie Eisenhower, wife of President Dwight D., meanwhile, elevated birthday celebrations to a new level with televised celebrity-studded parties and fundraising galas (Mamie was associated with the Women's Republican League of Washington), and traditionally, her favourite carnation cake, which was made for her by the White House chef in 1955 and every year thereafter. It was an orange-spiked vanilla cake with a lavish fondant icing, and decorated with pink carnation flowers made from intricately moulded almond paste. Mrs Eisenhower also keenly observed her family's birthdays, and those of her household staff too, each of whom was baked a cake during her time in the White House.

The early presidents of the United States left less of a mark when it comes to birthday celebrations, and although there is an annual Presidents' Day holiday on the third Monday in February (in honour of Washington's birthday, although Lincoln and any number of other presidents are now also included in the commemoration), there is no specific cake associated with the occasion. There are cakes named for Washington, Lincoln and Jefferson, all first recorded in the late nineteenth century, but usually not created until after the deaths of their namesakes. We can fondly speculate that George Washington enjoyed one of the cake recipes from his wife Martha's family cookbook; they were known for serving a fruited 'great cake' at special functions. Another First Lady, Mary Lincoln, was, meanwhile, a self-taught cake-baker, learning from books like Eliza Leslie's (the Lincoln household was apparently a big consumer of sugar). Lincoln is said to have declared his wife's vanilla almond cake the best he had ever tasted, while James Madison's wife Dolly was famed for a caramel-frosted layer cake. And John Adams, second president, served cakes baked in new ovens on either side of the fireplace at the official opening of the White House in 1801.

Washington and Lincoln might be surprised to find that they have left a legacy in cakes named after them, but others were able to rejoice in that honour during their lifetime. Some even created their eponymous cake themselves. A birthday cake is not the only sort of cake which makes you feel good about yourself, after all.

We've already met some of the cakes which carry someone's name: Sally Lunn, Lady Baltimore, Robert E. Lee and the Lane cake, to name but a few. In the first two cases we don't know who the original inspiration was, if they existed at all. Robert E. Lee did not have any say in the choice of his commemorative cake: it was picked (like Washington and Lincoln's cakes) after his death, but the Lane cake was named proudly by and for its creator. Cakes like the latter can produce a lot of argument. While no one else claimed to have invented the Lane cake, there is suspicious muttering that it was not the first cake of its sort. In the case of the Austrian *Sachertorte* the muttering took the protagonists all the way to the law courts in a battle which lasted over thirty years.

The *Sachertorte*, a single-layered, dry but intensely chocolatey cake with an apricot glaze and a glossy, hard chocolate topping, is one of Vienna's most famous foods. It was invented by a young Franz Sacher in 1832 for his employer, Prince Wenzel von Metternich. So far, so clear. The cake was popular but did not receive undue attention, and Sacher went on to a successful career as a baker. The trouble arose when his son, Eduard, who had tinkered further with the recipe while working at Vienna's Demel bakery, started to serve it at his current establishment, the Hotel Sacher. Just to make matters more complicated, Eduard's son, also called Eduard, subsequently sold the rights to the *Sachertorte* to Demel's. By the 1930s, the two institutions were locked in fierce argument about who could claim to offer the 'original' *Sachertorte*, and what, exactly, that might be. The matter was not resolved until the 1960s, when the Hotel Sacher was awarded the rights to call their cake (which contained a layer of jam in the centre) 'the original *Sachertorte*', and Demel (whose version now has jam on top of the cake and under the chocolate topping) the *Eduard-Sacher-Torte*. The 'original' version can now be tasted worldwide thanks to the hotel's mail order service; but the recipe remains a closely kept secret.

There are many European cakes which are named after their creators, and we will meet more of them in the next chapter; it goes with having a skilled labour force of pâtissiers keen to make their mark on the pastry world. One beautiful and painstaking example from Hungary is the Dobos torte, which consists of many layers of thin cake sandwiched together, topped with a chocolate buttercream frosting and coated in chopped nuts. The top is then adorned with shaped wedges of caramel-soaked cake.

The Dobos torte is a beautiful expression of the European pâtissier's art, but it has a pleasing tale to go with it too. Its inventor, József Dobos, was a showman of the highest order as well as a gifted baker. His shop in Budapest stocked exotic and imported foods at a time (the late nineteenth century) when this was very rare. He travelled widely, wrote cookbooks on French and Hungarian cuisine, and had a fame which extended well beyond the bounds of his home city. It was on one of his journeys that he came across the recipe for buttercream, which was not yet really known in Europe, where creams and custards were still the more popular cake fillings. It was this that really made his many-layered cake – which, with the typical pâtissier's immodesty, he named after himself – stand out, both for its distinctive taste and finish, and also for its keeping qualities. With so many layers, the buttercream preserved the cake's freshness for much longer than many of the other somewhat dry European cakes of the time. He exhibited his new cake at the 1885 National General Exhibition in Budapest and it became a favourite of the Emperor Franz Joseph I and his wife the Empress Elisabeth of Austro-Hungary. All this only increased its cachet even more – as did the fact that, like the Sachers, Dobos refused to share the recipe. The recipe for a fashionable and exclusive cake, it turns out, is worth more than its weight in gold. He did not reveal his secret until after his retirement, but in a remarkable piece of business innovation for the time, he did make his cake available via mail order (using a special box to guarantee its safe passage) and also toured with it to ensure that its popularity remained high. The cake became so famous and so intimately linked with its birthplace that a city-wide celebration was held in Budapest for its seventy-fifth anniversary in 1962. Sadly, Dobos himself died in poverty in 1924, his financial investments gone awry.

The American speciality German chocolate cake is another layered chocolate cake, but its links with European culture go no further than its name. It sports a characteristic caramel coconut-pecan frosting and filling, and is named after the man who inspired it: Sam German, a British chocolatier. He came up with a new type of sweetened dark baking chocolate for his employers, the American brand, Baker's Chocolate Company which was launched in 1852 as Baker's German's Sweet Chocolate. It was a popular baking ingredient in the Southern states of America, but it shot to national fame as a named cake in a 'reader recipe' in a Dallas newspaper. This was not until 1957, however: a good hundred years after the launch of German's chocolate. The cake, which was flavoured with the chocolate, was picked up by other newspapers and caught on, boosting the sales of the brand significantly in the process. The name was soon simplified to German chocolate cake, pushing poor old Sam German's inspiration into the background, and suggesting for ever a further flung history than it really had.

Two of the most famous cakes of the Antipodes have a closer tie to their namesakes: the Pavlova, named for the Russian ballerina Anna Pavlova, and the Lamington, which honoured the late-nineteenth-century governor of Queensland, Baron Lamington. The Pavlova scarcely needs an introduction, so famous has it become: essentially a pillowy, tutu-like cloud of meringue made from a combination of egg white, cornflour and vinegar, topped with fruit and cream, and created in tribute to Anna Pavlova's tour to Australia and New Zealand in 1926.

A CAKE JUST FOR YOU

The honour of being its creator, though, is yet another of those hotly contested baking tales, this time drawing on national rivalries between the two Antipodean countries. Both Australia and New Zealand claim to have been the originator: the Aussies say that it was invented in 1935 at the Esplanade Hotel in Perth, Western Australia; the Kiwis that it was created at a Wellington hotel in the year of Pavlova's tour, although not given its name until the 1930s. This is probably one of those contests which will never be resolved, but the 'Pav' remains a traditional dessert in both countries, where it often graces a hot Christmas day dinner.

The Lamington, on the other hand, has a much more secure history, but plays instead into another sort of common culinary birth story: the happy accident. According to the self-styled Australian Lamington Official Website, the little cubes of chocolate- and coconut-covered cake came into being when one of Lord Lamington's maids accidentally dropped a sponge cake into some melted chocolate. Lord Lamington himself apparently suggested coating it with coconut to make it less messy to eat, and a new national treat was born. A possibly more plausible alternative is that the Lamington was deliberately created as a teatime novelty, or that it was thought up as a way of using up stale cake. Another theory still places its creation at the hands of a noted Queensland baker and cookery book writer, Amy Schauer. Whatever its origin, the recipe was soon published in the *Queensland Ladies Home Journal* as 'Lady Lamington's Chocolate-Coconut Cake' and rapidly became universally popular. Now there is even a National Lamington Day in Australia on 21 July.

There are many other cakes named for specific national heroes but little known outside that country: the tall, almond Finnish Runeberg cake, for example, which is topped with jam and was the favourite breakfast cake of the nineteenth-century poet Johan Ludwig Runeberg. The cake was apparently invented by his wife, Fredrika, and they are traditionally eaten on Runeberg Day on 5 February. The Lady Kenny, a fried cake with a raisin filling, is an Indian favourite named after Lady Charlotte Canning, a lady in waiting to Queen Victoria, and wife of the governor general of India; another is the Bobby Deol, named after a Bollywood star, and a portmanteau affair of brownie, chocolate mousse and cheesecake, covered with chocolate ganache and decorated with a marzipan puppy on the top. All, needless to say, are favourites of Deol himself. And Brazilians enjoy a Marta Rocha torte, which is another cake of unctuous proportions, consisting of layers of white and chocolate cakes, custard, meringue and a topping made from sugar and egg yolk, spun out into threads. This cake has a particularly charming story though: it was named for 1954's Miss Brazil, who lost out on the Miss Universe title apparently because of the (too large) size of her hips. Female bakers back in Brazil created the calorie-dense cake in tribute to this ridiculous slur on female beauty.

We could go on and on, but we will draw this discussion to a close with the Battenberg; one of the most beloved of British cakes, and one named for a commemorative occasion – or was it? The most distinguishing feature of this cake is its chequerboard appearance, made up of four small squares of gold and pink sponge, all wrapped in a thin layer of marzipan. The usual story is that it was named in honour of the marriage of Princess Victoria of Hesse-Darmstadt (one of Queen Victoria's granddaughters), to Prince Louis of Battenberg in 1884. The four panes are commonly thought to represent the four Battenberg princes, and the alternating colour may be a homage to German marble cakes.

Food historian Ivan Day has done some more research on what he notes should rightly be called the Battenburg cake (Battenberg is the modern spelling) and uncovered some very interesting facts. Firstly, there seems to be no evidence at all to support the theory about the four princes; in fact, many of the earliest recipes call for nine squares, not four. Secondly, he found several other recipes from around the same time – the 1890s – for similarly constructed cakes with other names, including a Neapolitan roll and a domino cake. The former looks much like the Battenberg but is coated in pink-tinted coconut – much like the Lamington, in fact. Thirdly, the checked or striped appearance was a common device in late nineteenth-century recipes, appealing to the same love of colour and novelty as we saw in nineteenth-century America. In fact, Day strongly suspects that the original Battenberg was concocted by a cookery author called Mrs Marshall twelve years after the royal wedding. Since she called it a domino cake, the whole connection with Victoria and Louis – and hence the Battenbergs – may be spurious. This is unlikely to bother the many British lovers of this cake, however, who count it among their guiltiest of pleasures.

'Guilty pleasures' is a fitting theme with which to close this survey of 'cakes that make you feel good'. Here, we are talking about the shop-bought pleasures many of us like to indulge in at the end of a hard week or as a special treat; brands which are beloved nationwide – and often not heard of at all in other countries, or even regions. One of the top favourites among these in Britain is a Battenberg Slice (to return to its modern spelling). These were being mass produced before the Second World War, but the iconic brand most people think of today, Mr Kipling, is considerably more recent than that.

Mr Kipling, whose tagline is that he makes 'exceedingly good cakes' is a prime example of the cachet lent to a cake by nostalgia and tradition. The unfussy logo, the kindly and mature voice-over, the depiction of an old-fashioned bakery in TV adverts, all speak to a family business steeped in tradition. In fact, like so many other marketing endeavours, this could hardly be further from the truth: Mr Kipling himself is a fiction, and the company which bears his name was only established in 1967. The brand has been owned by a series of big companies, founded by Rank Hovis McDougall, the flour people, and purchased by Premier Foods in 2007. But consumers still like that sense of heritage; when the packaging was rebranded in 2001 and again in 2004 featuring a more modern logo and a simpler look to the boxes, sales fell. The following year the pictures of the cakes were restored to the front, and the fall-off in sales declined.

Mr Kipling (let us keep fooling ourselves that he exists) has a wide range of cakes and slices in his portfolio, but two of the most beloved are the Mini Battenbergs (about an inch wide and two and a half inches long), and the square, buttercream-topped and pastel-tinted French Fancies, which are a cleaner – may we say it? – more elegant version of a Lamington. The appeal of both seems to lie at least partly in their snack size; they are a treat without being a complete indulgence. Perhaps most importantly for many consumers though, is the fact that they are associated with childhood treats – many snack-buying adults were children when the brand was launched.

When I asked my (British) friends via social media what were their favourite bought snack cakes, the Battenberg came out top. Coming up fast in second place, however, was another supermarket favourite: Jamaican Ginger Cake, manufactured by McVitie's. McVitie's is a Scottish baking company which dates back to 1830. Unlike Mr Kipling, the McVities were a real family whose business started with a single shop in Rose Street, Edinburgh. Gradually the business, still in family hands, was enlarged, and started to focus exclusively on baked goods. In 1892 one of the business associates came up with one of the firm's most beloved and signature products, the digestive biscuit. In 1893, and by now known as McVitie & Price, their credentials as bakers were confirmed when they were asked to bake the wedding cake for the future King George V's marriage. In the 1920s two more leading products were born: in 1925 the chocolate digestive (then known as the Homewheat Chocolate Digestive), and in 1927 the

Jaffa Cake. In 1947 the company made the two-and-a-half-metre high wedding cake for Princess Elizabeth and her consort Lieutenant Philip Mountbatten; a descendant of the Battenbergs, the family name now anglicised.

McVitie's, then, *can* lay claim to all of the attributes of Britishness and heritage that Mr Kipling evokes but can't quite live up to. It is no longer strictly speaking a family firm; since 1948 it has been part of the huge United Biscuits Group. In 2013 it was named one of the most popular brands in Britain, bought by four out of five British households. And although its most popular lines are its chocolate digestives, wheaty chocolate Hobnobs and the Jaffa Cake, the Jamaican Ginger Cake is much beloved for the sticky exterior and dark, tangy flavour which can never quite be recaptured in any home-made version (though Catherine Beechor's sponge gingerbread came close).

The companies who manufacture these products have to tread a fine line between retaining the loyalty of their established customers and attracting newer generations. Fortunately, the nature of childhood nostalgia means that adults who loved these cakes in childhood are likely to give them to their own children too; not only Jamaica Ginger Cake and Battenberg Slices, but also the domed and chocolate-covered Tunnock's Tea Cakes (launched in 1956 and sporting the legend 'Still a family business' alongside a Scottish flag on its packaging), Mini Swiss Rolls and infamous Snowballs. And while many of the companies making these cakes have a presence in foreign markets, they are still predominately British treats. Mr Kipling is now stocked in Coles supermarket in Australia, but a real market presence is said to be difficult to establish – except, presumably, among expats.

The market for snack cakes in America is completely different – full of novelty and with little regard for the 'wholesome, home-baked' image which British brands play up to. In fact, it seems that where snack cakes are concerned, the more fantastic and synthetic the better. So it's both amusing and ironic to discover that many of the most beloved American brands actually have a longer pedigree than Mr Kipling: the iconic Twinkie dates back to 1930. What remains the same, however, is the association with nostalgia and childhood treats. When Leandra Palermo, a writer on the food website Serious Eats, asked readers about their favourite snack foods in February 2014, she attracted seventy-one comments, all full of fervour for particular brands. The names Palermo subsequently drew up into a 'Very Unofficial Snack Cake Field Guide' reads like a list of futuristic food substitutes marketed to children with no regard for spelling: Twinkies (of course), Ho Hos, Ding Dongs, Suzy Qs, Chocolate Zingers and Krimpets among others. What is really noticeable about both her articles and the comments they attracted, is the affection people have for their favourite manufactured cakes – and much of this stems from the fact that they were childhood treats. One commenter thanked the author for the 'trip down memory lane', while others weighed in on the occasions they had eaten their favourite cakes (in lunch boxes, at summer camps and as snacks at home), and also *how* they had enjoyed eating them (variously unrolling, squishing and removing prized layers to eat separately). Many also said that they had not eaten the cakes for years, and that they came from a time when parents weren't too worried about additives and synthetic ingredients.

The best known of this baffling array of creatively named treats is the Twinkie – its fame extending well beyond the States and to places where Twinkies are only to be found in speciality import shops. They are yellow oblong sponges (and very spongy at that), filled with a synthetic sweet cream and sealed into small packs of two. They were invented to make year-round use of the moulds owned by their parent company for making summer strawberry shortcakes, perked up with a banana-flavoured cream filling (this was switched to vanilla because of banana shortages during the Second World War). They have entered popular culture because of their extreme durability, high sugar content, and because they are a throwback to childhood. One of the most popular urban legends about the Twinkie is that it can withstand nuclear disaster (forty-five days is the official maximum shelf life). An episode of the animated cult sitcom *Family Guy* has the Griffin family set up a new community around a Twinkie factory after a millennium bug nuclear holocaust; and sure enough, the cakes have survived. Twinkies were famously invoked by a lawyer defending a San Francisco man from a murder charge in the 1970s, putting forward the theory that his client's high consumption of sugary foods made him unable to exercise proper judgement. It was persuasive enough that the judgement came back as manslaughter rather than murder (and gave rise to the phrase 'Twinkie defence'.) A proposed tax on high-fat foods and drinks in America in 1997 was quickly christened the Twinkie Tax. Also allegedly true is the legend that escaped baboons were lured back to the Ohio Zoo with Twinkies in 1976, while Jimmy Carter apparently had a Twinkie vending machine installed in the White House (this appealing story has been officially denied). President Clinton, however, did put a Twinkie in the 1999 Millennium Time Capsule which was designed to represent America at that point in history. It was later removed in case it attracted mice – although they would have had to be fairly hardy mice to get through the capsule's steel and titanium housing. And anyway, as we already know, Twinkies can withstand anything.

Twinkies are owned by Hostess, who also make another much beloved American snack: the Hostess CupCake. Much imitated by home bakers as well as by other brands, this is a chocolate cupcake with a glossy, solid chocolate layer of icing, and a distinctive 'squiggle' of similarly solid white frosting. It was launched in 1919 by the Taggart Baking Company of Indianapolis (also the manufacturer of another American convenience staple, Wonder Bread), although it did not gain either filling or squiggles until 1950 and was originally simply called the Chocolate Cup Cake. Needless to say, its claim to be the first commercially produced cupcake is disputed by at least one other company. Hostess Brands Inc. was, however, the first (and possibly only) company to give us a cupcake superhero: Captain Cupcake, launched, so to speak, in 1973. Twinkie, meanwhile, sported 'Twinkie the Kid', a lasso-bearing manifestation of the snack cake, who sponsored the prime-time family *Howdy Doody Show* in the 1950s – another reason, no doubt, for the fondness for the snack among those growing up at the time.

So entrenched in popular culture are both the Hostess CupCake and the Twinkie that there was an absolute furore when Hostess Brands filed for Chapter 11 bankruptcy in 2012, citing a range of business factors from unsustainable labour costs to structural inflexibility. However, although this was not cited, sales had also been falling slightly for several years. It was actually the second brush with the bankruptcy courts for Hostess, who had been there already in 2004, under the name Interstate Bakeries. This time round, however, Twinkies disappeared from supermarkets in the States, although not in Canada where they were owned by a different company. This was horrifying news for those who loved them, whether they actually still ate them or simply liked the reassurance that they were out there somewhere. Snack lovers across the States breathed a sigh of relief when they were relaunched (as the 'Snack Cake Golden Child') with huge fanfare and new financing in 2013, now with a market of eighteen- to thirty-five-year-old men in mind (and with the original banana filling available once more). It might be worth noting that eighteen- to thirty-five-year-old men are precisely the demographic most likely to have a bit of disposable income, least likely to have family commitments, and be most receptive to synthetic child-like snacks with a high calorie load. The relaunch of the banana-filled version is also a savvy nod to the nostalgia factor. However, despite their rebranding as 'dude-food', the latest incarnation of Twinkies has retained the slimmed-down size that preceded the bankruptcy. Representatives of the brand say that even smaller versions are in the pipeline, marketed – inevitably – as snacks for women.

Leandra Palermo's Field Guide identifies three other big players in the American snack cake market: Drake's, TastyKake, and Little Debbie. All are notable for the longevity of their brands. Drake's was founded by Newman E. Drake, who started off selling pound cake by the slice in 1888. He moved up to selling whole cakes from a bakery in Brooklyn, and his sons in turn specialised in single-serving snack cakes. The Devil's Dog (essentially an éclair-shaped chocolate sandwich much like the whoopie pie we will meet in Chapter 9) was launched in 1923, although other favourites like Ring Dings (described on the company's website as round devil's food cakes, with the usual cream filling) did not follow until the 1960s. Drake's products may not be as universally well known as Hostess's (they are found mainly on the east coast) but they are still a cultural reference point: Seinfeld uses an individual Drake's Coffee Cake as a bribe in one episode of the eponymous show – a clear sign that the American public knew exactly what that flat round circle of cake signified to the hungry sugar lover, Newman. The Tasty Baking Company, owners of TastyKake, is another brand with its roots in a small family business. Their own best-known line is the Krimpet, which was born in 1927 and named for the 'crimping' on the top, which was an expedient to make the icing stay on the cake. The company shipped Krimpets and Tandy Kakes out to the forces serving in the Second World War, and in 2004 Kandy Kakes, the peanut-butter-flavoured most popular line, received an extra boost when they were declared to be kosher (unlike the Twinkie, which contains beef fat).

Little Debbie, meanwhile, has the distinction of being named after a real person – the granddaughter of the founders. Little Debbie has a huge range of lines, from striped Zebra Cakes to Swiss rolls in a variety of flavours, all aimed at the more discounted end of the market.

Finally, one other iconic snack food deserves some attention, and that is the doughnut, and particularly, the Canadian doughnut. Doughnuts are not classic cakes, as they are fried, but they include the same base set of ingredients and arise from the same family, albeit its breadier branch. But what makes them interesting in the present context is the fact that they form such an iconic part of Canadian culture, much more so than the Twinkie or the Battenberg do in their respective homelands. In fact, they are a rare example of a snack cake taking on the status of the American apple pie, or the British meal of fish and chips. Which leads us to ask: why on earth has a sugary, fatty snack become an icon of national identity – 'snackfood nationalism' as the leading doughnut scholar, Steve Penfold, has put it?

Penfold answers this question by claiming that the doughnut, which was originally imported into Canada from America, became popular just as the country was feeling the lack of a distinctive cultural identity. The doughnut became a symbol of blue-collar pride, democratic values, ordinariness, and (by the late 1970s) something which set the country apart from its gourmet-coffee drinking southern neighbour. Eaten at ice hockey games through the famously cold Canadian winters, it became an integral part of national identity, especially when ice hockey player Tim Horton entered the market and started on its domination. Today, Tim Hortons (no apostrophe: it was removed for fear of contravening Québécois laws on language: the possessive apostrophe is an English grammar rule which is superfluous in French) is so ubiquitous that it is used as a generic label for the snacks. It now has more outlets than McDonald's in Canada. In 1976 the genius Timbits were launched: doughnut 'holes', or small, round bite-sized doughnuts; not an innovation in the market, but one which again, entered the language like 'Hoover', 'Sellotape' or 'Kleenex'. Stopping for a coffee and a snack pack of Timbits is an intrinsic part of any Canadian road trip. The doughnut is now ubiquitous worldwide but it has achieved that rare accolade of a snack cake of becoming, in Penfold's words, an 'edible symbol' of nationality. There are few other cakes which could make such a claim.

Tim Hortons' doughnuts, then, could be said to make Canadians feel good about themselves; that's certainly what the chain's advertising would like us to believe, anyway. And it seems that Twinkies, Hostess CupCakes, TastyKakes, Ding Dongs and Ho Hos give Americans a surge of patriotic nostalgia, whether they actually like the things or not. Mr Kipling's cakes and the coconut-covered Lamingtons do the same thing for Brits and Aussies, while one imagines that József Dobos, like Franz Sacher and, for that matter, Southern baker Emma Rylander Lane of Lane cake fame, would feel a certain pride in knowing that the eponymous cakes were still bearing their name many decades after their deaths. Meanwhile, a birthday cake makes each one of us feel special for a day in our turn, whether it's one shaped like a football, a clown or a dog (even one baked for a dog); whether it's topped with pink sugarpaste carnations, the presidential seal, or made by Mr James Middleton, uncle of Prince George.

And the reason for all this? A mixture of endorphins, national pride and nostalgia, it seems. Cake naturally makes us feel good; we've seen that already in its frequent inclusion in definitions of comfort food. But there is something particular about cake which marks out one person as worthy of celebration, whether you're treating yourself to the guilty pleasure of a Twinkie, or on the receiving end of a home-baked candlelit birthday cake. And that, in turn, is deeply rooted in the foods that formed part of your childhood. It explains why young adults remain fond of the cakes of the 1970s and '80s, even when they contain an ingredient list which would make many modern parents shudder. It's why when people talk about small snack cakes, they also talk about lunch boxes, family teas and visits to grandparents. Sociologist Pierre Bourdieu said as much in his famous study of taste and culture first published in 1979: food more than almost anything else reflects the lessons we learned as infants. The food we encounter as children, in short, is weighted with memories of our early lives, and when it's sweet and made especially for you, well that makes it more likely to be a happy memory: the start of your own personal foodway, if you will. But lest we get too sentimental let's turn to special occasion cakes on a much grander scale.

8

THE ORIGINAL SHOWSTOPPERS

It was quarter past six on the morning of Monday, 7 September 1891, and Paris was already alight with excitement. The newspaper *Le Petit Journal* reported that the streets were black with the coats of thronged spectators, all keen to see the start of the inaugural 1,200-kilometre Paris to Brest cycle race. Cycling was newly popular in France, and the old, large and precarious penny-farthing bicycles with a huge front wheel and a small back one were on their way out in favour of the new style of the diamond-framed machine with two evenly proportioned wheels. This new race was designed as an opportunity for French cyclists to show their worth. The day dawned bright and sunny as 206 male contestants, amateur and professional, lined up on the rue Lafayette, including a few stalwarts on tricycles, tandems, and even one anachronistic penny-farthing. The riders moved off to a fanfare until they reached the avenue de Bois-de-Boulogne where the official start signal was sounded. Within minutes they had separated and disappeared into the woods. For the next few days, *Le Petit Journal*, whose editor was the brains behind the race, covered every stage in enthusiastic and breathless detail, reporting on the times achieved by the leading riders as they came through each town and village, the few

attempts to unseat them with sharp objects thrown in their path
(several of the professionals were riding on the new pneumatic tyres
manufactured by Dunlop and Michelin; the eventual winner completed
several stages riding on the rim of his wheels because his tyre had had
a puncture), and the much more frequent stories of huge crowds,
fanfare and excitement.

The race west soon became a finely balanced contest between the
professional cyclist Charles Terront, and the amateur Pierre-Joseph
Jiel-Laval, the highest-ranking Frenchman in the first Bordeaux–Paris
race earlier the same year. At the turning point, Brest, on the Breton
coast, the town was in a frenzy of anticipation. At 16.07 on 8 September
the assembled throng was thrilled to see Jiel-Laval come in first in 'bon
état'. To their extreme surprise and no doubt disappointment, he
paused only to eat a few pears and drink a bowl of bouillon before
setting off immediately on the return leg. The second, Terront, did
likewise. The third, Corentin Corre, the leading Breton rider, arrived
in poor shape and stayed to rest for some hours.

By 9 September the paper was reporting a thrilling reversal at the
head of the race: while Jiel-Laval caught a three-hour stretch of sleep,
Terront had pushed on through the night (turning off his bicycle
headlamp so as to avoid alerting Jiel-Laval's team), relying on loud
bells rung by his ear and slaps from his team to keep him awake. He
was borne in to the final strait by the crowd, his left arm held high in
a victory salute, and let out a cry of triumph. He had completed the
course in an astonishing time of 71 hours and 22 minutes (the
maximum allowed was and remains 90 hours). Only 106 of the
starting riders had got to the halfway point at Brest, the others defeated
by the distance, the pace and the gruelling lack of sleep. Ninety-nine
reached the finish line.

The Paris–Brest cycle race still runs every four years, albeit along a
different route to Brest and back, and with some different rules;

nowadays it is strictly for amateurs, and since the 1930s women have competed too. For those wondering why it is at all relevant to the topic at hand, it is because the French soon married their love of cycling with another national predilection: pâtisserie. A victory cake was allegedly commissioned in the first year that the race was run, but posterity tells us little more than this about it. In 1910, however, a skilful pâtissier named Louis Durand, whose shop lay along the main race route, was commissioned by the organisers to come up with a new delicacy to commemorate the event. His cake was made from puffy choux pastry shaped like a bicycle wheel with its air-filled pneumatic tyres, split horizontally, filled with a praline-flavoured cream, and topped with slivered almonds. It was called, simply and fittingly, the Paris–Brest. The original recipe is a secret and has been passed down through generations of Durand pâtissiers ever since.

The Paris–Brest is still a very popular cake in France. It can be found in most pâtisseries and is a favourite family dessert. It comprises one of the items demanded of contestants in the annual contest for the best French pastry chef, the Trophée de la Meilleure Pâtisserie Francilienne (alongside an éclair, a lemon tart and an opéra cake). It has been updated by several enterprising pâtissiers in recent years, the most notable example being the one named best Paris–Brest in Paris in 2010, by Philippe Conticini of the much noted Parisian Pâtisserie des Rêves (Pâtisserie of Dreams). It contains a controversial but much applauded liquid praline in the centre. Other bakers make them very large, with spokes like a bicycle wheel radiating from the centre; one recent finalist on *The Great British Bake Off* even made a Paris–Brest shaped like a whole bicycle (and won the weekly star baker award for it).

Novelty aside, the Paris–Brest sums up many of the most distinctive attributes of Continental European baking. First, it is beautiful to look at and, second, it is painstaking to create. The baker must achieve the

requisite rise and puff in their choux pastry (a notoriously temperamental beast, and one of the foundation classics of French pâtisserie,
made by heating water, butter and salt, adding flour and whisking
like the proverbial demon until it forms a paste, then adding eggs
and stirring until the correct glossy and stiff texture is achieved for
piping and baking – a skill which has, as yet, always defeated me).
Not only that: they also need to make a hazelnut cream, which in
turn means first whipping up crème pâtissière (a thick pastry cream
made from eggs, sugar, flour and warm milk) and then adding butter
and ground almonds to it. Finally, the fragile choux ring must be split
in half, filled with the creamy mix, and the whole coated in slivered
nuts and icing sugar. It is most decidedly not a recipe for the faint-
hearted, which brings us to points number three and four: it is usually
bought from a pâtisserie, not made at home, and it is usually thus
made by a craftsman.

These traits of elegance and sheer skill mark much Continental
baking out from the Anglo-American tradition. While in Britain, North
America or Australia, the gift of a home-baked cake is usually received
with considerable pleasure, in France or Belgium this is not the done
thing at all. Instead it is a beautifully boxed shop-bought cake which
indicates the value you place on your host or your guests; home baking
is a strictly family affair. Even in Germany, where home baking is
much more common, it co-exists with a long history of bought café
cakes; in fact going out for kaffee und kuchen has culturally iconic
status in many central and Eastern European countries.

The Paris–Brest is just one example of this type of cake: in France
alone there are many, many others, including the choux-ring, crème
pâtissière-filled, profiterole- and caramel-topped St Honoré cake,
named for the patron saint of bakers; the tall and conical croquembouche, made from a heap of glazed profiteroles; the sponge and
buttercream fraisier, with its ring of cleanly cut upright strawberry

slices displayed around the outside; and the delicately layered coffee-soaked almond sponge opéra, its sides left exposed to show off the skill of the baker. There is also the array of small beauties known as petits fours, or 'small oven', named partly for their size and partly because they went into the oven in its final stages of cooling (the Italian equivalents are called *pasticceria mignon*). Each one of these is painstakingly crafted and made for the refined tea table. In Austria and Germany you will find cabinets of glossily iced cakes and torten, featuring chocolate, fruits and nuts. In Italy fancy cakes are so rich in dairy creams, fruit and nougat that they must be eaten on the day they are made.

The collective term for many of these cakes are, respectively gâteaux and torten. The former is derived from the old French *guastrel*, which is also the origin of the old English 'wastrel' meaning the finest flours used for bread-making. In England the word gâteau was used for baked and moulded puddings and savoury dishes, and it wasn't until the second half of the nineteenth century that it came to be attached to fancy cakes which were often ornately iced and decorated. In France, too, the word can be used for savoury tarts and cakes, but much like the German torte it more commonly means a sponge layer cake, filled with whipped cream or crème pâtissière, and decorated with piped chocolate, cream or fruit. Some combine cake with pastry or meringue; others have little in the way of conventional cake components, but together they form a beautiful collective of baking and pastry work.

Across central Europe fancy cake-making is an art, part of a tradition of craftsmanship whereby any aspiring pastry chef must pay his dues and create his 'masterpiece' to gain entry into his (only exceptionally 'her') official guild. These guilds were not birthed painlessly, however. Bread was such an important commodity in medieval and early modern times that its manufacture and trade were strictly controlled; we have already seen how the English Assize of Bread set out precise guidelines for the size and price of a loaf. In France, the quality and availability of bread continued to be critical for social order well into the eighteenth century (witness the Flour Wars in the 1770s when people despaired of their basic subsistence), and so the diversion of precious flour into frivolous cakes was a real issue for the authorities. Sweetened and enriched breads could generally not be sold without the permission of the municipal authorities, and in 1740 French bakers were forbidden to use flour to make *gâteaux des rois* during Epiphany because of flour shortages. But already by 1440 the demand for sweet and rich flour products had grown to the extent that the Parisian authorities endorsed the formation of a pastry guild, an important development giving pastry-makers a professional identity and exclusivity. In 1566 a new charter was granted by King Charles IX, awarding them the privilege of measuring out and select-ing their own wheat at the corn market. This was a significant concession which was probably linked to the fact that it was the pastry-makers who made Communion wafers.

Choux buns, piped meringues and crème au beurre were a little while longer in coming. Meanwhile the real pastry stars of Europe were the Italians; in fact it is thought that choux pastry was invented in the sixteenth century by the chef to Catherine de' Medici, the Italian noblewoman and consort to the French King Henri II. It was not until the seventeenth century, however, that cake- and pastry-making really took off in France. One factor was the flowering of lavish entertaining and spectacle under King Louis XIV, the 'Sun King' of Versailles, whose long reign lasted from 1643 to 1715. The excess and display of his court inspired chefs and their aristocratic employers to create new novelties that were as good for the eye as for the palate. And while the French Revolution of 1789 left many renowned chefs kitchen-less and their aristocratic patrons scattered, exiled or worse, this displacement also prompted the abolition of the old guilds and the rise of restaurants and pastry shops. It also, of course, gave rise to one of the most famous cake-myths of all time: Queen Marie Antoinette's proposal that her hungry Parisian subjects eat cake (in fact the story predates the Queen's birth by some considerable time). With the return of the aristocracy and monarchy after the fall of Napoleon in 1815, a new and glittering world of culinary patronage was also restored.

One such epicurean aristocrat was Charles Maurice de Talleyrand Périgord, a master bureaucrat and diplomat who held high office under King Louis XVI, through all the revolutionary and Napoleonic administrations which followed save for a brief exile in the 1790s, and under the restored monarchy too. He was known for his table perhaps almost as much as his diplomatic skills: Napoleon Bonaparte, a notorious anti-gastronome who apparently became bored by meals which lasted for more than twenty minutes, frequently asked Talleyrand to depute for him in entertaining foreign notables. In 1798 Talleyrand's attention was drawn to a young pastry chef who was displaying truly awe-inspiring creations in confectionery in a local pastry shop window. His maitre d' was authorised to engage this young master to do custom work, and a reputation was born: Talleyrand's as the master of a truly fabled table, and the pastry chef's as the rising star of French cuisine – some might even say its creator. The latter's name? Antonin Carême.

Carême's name is still revered in the French culinary hall of fame. He was the first person to codify the hallowed family of French sauces and the first to wear a stiffened white hat and a double-breasted white jacket in the kitchen – a reflection of the discipline he demanded in his staff. He invented the technique of piping meringue, vital to many now quintessentially French cakes, and he wowed Europe with his stunning cake-and-sugar-work table centrepieces or *pièces montées*. By the time of his death in 1833 from the effects of a lifetime's exposure

to carbon monoxide fumes over the stove, Carême had worked for
many of the most influential leaders in Europe: Napoleon, Tsar
Alexander I of Russia, Britain's Prince Regent (later George IV), and
Betty and James Rothschild. He was, in essence, and as his many
biographers are keen to stress, the first celebrity chef. He was not born
to mingle in such circles, however; he was the sixteenth child in a
family of possibly twenty-five offspring, born in a slum neighbourhood
in the Left Bank of Paris, and abandoned to make his own way at the
age of twelve – or so biographers think; records are scanty and
Carême's own writings cannot necessarily be trusted on the details
of his inauspicious personal history. Luckily for the later history of
French cuisine, he found work in a kitchen, graduating at the age
of sixteen to the Parisian pastry shop where he came to Talleyrand's
attention. There, he started to study architectural drawings in his free
time and to reproduce them in pastry work and marzipan. He famously
said that confectionery was the principal branch of the art of architecture. No one who saw his pagodas, pyramids, follies and fountains
could doubt it.

Everything about Carême's work was about spectacle. The *pièces
montées* were designed to be seen, drawing the eye with their beauty
and height, which stretched to several feet. For much of Carême's
career it was still traditional to serve almost all of the dishes at the
same time, with guests eating whatever they happened to be closest to.
Appearance and symmetry were thus a vital part of food presentation.
Carême delighted in showing off his prowess in spectacular fashion –
plunging one hand into freezing water then straight into a pan of hot
sugar syrup, pulling and moulding the strands to make spun sugar
pagodas and colonnades before relieving it in cold water again. The
window of his own Parisian pastry shop was a magnet for lovers of
sugar, beauty and showmanship. In truth, relatively little about his
masterpieces was actually there to be eaten: the entire framework was

made from hardened pastry, or even gum paste and mastic, was painted with oils, and could be reused several times over. Some were very long-lived and would no doubt have lasted longer had they not fallen casualty to the siege of Paris by the Prussians in 1871.

Carême's confections were not a total innovation; remember the sugar-work table centrepieces or subtleties which we met in Chapter 1, but he took them to a new level of inventiveness and skill. His creations ranged from an imaginative collection of tributes to famous buildings like the Russian Hermitage, to whimsical follies and classical ruins. In 1821 he provided four large pieces for the christening dinner of his current aristocratic patron's baby son, George Henry Robert Charles William Vane-Tempest-Stewart. These were a Roman villa and a Persian pavilion, both situated on rocky outcrops, together with a Venetian fountain and an Irish pavilion. In 1829 he created a temple standing in a rockery made from hand-painted almond paste, and decorated with meringues and choux buns for a banquet at the Rothschilds'. He was also called on to make the cakes for several momentous society events despite by this time being a famous all-round chef: Napoleon's wedding to his second bride, Marie Louise Hapsburg in 1810 for one, and the christening cake for the couple's son the following year. He failed to describe the wedding cake, but the one he made for the christening was shaped like a gondola, complete with sugar waves, alongside a pavilion decorated with meringues and truffles. He also created a range of tiered cakes for young George Vane-Tempest-Stewart's christening (genoises, meringues, nougat and the enticing-sounding iced tiaras); and cakes aplenty for the gourmand-ising and gluttonous Prince Regent, including small genoises flavoured with George's favourite liqueur, maraschino. At another event for the Parisian army he made 100 cakes decorated to look like military drums. On top of all this he wrote several authoritative books on French pâtisserie and cuisine, and several books on architecture. His

fame was so great that he was able to negotiate staggering salaries
(£2,000 a year from the Prince Regent, or well over £100,000 in
today's money) with time off to write built in.

Carême's impact on French gastronomy was immense, thanks to
his skills and his dedication alike. One of his protégés (and renowned
pastry chef in his own right), Jules Gouffé, chef de cuisine of the Paris
Jockey Club, wrote in his own book *Le Livre de Pâtisserie* in 1873 that
a good pastry chef needed quickness and intelligence, a 'lively and
inventive fancy', skill in drawing, sculpture and architecture, good
taste, and eight to ten years of practical experience with pastry
(experience Gouffé himself had gained in his father's Parisian pâtisserie
before becoming Carême's pupil at the age of sixteen; in fact, legend
has it that it was in the window of this shop that Carême first spotted
the young Jules' potential). The aspiring pâtissier also had to be able
to govern the imprecise and temperamental brick oven, a vital point
when making delicate pastry work which required a certain degree of
puff, colour or crispness. Gouffé's method of testing oven temperature
was a more methodical version of some of those we have met before:
the piece of paper test. If it immediately catches fire, the oven is too
hot; if it chars, it is still too hot; if it scorches to dark brown but does
not catch alight, it is the correct temperature for small pastries; light
brown is suitable for vol-au-vents, choux buns and pie crusts; dark
yellow for large pieces of pastry, and light yellow for cakes and
meringues. Finally, the pastry chef needed to oversee all of the usual
pounding and sifting of sugar, nuts and dried fruit; to direct the
colouring of the accoutrements to the *pièces montées*, using ingredients
like spinach and watercress; and commission the stands and ornaments
for displaying the finished items. Gouffé gave many examples of such
items from his own career in his books, including a beehive made
from meringues, and featuring bees crafted from pistachios with a
currant for a head and almond slivers for wings.

Clearly Carême's showmanship and demands for exactitude and flair had been the start of something new. These attributes were taken to new heights of extravagance by another famous French chef, Alexis Soyer, who was a young man of twenty-three when Carême died. Like his predecessor, Soyer also came from humble origins, a fact which continued to rankle all his life. He had a fascination for the theatre which is plainly evident in his person, his food and his kitchens; the custom-built kitchen at the new London Reform Club – one of the first to feature gas stoves – where he worked for thirteen years was open to visitors, and he was always meticulous in his chef's whites (outside the kitchen he was noted for his flamboyant costumes). Also like Carême, Soyer was the author of many cookbooks, pitched variously at every social group from high society to the near-destitute (he had a lasting interest in assisting the poor and toured Ireland with his patented soup kitchen). He was a man of extreme passions, on the one hand brushing up against death during a trip to the battlefields of the Crimea where he had gone to supervise and improve upon the field kitchens, and on the other setting up a wondrous but ultimately ill-fated restaurant-cum-spectacle that he called his Universal Symposium opposite the new Crystal Palace. The latter, it might be noted, was conceived after he failed to win the official catering contract for the 1851 Great Exhibition (he also submitted a design for the building). He made money and lost it, counted Thackeray and Florence Nightingale among his friends, and patented a series of drinks, sauces and gadgets which he endorsed in his bestselling books. Unlike Carême, who was never happy in England, Soyer settled there and made his name catering sumptuous banquets, although he could never write in English and used an amanuensis to write his cookery books.

Soyer was not, like Carême, a pastry chef by training, but his banquets were equally well known for their cakes and desserts (remember his haunch of lamb made from cake?). In 1846 he created a two-and-a-half-foot tall, pyramid-shaped cake made from meringues and decorated with cream and fruit to flatter the army commander and son of the ruler of Egypt, Ibrahim Pasha. On the top was an edible portrait of the Pasha's father. He even used cake to tell a typically self-promoting story in one of his most popular cookbooks, *The Modern Housewife*, published in 1849. This book was set out as a series of letters between two ladies of leisure, Hortense and Eloise. In them the ladies exchanged an edifying and instructional set of recipes and household tips. In one letter, Hortense recounted an extraordinary dream in which she had been commissioned to make a 'monster cake' for a lunch party attended by Queen Victoria and her young family: four feet high, three feet wide, and covered in crystallised ornaments. It sat at the centre of a beautifully decorated and lavish tea party, watched by hundreds of child guests including the young royals. Hortense, the baker, rose to make the first cut. Just as she lifted the knife, however, she was rudely woken by her young son calling her for dinner. Fortunately, Hortense's dream was so detailed that she was able to recall the recipe and she included it in her letter (a large, ten-egg affair containing pistachios, angelica, liqueur and cream, which had to be sent out for an hour and a half's baking in a commercial oven). So accurate was the dream-recipe that it was recreated at a family christening, supervised by none other than famous society chef, inventor and philanthropic do-gooder, Alexis Soyer. Naturally the story (as well as Hortense and Eloise) were a fiction. We don't know whether Queen Victoria ever tried the yeasted 'Queen Victoria's Cake' he included in the same book either.

Carême and Soyer were both gifted chefs who were responsible for the shift towards haute cuisine. They, like that other famous influence on French cooking, George Auguste Escoffier (1846–1935), joint founder of the Carlton Hotel and the Paris Ritz, reformer of the London Savoy and author of the famous *Guide Culinaire*, were both firm advocates of order in the kitchen and in one's person: neatness and care bespoke an organised mind and an organised work station. Carême's classification of the four 'mother sauces' of French cooking, which was later updated by Escoffier to five, is a reflection of this love of order. Many pastry chefs since then have tried to do the same for pâtisserie's 'mother recipes'. Let us see what they have come up with.

The first thing that becomes clear from a perusal of any master pâtissier's reference work is that the cake holding up the foundation of all pastry work is the genoise. This is perhaps the simplest cake imaginable in terms of ingredients: the classic true sponge consisting of eggs, flour, sugar and no or very little fat, and with no raising agent save well-whipped eggs. The lack of chemical leavener does make the method a little more taxing than a Victoria sandwich, and the eggs are whipped with the sugar over heat in order to maximise the introduction of air into the batter. Precise temperature is thus as critical as precision in weighing and baking; the renowned modern pastry chef Pierre Hermé states generously in his book *Desserts*, that the mixture can be 'temperamental'. That said, the genoise is very amenable to flavourings and soaking up syrups, hence its huge versatility: it is the basis of Swiss rolls (including the Christmas *bûche de Noël*), the *fraisier*, the memory-evoking madeleine, and the *café Liégeois* (layers of genoise alternating with coffee ice cream and cream), among others.

The wide range of French pâtisserie means that the baker needs to know a few other base recipes to perfect the classics: pastry from choux to sweet, *sablée* and puff, meringues cooked and uncooked, yeast-raised doughs from baba to savarin, and a family of fillings: crème pâtissière, crème Chantilly (sweetened whipped cream), crème au beurre (crème pâtissière with butter added to it), crème legère (crème pâtissière with double cream), and crème anglaise – a classic English custard. A further subset of mousses make up the base of most French gâteaux and pastry.

So far, as they say, so good, but let us see just one of the classics of French pâtisserie in action to see just why they are so often shop-bought rather than home-made (despite the intentions of the cookbook-publishing pastry chefs): the croquembouche. This dessert is, quite simply, a showstopper, clearly designed for maximum visual impact. Unsurprisingly, therefore, it is attributed to Antonin Carême. It consists of a pyramid of cream-filled choux buns, several feet in height, stuck together with caramel, and covered with spun sugar. It is made in a conical mould not unlike a tall traffic cone, and requires significant skill, not only in making the component parts, but in achieving the necessary structure and heft to stay upright once unmoulded. It is a temperamental beast too, and must be eaten the day it is made; more than half a day in the fridge and it will become soggy. Its name means 'crunch in the mouth', a reference to the brittle caramel, and it is a common sight at weddings, christenings, and other special occasions.

Today, the conical shape of the croquembouche is one of its most distinctive characteristics but in Carême's hands it was a much more flexible vehicle. We have already seen that he used choux liberally in many of his creations, and whole croquembouches were put together in the shape of colonnades, baskets and shrubberies, decorated in different colours and with different fillings and coverings. In fact, Carême's disciple Gouffé described a large number of croquembouches in his 1873 *Livre de pâtisserie*, some of which did not contain choux at all, but were instead made from rounds of shaped fruit paste, actual sugared fruits or meringues.

There is something very macho about much of Carême's show-manship: the hands dipped in boiling sugar, the long hours, which eventually cooked him to death in the fumes from his stove, the circles of male patronage – although in Betty Rothschild he had at least one very influential female patron too. And while pâtisserie is now one of the very few courses at the Culinary Institute of America which is split evenly between men and women for reasons we will go on to consider, in Carême and Soyer's times things were very different. This was partly, of course, because it was very difficult at that time for women to gain entry to the inner circles of training and apprenticeship. However, it was also due to a conviction that is only slowly being overturned today, that professional cooking at a high level is the work of men: women are cooks; men are chefs. Or in other words, a family sponge is made by a woman; a croquembouche by a man. Even the French word *chef* is a specifically masculine one; the feminine version is *cuisinière*, with all its connotations of kitchen worker rather than boss in charge. What was different in France compared to Britain and America was that this culinary 'closed shop' extended to professional cake-makers too. The tradition of food writing illustrates this: while much of the trade in printed cookbooks in Britain and America was based on the work of female authors (with a strong emphasis on making cakes), in France it was always dominated by men, often producing authoritative encyclopaedic tomes – including several on the art of pâtisserie – rather than 'how-to' guides. Naturally this was partly the result of different traditions in writing and publishing (not for nothing did France produce the famously comprehensive *Encyclopèdie* in the second half of the eighteenth century, edited by Diderot), but it both confirmed and perpetuated an understanding that professional chefs, including pastry chefs, were men. Even today, most of the most renowned pastry chefs are male; a 2011 list of the top French pâtisseries in the *Guardian* included only one run by a woman (Claire Damon of Des Gâteaux et du Pain in Paris) and noted her to be unusual in a male-dominated field. And while Carême's contemporary Gouffé made the interesting observation in the preface to his work on pâtisserie that pastry was an important part of female training, and even stated that his book was intended for women as well as men, he then went on to talk in some detail about the training required for professional male pastry chefs.

The fact that it was professional men who wrote the cookbooks in France means that our view of French cooking and baking is one of the professional world. In Britain and America, in contrast, the likes of Mrs Beeton, Eliza Acton, Catherine Beecher and Eliza Leslie – even Elizabeth David and Jane Grigson, who managed to cross the line into gastronomy as well as recipe writing – depict the more private world of domestic cooking and eating. Even Julia Child, who had trained at the Parisian Cordon Bleu school of cooking, always called herself a cook and not a chef. And while Soyer actually gleaned many of the recipes he published from one of his female employees, she did not get credit, because her gender made her, relatively speaking, unimportant. Nonetheless, this national divide is heightened by the fact that French pâtisserie is a different type of art from its Anglo-American counterpart. That's not to say that British and American bakers are not skilled (or that French women don't bake); but more to stress that French pâtisserie makes a unique type of demand on presentation, precision and a range of classic skills which require long apprenticeship or specialist training.

Interestingly, the range of required skills for a pâtissier (in contrast with those of many other branches of cookery) includes many that, for good or ill, are associated with what are often perceived as natural *female* specialities. Pâtissiers must be risk takers who function under high pressure, but they must also have artistic flair and a high level of attention to detail. These latter attributes were among those most frequently cited by the women contributing to Beverly Russell's 1997 study of influential female chefs in modern America, alongside cooking by instinct and cooking 'with love' (of course the latter is one of the key reasons given for baking cakes by amateurs, too). But many of these so-called 'feminine' skills do not fit in well with the traditional restaurant kitchen, which tends to be built on the French model laid down by Carême and Escoffier. American chef Anthony Bourdain describes with some delight in his 2000 autobiography *Kitchen Confidential* the high-octane environment of the kitchen with all its ribaldry and profanity, linking his success with his own qualities of machismo. He admits candidly that power and prestige are for him important (testosterone-fuelled) rewards for doing well in his field, and that a shaming insult early in his career inspired him to succeed. This is accompanied by what comes across as a frankly misogynistic attitude to many of his kitchen-based female employees, who are apparently mainly disposed to cry and buckle under pressure. At best they are a 'civilising' influence' on the men. For him, pâtisserie is too close to an art than a craft to appeal; he does reserve a few words of praise for the skill of his female pastry chef, but still revealing an underlying assumption that pastry is a less-demanding field than other areas of kitchen work, both physically and emotionally. Pastry chefs, after all, do the majority of their work in advance of service, making their hours potentially shorter and less frenzied with the business of an ongoing service.

Things are changing even at the top though: in November 2014 the White House announced that it was employing its first female pastry chef in Susan E. Morrison (joining the first female executive chef, Cristeta Comerford, who got the job in 2005). One of Morrison's first tasks was to make the annual festive gingerbread White House; she is also a keen apiarist and is in charge of the presidential beehives. But Sarabeth Levine, named the James Beard Pastry Chef of the Year in 1996 is frank about the arduous work it took to reach the top. She spent ten years putting in eighteen-hour days starting at 4.30 a.m. – just like the men. Women now have their own culinary guilds and fraternities too, like Le Petit Cordon Bleu, founded by Diane Lucas and Rosemary Hume in New York City in 1942, and Les Dames d'Escoffier, an international and invitation-only body of professional women working in the food and hospitality industries. The first recipient of its Grande Dame award, created in 1977, was Julia Child.

Carême and Soyer claimed that they wanted to share their expertise with the public, though the exacting requirements of their recipes make one doubt how likely people really were to emulate them. The new modern masters of pâtisserie are bringing a somewhat more relaxed attitude to the discipline, and 'how-to' guides to the fundamentals of the discipline are now legion. Gaston Lenôtre, Pierre Hermé, Richard Bertinet and Eric Lanlard have all published cookbooks containing the familiar set of base recipes as well as their own creations. Bertinet even called his book *Pâtisserie maison* to make it clear that the recipes could be made at home (although most do still require a range of specialist items from special tins to sugar thermometers and piping tips). Nonetheless, it's worth noting that they – and the female authors of works on pâtisserie too – all have classical French training, unlike most of the female domestic goddesses.

The home baker attempting the French classics is participating in a world Carême would recognise. Appearance, structure and show-stopping presentation are all important attributes even in the scaled-down cakes and pastries on view in pâtisserie windows in every French, Belgian and Swiss town. No wonder that they bring a sense of occasion: many families make a tradition of the weekend pilgrimage to the pâtisserie to choose their lunchtime dessert, taking them carefully home in an elegant cardboard box.

If the French are known for their pâtisseries, then the Germans and Austrians can lay claim to the noble tradition of the coffee shop *kaffee und kuchen* – a slice of a fancy cake accompanied by a cup of coffee. And nowhere more so than in Vienna, where coffee shops have traditionally been places where political movements took shape, the arts were laid down, and philosophy was ardently discussed. In 2011 'coffee house culture' was even listed as part of the Viennese 'intangible cultural heritage'. Trotsky, Klimt and Herzl were all coffee shop regulars. Sigmund Freud favoured the Café Landtmann on the famous Viennese Ringstrasse, Mozart performed at the Café Frauenhuber on Vienna's Himmelpfortgasse, and Hitler hung out at the Café Sperl, near the Academy of Fine Arts. And we have already heard about another famous Vienna kaffeehaus: the café at the Hotel Sacher.

The first coffee house in Vienna opened in 1685, but they really flowered from the start of the nineteenth century, around the time that pâtisseries were taking off in Paris. They were strictly male spaces though: women were banned until 1856. But what *kuchen* would regulars find to accompany their *kaffee*? On the whole, the cakes of Germany and Austria tend to be richer in butter than British or American ones, and contain less sugar, less height and fewer show-stopper adornments than French pâtisserie. Instead, they tend to be single-tier round or square bakes, often featuring fruit, nuts, chocolate and the traditional streusel topping of sugar, spice and nuts. Fillings are often custardy or cheesecake-like, sometimes based on the tangy quark soft cheese. These are cakes designed to be eaten with a fork, inviting with their sheer unctuousness, although many are also beautiful to the eye.

The showier branch of this cake family tree consists of the torten, which are broadly akin to the French gâteaux. They can be a single cake or layered, frequently feature whipped cream, jam or buttercream fillings, can be spiked with alcohol, and are often beautifully decorated with chocolate ganache, fruit, cream or piped chocolate work. Originally a torte was always baked in a pastry case and could be either sweet or savoury, like the Austrian Linzer torte which with a seventeenth-century birth date is the oldest of the sweet versions still around today. It consists of a nutty pastry base holding a filling of jam (traditionally raspberry) and covered with a lattice of thin pastry strips.

By the early nineteenth century the varieties of torten were only held back by the imagination of their bakers: one book on German confectionery dating from the 1820s described 101 different varieties. The pastry base had given way to sponge cake, often with a jam filling and a simple water icing. This is the foundation of the famous Sacher torte, updated with a chocolate sponge and a chocolate ganache; also the Dobos torte, which is made from many thin layers of batter. An even more classic example is the Black Forest gâteau, or *Schwarzwälder Kirschtorte*, described by Alan Davidson in the *Oxford Companion to Food* as 'a baroque confection of layers of chocolate cake, interspersed with whipped cream and stoned, cooked, sweetened sour cherries'. It became popular in Britain in the 1980s perhaps because of its lavish decadence and suitability for dinner party extravagance (it also celebrated the growing market in frozen convenience foods – no one seems to remember actually making one from scratch), but the recipe in any case goes back no earlier than the 1930s. As its name suggests, it was created to celebrate the produce of the Black Forest region of Germany where sour cherries grow, and where the cherry brandy kirschwasser is made.

The German-speaking lands are also not without their own version of the French petits fours; those small and beautiful dainties made for the tea table. These are often individual-sized slices not unlike the British favourite the Battenberg Slice, or small versions of the classic torten. Their component parts are as varied as their names: some are based on cake, like the Austrian *punschkrapfen* which looks like a fondant fancy, doused in alcohol and with a cherry on the top; others on a yeasted batter like the *bienenstich* (or bee-sting slices, named presumably for the honey in their nutty topping); others still on pastry, like the German *brasselkuchen* which consists of puff pastry with a butter streusel topping; or the *Napoleonschnitten* (Napoleon slice) which is much like a French millefeuille. Not for nothing did Carême spend some of his working life in Vienna, and news of fashionable treats travelled fast in this world of the Grand Tour, publishing and letter-writing.

In the pantheon of German cakes there are two which deserve a particularly special mention because of their sheer uniqueness: the *baumkuchen* and the *rehrucken*. The former, its name literally meaning 'tree cake', is an astonishing labour to make and certainly not one for the home kitchen. It consists of layers of batter which are poured over a long revolving spit placed in front of a set of electric or gas elements. As the spit turns, the cooking batter is shaped by the baker so that it sets in the shape of a series of wide bands with narrowed rings in between them. The finished cake can be many feet tall and is often covered with chocolate and decorations, and a slice through one of the bands reveals each of the layers of batter baked into a distinct ring – just like those on a tree. The recipe apparently originated in German monastery kitchens in the fifteenth century and was recorded in a cookbook of 1581. Although it seems not to have survived in the British baking tradition there is also a fourteenth-century English recipe extant for a similar cake.

The equally traditional *rehrucken* is similarly shaped to resemble something else: this time a saddle of venison. This apparently unlikely shape for a cake is achieved by using a special pan which contains grooves to resemble the ribs of the joint of meat. The cake itself is a chocolate-almond one, covered with chocolate icing, and with whole almonds studded all over it to resemble the bacon used for curing a real saddle of venison. As to why the Austrians felt the need to recreate a meat dish in cake – well we can only assume that it was a culinary joke, much like Soyer's haunch of lamb.

One very striking feature of German cakes is their use of yeasted doughs. We know that yeast was the starting point for the European tradition of cakes, and that it lives on in some of those we have already met, from Mardi Gras king cake to the old American election cake. It is in German baking that this tradition has been kept most alive though, both in the use of yeasted batters for baked goods that look like traditional cakes, and also in a variety of cake which show their common origins with bread more clearly – like the Christmas stollen which we met in Chapter 2. In between are very light and tall cakes like the *kugelhopf* and its close relation, the Italian panettone, which are made from enriched and sweetened bread doughs (and make a surprisingly good base for a decadent Christmas trifle).

Jews hailing from northern Europe and residents of the Germanic areas of the United States alike will be most familiar with the first category of yeasted cakes: the *kuchen*. My grandparents lived in north London when I was a child, and no trip to the kosher bakery was complete without a mouth-watering glimpse of these unctuous cakes, often pre-cut into large squares. My great-aunt had a signature recipe for a *pflaumenkuchen* or plum cake, but my grandmother's favourite was a shop-bought box of *rugelach* – small twisted crescents of dough containing a chocolate filling. *Kuchen* are traditional coffee cakes with a long history in home baking and strong roots in local foodways. Wherever people were making their own bread it was easy to save some dough and make these not-too-sweet cake treats to eat with the morning coffee, filled with whatever local fruits and nuts were on offer. Every housewife would have her own recipe, and this is another reason that they were so treasured.

The *kugelhopf*, which falls into our second category of 'breadier' cakes has a more troubled past. Known variously as *kugelhopf*, *kugelhopf*, *kougloff* and *kougelhopf*, it is a favourite in Germany, Austria, Alsace and Poland, all of which places fight possessively over its heritage. It is a favourite breakfast cake, made from a yeasted 'sponge' of flour and warm milk, enriched with eggs, sugar and softened butter, and spiked with lemon and dried fruit. The *kugelhopf* is baked in the distinctive turban-shaped, fluted ring mould which eventually became known as a Bundt tin in America. One legend says that it was created to honour the Wise Men who attended the birth of Jesus, as they wended their way home (somewhat mysteriously) through north-eastern France (they left another trace of this unlikely detour in the French *galette des rois*, or kings' cake). Another, Austrian, tradition holds that the shape is to commemorate the defeat of the Turks at the gates of Vienna in 1683 (this is allegedly also when coffee first became known to the Viennese). The word *kugel* means round, which may be a more prosaic origin of the name. Huge, decorative moulds remain in the museums in Alsacian towns like Strasbourg and Nancy, and according to Elizabeth David, the town of Ribeauvillé in Alsace hosted a *kugelhopf* fête every year which includes a prize for the best example made by a local housewife. Sadly this has fallen into abeyance in recent years but other towns in the region do still have an annual festival to celebrate their local cake. The Italian panettone ('big loaf') is similar, although baked in a dome rather than a ring shape, and traditionally made for Christmas. At Easter they can be found (minus the raisins) baked into the shape of a dove, when they are called *colomba di Pasqua*.

The French have their yeasted favourites too, illustrating again the close ties within the family tree of Continental baking. Their love of breaded pastries like croissants and the enriched bread brioche is one of their defining culinary characteristics, but the lesser-known savarin and baba are more cake-like. Savarins and babas are made from an identical dough, but they are shaped and served differently. Savarins are ring-shaped and are usually served with fruit, crème pâtissière or Chantilly cream. Babas are baked in small cylinder moulds and are served with whipped cream. The latter may also contain dried fruit and come with an apricot sauce. Both are soaked after baking in an alcohol-spiked syrup, traditionally rum.

The birth story of the two cakes is more universally accepted than many, but is no less colourful for that. It seems clear that the baba came first, another case of rescuing a bake gone wrong, this time a sponge-like cake made for the deposed King Stanislaus of Poland, then living as a nobleman in France. The overly dry cake was perked up with the addition of rum, and a new dessert was born. The savarin came some time later and is named for the famous philosopher and writer on food, Jean-Anthelme Brillat-Savarin (1755–1826). It was he who coined the much repeated aphorism, '*Dis-moi ce que tu manges, je te dirai ce que tu es*' ('Tell me what you eat and I will tell you what you are'). In this case, we know that Brillat-Savarin himself did *not* eat a Savarin; it was not created until after his death.

In this chapter we have met some of the most distinctive cakes of Continental Europe, and the cultures that they embody: the skill and spectacle of the French pâtisserie; the sociability and luxury of the German *kaffeehaus*. We have also seen their origins in a very male culture of creation and consumption, where gâteaux honour their creators and patrons, and pastry work shows off training and creativity. On the other hand, in the German-speaking lands especially, women embraced a tradition of domestic sociability. The *kaffeeklatsch*, or coffee break, is still an important pause for cake and chat, whether with friends or simply among family, and many of the *kuchen* and yeasted cakes are still made at home. You are as likely to be invited to a friend's home '*zum Kaffeetrinken*' (coffee and cake) as for lunch or dinner.

There are also obvious connections and similarities between many of the cakes of Continental Europe which reveal a much bigger family tree. Viennese cakes share traits with traditions further east, and also hint at their historic place between east and west. The Ottoman Empire came right up to their door after all (remember the siege of Vienna, which may have inspired the turban-shaped *kugelhopfs*), and it is seen in the poppy seeds, marzipan and layered pastry cakes in Austrian, Polish, Ukrainian and many other Eastern European countries. The Arabs are thought to have been the first to experiment with layers of pastry, producing the filo baklava which is still so popular today. It's easy to see now why German-speakers, with their rich tradition of home baking and the sociability attached to cakes, were so keen to take their recipes with them as they dispersed across the world. There are places in America where the coffee break is still called a *kaffeeklatsch*, and where the cake in question is a *kuchen* or a torte. And it was, of course, the Germans who introduced us to that most honoured of sociable cake traditions: the birthday cake.

We cannot end this chapter, however, without noting that things are starting to change in the pâtisseries and kitchens of Continental Europe. On the one hand, master pâtissiers are fêted as never before: queues form for the latest flavour of Hermès macaron and the newest invention at the Pâtisserie des Rêves. But a few women are also getting to the top of this traditionally male world. On the other, home bakers are tackling the hallowed craft of pastry work. A recent poll showed that 71 per cent of French people bake their own cakes at home between once a week and once a month; 84 per cent say that they would like to be better at pastry work. *Le meilleur pâtissier*, the French version of *The Great British Bake Off*, places a strong emphasis on intricate and skilled pastry challenges (the host, Faustine Bollaert, famously said that the cakes baked on the British show made her feel ill with their overload of sugar and lack of refinement). The winner of the first series claimed the trophy with a *gâteau St-Honoré*, though we might note that the stakes are being raised in the baking contests everywhere; the winner of the Australian version in the same year made petits fours and profiteroles in the final, and the British contestants regularly tackle complex European bakes. Furthermore, several male cookbook writers are claiming their credentials as homey, domestic bakers rather than skilled professionals. Even the professionally trained Eric Lanlard, whose recent television programme showed him recreating some of Carême's signature bakes, goes under the much less ostentatious moniker of 'Cake Boy'. Quite suddenly, the hallowed art of the pâtissier and the German equivalent, the *konditor*, is being democratised, and bakers everywhere are prepared to tackle the complex bakes usually reserved for pastry shop windows. If Brillat-Savarin was correct, what does this show us about what we are becoming? Confident entertainers, rooted in our collective culinary heritage? Or fashion-chasers, keen for a new challenge? We will examine the latter suggestion in the final chapter.

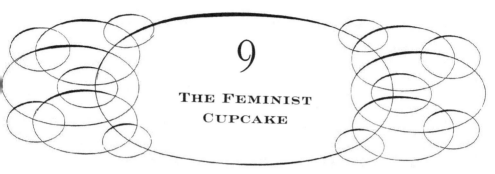

9

THE FEMINIST
CUPCAKE

Four aproned contestants glower at each other over their counters. Three judges settle in for a show. The host counts down the seconds and . . . let the cupcake wars commence! On food channels everywhere, cupcake baking has become fiercely competitive. It is no longer enough to pile some vanilla-flavoured batter in a paper case and drizzle on an icing sugar glaze when it's done. Now, to hold its (frosted) head up high, a cupcake has to be the size of your fist, piled with a sculpted mountain of buttercream, flavoured with Earl Grey tea, beetroot, ginger or banoffee, and spiked with chunks of Oreo cookie, a mini tuile or a hand-crafted sugar paste animal.

But cupcakes were not always this way. Their British antecedent, the fairy cake, was apparently named because they were small enough for a fairy to eat. How, then, did they get so big and blowsy, so ostentatious and fashionable? And what of their other small, chic friends, the delicately tinted macaron, the unapologetically flat and gooey-looking whoopie pie, or the cutesy cake pop, dandering on its stick? Why are we so taken these days with cakes that are (mostly) small and cute? What do they say about our culture and our tastes?

Before we get going in answering these questions, the first thing to note is that although they are all the rage now, our taste for small cakes is actually not so new. Recipes for small 'Queen cakes' baked in tin moulds, cups or pans survive from the eighteenth century. We've already seen that the French petits fours, of which the macaron is one, also have a long, distinguished and beautifully turned-out history. They have in turn spawned international cousins: the British fondant fancy, the coconut-coated Australian Lamington, and the Austrian *punschkrapfen*. As these examples show, small does not mean simple. The Spanish have their *madalenas*, which are similar to fairy cakes, but made with olive oil. They are quite dry and tend to be dunked in coffee for breakfast or an afternoon snack. The Swedish enjoy miniature versions of their pristine, dome-shaped and green-hued classic *prinsesstarta* (named after three princesses who particularly enjoyed them: Margaretha, Martha and Astrid, all born around the turn of the twentieth century), sometimes decorated to look like a frog for kissing, while a similar looking green-tinted small cake goes by the name of frog cake in Australia, complete with wide open mouth. These are so classic in Adelaide that they have been named as a South Australian Heritage Icon. And we probably shouldn't even get started on the French scallop-shaped madeleine, made famous by Proust as a gateway to times past.

All of these small cakes share many traits with the modern whoopies and pops: they are eye-catching, they are pretty and they come in portable, one-portion sizes. Perhaps that is why the old-fashioned and understated English fairy cake is a popular stalwart at children's birthday parties – where they are also ideal for young children who are disinclined to share! Not all small cakes have allusions to the stylish beauty of the macaron: think of those rugged British rock cakes, the oily oblong doughnut known as a yum yum (which probably started its foodway in Holland), and its Canadian counterpart the beavertail. But in this crowded market of individual treats, it is the cupcake which is queen, and despite rebellious murmurings from critics and attempted coups by new upstart baked goods, her supremacy remains intact.

The origins of the cupcake are somewhat mysterious, partly because it depends on when you start to call any small cake a cupcake. The two clearest indications lie in recipes which direct the baker either to measure their ingredients in cups (a calibration devised by Fannie Farmer in her 1896 *Boston Cooking School Cookbook*) or to bake them in cups – the latter, of course, being closest to our modern usage. According to Ivan Day, food historian and blogger at 'Food History Jottings', the name 'cupcake' did not appear in recipe books until 1828; before that, small cakes were known as 'queen cakes' or 'queen's cakes'. The earliest recipe he has found for such a little queen cake appeared in a 1724 book called *Court Cookery* by one R. Smith. It was loosely based on a pound cake, but used only five egg whites to ten yolks, making a richer cake. It also included the then habitual currants, mace and orange-flower water. With domestic goddess Maria Rundell's recipe for queen cake of 1806, we take a step closer to our cupcakes, as she directed that they be baked in a tea cup, or alternatively a saucer, a small tin or patty pans, which were by then available in many moulded shapes from hearts to clubs. Elizabeth Raffald also wrote about little 'Plum Cakes' in her 1806 *New System of Domestic Cookery*, which were in a similar vein. Day, who specialises in practical cookery from historic recipes, reports that most of the early recipes for queen cakes would have produced a cake with a domed top, much like the traditional cupcake (today, a flat top is often preferred as it gives a better surface for what many feel is the real deal: the frosting). However, it was mince pies which were originally made in those little tin moulds; another flashback to the British fondness for heavy, fruited baked goods before they took the step to lighter, sponge-like varieties.

Day's research into cupcake history places its truest origins, appropriately given its recent history, in America. Amelia Simmons, the first woman to publish an American cookbook, in 1796, included a recipe for 'a light cake to bake in small cups'. This was a yeasted batter (one of the ones using the distinctively American term 'emptins' that we met in Chapter 4), so not yet quite the sort of cake we now think of as making a cupcake, although she also included a recipe for small spiced queen cakes. But by the time Philadelphia legend Eliza Leslie published her *Seventy-five Receipts for Pastry, Cakes, and Sweetmeats* in 1828 something actually called a cupcake seems to have been born. This one wasn't named for the receptacle it was baked in, but for the way the ingredients were measured out in teacups. It's possible this was even what started off the American tradition of measuring in cups, albeit not yet ones of a standard size, and also the 1-2-3-4 cake (one cup of butter, two of sugar, three of flour, and four eggs). Leslie's recipe was not quite so easy to remember: two cups each of brown sugar, molasses and butter; one of milk; five of flour; and half each of allspice, cloves and ginger. Its flavours would make it not out of place in a modern bakery, where all sorts of cakes have been scaled down to cupcake size. It's hard to say whether the cupcake was then exported back to Britain or whether it was developing concurrently there, but it had certainly caught on by the middle of the nineteenth century. By this time, the most defining feature as far as Day is concerned – the pleated paper case – was also in common use for all sorts of little cakes and biscuits.

The presentation of little cakes in their own paper cases perhaps give us an idea as to why they were becoming popular: they were fashionable and well turned out. Teatime was well bedded in as a social occasion by this time, and small treats, neatly encased in their own wrapper, were easy and tidy to eat. They also catered for a new sort of femininity, one which put ever-increasing emphasis on appearance, dress and physical beauty – including, from the 1840s, the desire to stay trimly corseted into an hourglass shape. Perhaps it is no coincidence that the small and dainty cupcake became popular in Britain at the same time as mass production of the corset.

We should probably not read too much into this theory, however, appealing though it may be. The little queen cake and mince pie moulds from earlier decades indicate that small cakes had long been popular, and the cupcake seems to have survived the move to 'rational dress' popularised by the likes of Amelia Bloomer and her wide-legged trousers. The point about daintiness remains, however, and is still a factor in the popularity of cupcakes today, as is a link with femininity – a point we will expand on later. A cupcake is a predetermined portion, and guarantees that you cannot be labelled as consuming unseeming quantities of cake (assuming you stop at one, that is). There is also a more practical reason for their popularity: small cakes were more amenable to cooking in a cooling oven than large ones, a fact demonstrated in the name of the French treats: petit four, or 'small oven'.

Irma Rombauer fully understood the appeal of cupcakes when she wrote her bestselling *Joy of Cooking* (first published in 1931). She noted, firstly, that they are both easy to bake and easy to serve; an appeal that endures today and another reason that they are good for entertaining. She even pre-empted the cutesy look so popular today by suggesting that the baker use the new frilled paper cups which should be filled only a third of the way. This would ensure that the cakes rose to just beneath the top of the frilled edge, leaving a neat and attractive border and, perhaps not coincidentally, an excellent space for decoration with butter icing or icing sugar, and garnishes like nuts, cherries or dried fruit. An alternative way to serve them was to remove a 'lid' from the top, fill the space with a ganache or buttercream, replace the lid and frost the top – another stylistic touch still used today. Most of her cake recipes could be used to make cupcakes, including the Queen Mary's sponge which we met in Chapter 4 (the favourite of King George V), a gold cupcake, using egg yolks, and angel cupcakes with the whites – the American fondness for contrast and balance again. She also offered a whole host of other flavour suggestions from gingerbread to pineapple or peanut butter. Attractive combinations included daffodil cupcakes, which were white or yellow cakes with orange or lemon filling and an orange or lemon icing. This is not dissimilar to that other British cupcake derivation, the butterfly cake, in which the sliced-off top is cut into two 'wings' and placed back atop the buttercream.

Cupcakes, then, are easy to bake, amenable to the tail end of the oven heat, modest in size, and pretty to look at. These are all powerful reasons for their enduring success, especially when we consider that we are dealing here with a category of food which is essentially a treat for a special occasion, not a main meal. Instead, they feature at occasions where the food is part of feeling the specialness and happiness of the occasion.

We could add another word to this list of important attributes: nostalgia. This is cited as one of the key reasons for the rebirth of the cupcake phenomenon in recent decades in many Western countries. Put simply, cupcakes remind us of childhood, and especially birthday parties and family treats. Cupcakes are often the first sort of cakes a child bakes with an older relative, laying down personal memories of family bonding and shared accomplishment. And, by extension, they remind us of a simpler time of life, of being loved in the straightforward way that one hopes parents and grandparents love their children, and of when a small iced fairy cake in a plain white paper case, covered with a little glacé icing and a few sprinkles, meant happiness. It's a big role for a small cake to play, but it crops up time and time again when cupcake fans, bakers and market analysts alike try to explain the enduring popularity of the little cakes.

Whether it's nostalgia or novelty, we are certainly eating more and more small cakes. A Mintel survey of 2013 found that sales of small cakes in the UK had eclipsed large ones, taking 44 per cent of the market share compared with 37 per cent for the larger varieties, and representing a growth of 19 per cent between 2011 and 2012. And what's more, a quarter of Brits in this cake-eating survey said that they would like more one-person-portion cakes on the market. Analysts pointed to the penchant for snacking as one explanation, which had led to the growth of sales in cupcakes, muffins and cake bars. In total, Mintel estimated that only 6 per cent of Brits *hadn't* eaten cakes or cake bars in the previous six months.

The cupcakes we reach for today are not, however, the small and childlike ones of memory. Rather, the trendy option is the chic-yet-retro gourmet cupcake. Its explosion on to our high streets and into our popular culture is credited to a scene in *Sex and the City*, which was first aired in 2000. In it, the main character Carrie and one of her best friends, Miranda – both forty-something, sometime single career women and affluent consumers – were shown eating vanilla cupcakes with pink frosting outside Magnolia Bakery in New York City. The scene lasted not much more than a minute, but became a defining moment in consumer culture. Viewers might not be able to aspire to Carrie's clothes, lifestyle or – most likely – her shoes, but they *could* afford a cupcake from Magnolia Bakery, and they did, in droves. Fifteen years on, and the shop is still on the official *Sex and the City* tour of New York.

What *Sex and the City* actually did for Magnolia was to hugely popularise an existing craze. The bakery was opened in 1996 by two friends, Allysa Torey and Jennifer Appel (Appel subsequently left the chain and set up on her own). In 2003 they were reported to make $40,000 a week just from cupcakes, and they frequently had queues running round the block. When Magnolia's latest branch opened in Tokyo in June 2014 there was a six-hour wait to get in, and there are branches also in Moscow, Dubai, Abu Dhabi, Beirut, Kuwait City and Doha (we will return to this Middle Eastern fascination for cupcakes later). Magnolia's success was followed by the foundation of a wave of specialist gourmet 'cupcakeries', of which Sprinkles Cupcakes of Beverley Hills is said to be the first. This bakery opened in 2005 and is owned by Candace Nelson, who is also one of the long-time judges on *Cupcake Wars*. It was also the first cupcake chain to provide its customers with 24-hour access to baked goods, via a 'Cupcake ATM' which opened in 2012 at selected stores. There is also a travelling 'Sprinklesmobile' to take cupcakes even further afield.

Magnolia, Sprinkles, and more briefly, Crumbs, which was for a while the biggest player in terms of number of stores, but which met a sticky financial end in 2014, have been some of the highest-profile kids on the cupcake block, but they have been joined by droves of competitors. The frequently updated blog 'Cupcakes Take the Cake' listed sixty-one cupcake bakeries in New York City alone at the time of writing, but this isn't just a New York phenom-enon. Georgetown Cupcakes in Washington, for example, has a huge following because of its reality show *DC Cupcakes*, which tracks the two sister-owners through the challenges and comedies of run-ning a cupcake bakery. The show even covered the wedding preparations of one of the sisters, who got married in a dress which (in her own words) made her look like a cupcake, and whose special day – unsurprisingly – featured a huge tower of Georgetown wedding cupcakes. The bakery also holds the current record for the world's largest cupcake, set in November 2011, for a cupcake weighing 2,594 pounds and measuring 36 inches in height. This, too, was featured on the show.

The fascination for gourmet cupcakes has successfully transferred across the Atlantic, even though the British tradition of cupcakes is not much like the new gourmet product, while in other parts of Europe they have no native heritage at all. We can see this in the way that many of the big British players market themselves. Two of the market leaders, Hummingbird Bakery and Primrose Bakery, both in locations across London, make it clear that they are bringing American cupcakes to England. Hummingbird, which first opened in Notting Hill, west London, in 2004, describe their cupcakes as 'US style', and are known for their red velvet cupcake, which as we know, is a classically American flavour. Primrose opened in Primrose Hill, north London, also in 2004, again, aiming to bring well-known treats from America and elsewhere to the UK. Primrose had originally started out baking for the traditional children's market for cupcakes, but like so many other bakers had realised that they actually had much more potential as a product for adults. Children tend to be happy with chocolate or vanilla sponge and some sprinkles on the top (that is, the classic British fairy cake); adults, on the other hand, are ripe for a much greater variety of flavours, and will pay a lot more for an indulgent treat than they would for a children's party. Cleverly, Primrose still market their 'mini' cupcakes as ideal for children's birthdays, constituting 'approximately three bites' (whether three child bites or three adult bites is not specified). On the other hand, the regular daily specials offer a very British twist on the American theme, featuring beloved confectionery like Toblerone and Maltesers, as well as flavours like rose and Earl Grey (alongside peanut butter, banoffee and maple and pecan, which shout of their North American origins).

Cupcakes have also become popular in Continental Europe, but there they are even more likely to be marketed as fun imports from America or Britain. Lilicup bakery in Brussels describes its cupcakes as 'English style', and states that the two founder-bakers had had to look to Britain and America for models, as Belgium had no tradition of little patty cakes like the ones they had started to produce for children. The Anglo-Saxon influence is evident in English names for many of these bakeries: That's Bakery in Milan, Alice in Cakeland in Rotterdam, and Cupcake Corner Bakery in Krakow, which features 'Authentic American' cakes in flavours like peanut butter and jelly and red velvet. Since there is no tradition of childhood cupcakes in these countries, we can safely conclude that the little cakes have their own appeal which goes beyond nostalgia and familiarity. Their cute-yet-chic appearance and association with dominant cultures like America, bring them appeal where they were not known previously. That's not to say that they haven't been adapted to national tastes though: the Speculoos cupcakes named for the much-loved spiced biscuit in French and Belgian bakeries are a case in point.

Meanwhile, the taste for cupcakes travels ever further. Magnolia has a strong presence in the Middle East, and London's Hummingbird Bakery also has a branch in Dubai. The Westernisation of culture and the cachet attached to American and British goods has given the cupcake and its friends a sound introduction. They are making inroads into China, where appearance, novelty and 'cuteness' are important traits in the market, alongside more distinctive local preferences like a desire for individual packaging (thought to be more hygienic). Western chains like Starbucks have even given long-traditional Far Eastern cakes like moon cakes the miniaturisation treatment, in a range of both Eastern and Western flavours.

The gourmet cupcake craze has run and run (there is now a National Cupcake Day in the States – 15 December, if you're interested), but at first glance, there seems little reason why it should have succeeded. For one thing, as we've already noted, cupcakes are not hard to make. Why, then, are so many people happy to fork out upwards of $3 for one (or $21 for six via Magnolia's mail order service; they come frozen)? Some have cited the New York effect, where small kitchens, dense urban living, and one of the most cosmopolitan food scenes in the world combine to make baking at home a lot more hassle than eating out. But this doesn't explain the popularity of the gourmet cupcake in other parts of the States, and indeed, the world – even places where there is no tradition of baking them in childhood to tap into.

Secondly, cupcakes don't keep very well, at least not if bakeries wish to avoid using lots of preservatives. And this is one of the key features of the cupcake boom: although the best-known names belong to highly corporatised chains which spread across multiple states and even countries, they almost without exception stress their homey origins, and their use of old-fashioned methods and fresh ingredients; and many, of course did start as single-outlet businesses. Magnolia's website uses the phrase 'old-fashioned' to describe their baking process; Katherine Kallinis Berman and Sophie Kallinis LaMontagne, the owners of Georgetown Cupcakes, have written about the fact that they were inspired to open their business by memories of baking with their 'Grandma Babee', and that to them, cupcakes are a direct line to childhood and happiness. Susan Sarich, the founder of Susie Cakes, a California chain, started out with recipes written on index cards which had been passed on by her grandmothers (who also gave her her nickname, Susie). In fact, most of the bakeries stress the freshness of their ingredients, and the fact that they are made from scratch every day using traditional (i.e. non industrialised) methods. Thus although cupcakes may be easy to make and scale relatively well, they can be a labour of love. When Katherine and Sophie opened Georgetown

Bakery in 2008 they got up at 4 a.m. to bake 500 cupcakes and sold out within two hours. With customers still pressing at the door, they put up a sign saying they would be back with more, and frantically whipped up another 300 – which sold out in another two hours. Now their bakery produces more than 5,000 per day, presumably at a slightly more leisurely pace, but producing several different lines by hand every day cannot be easy work.

In this hyper-crowded market it is perhaps unsurprising that things got competitive. *Cupcake Wars* was launched on Food Network in June 2010 (the same year as *The Great British Bake Off*), with a prize of $10,000 on offer for the winning team each week. The format was deliberately tense and full of drama: four teams had to get through three rounds, creating and baking multiple variants on their cupcakes which reflected their flair, imagination and skill. The final round involved making 1,000 cupcakes in two hours to a specified theme, including all of the flavours already presented, and all displayed on a stand of their own design (manufactured in real time by the show's carpenters). The format placed a lot of emphasis on unique and imaginative flavour combinations, and also on presentation; however taste was by no means neglected. The two resident judges were highly qualified on this front: Candace Nelson of Sprinkles Cupcakes, and Florian Bellanger, previously named one of the best pastry chefs in America.

Cupcake Wars and *DC Cupcakes* show the two sides of the market in this buttercream-topped world. The former is all about proving skill and credentials; a win on the show opens doors and makes reputations. *DC Cupcakes*, on the other hand, is all about the joy and the madness of running a family business, set against the backdrop of that most unthreatening and feminine of products: the cupcake. Cupcake baking does not seem to inspire this sort of competition in the UK, however. True, there have been successful 'Iron Cupcake' competitions held in several British cities every month, modelled on an original in Milwaukee (now defunct), but they regularly attract considerably more people buying tickets to be judges than bakers, which must say something about people's interest in baked goods – and, perhaps, baking.

However, *Cupcake Wars* ended its run in 2013 after falling viewing figures. In 2014, the American chain of cupcake shops Crumbs closed all of its forty-eight branches and filed for liquidation after its shares became worth less than one of its mini cupcakes. Many have taken these events as signs that the gourmet cupcake is on its way out – that, as many writers were quick to put it, the cupcake bubble had burst.

Journalist and finance expert Daniel Gross had predicted such a shift in the market in an article which appeared in Slate.com in 2009. The cupcake market had, he said, become overpopulated, and consumers' fondness for a product which relied on so much sugar, at such a price tag, could not last. The cupcakeries were aimed at too specific a market; people do not buy expensive cupcakes every day, after all. As Joshua M. Brown, aka 'The Reformed Broker' put it on his blog, 'This is what happens when you extrapolate a passing fancy of the American people into a full-blown new category – and you believe that a $4 cupcake splurge will somehow become habit-forming enough to build a huge company around.' Forbes.com called the cupcake 'a fanciful luxury'. Gross himself never actually used the word 'bubble', which implies something inflating and then exploding; he did, however, predict a crash after the 'sugar rush'.

Gross's original article made some interesting suggestions about the reasons the gourmet cupcake had originally taken off. Just as 'hemline theory' shows that skirt length correlates with economic cycles (short skirts go with buoyant markets), so too, has the cupcake gone hand in hand with our recent travails and recovery. In the recession which started in 2008, Gross said, people were eager for small treats which would make them feel good without breaking the bank. Similarly, cupcakes were a good proposition for would-be business owners as they did not need large amounts of start-up, were relatively easy to make on a large scale, and catered to that bundle of needs for sugary comfort, served up with a side of nostalgic throwback to childhood and economic prosperity. Then, however, the market got over-saturated as copycat businesses jumped on board, producing a 'cupcake boomlet' of specialised products: organic, vegan, gluten-free, and so on. Finally, the market became awash with less well-funded projects and necessarily less unique products.

When Gross wrote his original, and much-cited article in 2009, the signs of wider economic recovery were not yet assured. With the benefit of further hindsight, others have refined his argument about cupcakes and hard times. As the economy improved, one might think that the fondness for gourmet cupcakes would only strengthen. Not so, says The Reformed Broker: 'Who needs sugar when you've gotten back your swagger?' The same thing happened to Krispy Kreme Doughnuts, he says: they became popular in the wake of the post-9/11 dot.com recession, but demand then fell off once things improved. Newly confident consumers in the first world economy are now looking for healthy treats like frozen yogurt and health-boost smoothies, and are getting their kicks in other areas than comfort food.

In fact, all reports of the demise of the cupcake seem extremely premature. Sales have been slowing slightly in recent years, but the market is still growing. The failure of Crumbs bakery, say more reflective analysts, was not due to a move away from cupcakes by consumers, but from unsustainable growth and a poor business model. Every season we hear predictions for the 'new cupcake', but increasingly, speculators are suggesting that the new cupcake is actually: the cupcake. Other trends have come and gone, but none has proved to be so enduring. Data on Google search terms illustrate this: first a gradual climb in searches for whoopie pies from 2009, and a veritable surge in 2011, then the macaron, which had a more sustained climb up to December 2013 and a particular hike in interest in December of 2012. After these came cake pops, which have had regular surges at the tail end of 2011, 2012 and 2013 (possibly indicative of home-made Christmas presents?). The search term 'cupcake', however, remains more popular than any of these, and sustained a high level of interest throughout the period 2012–14. We should probably wait a little longer before confirming any decline since then; the cupcake does seem to be the most resilient of sugary beasts.

The whoopie pie, which garnered so much attention from internet users in 2011, was a surprise contender for new cupcake status, especially when you think about how much of the appeal of the cupcake is its looks. A whoopie pie is, by contrast, and to put it bluntly, two flat splats of cake, sandwiched together with a buttercream or marshmallow filling. Aficionados would say it's much more than this: a gooey treat which should be eaten with both hands, with the cream which escapes round the sides of the cakes licked off the face afterwards. It's also not a new invention; like the cupcake it trades partly off its air of nostalgia and childish fun, although little is actually known of its origins. It is said to be a traditional Amish treat, but others cite European origins transported to the States by the Pennsylvania Dutch. Maine also makes strong claims to be its birthplace, and both Maine and Pennsylvania hold annual whoopie pie festivals. In a smart piece of one-upmanship, the Maine legislature voted the whoopie pie as Maine's official state treat in 2011 (it lost out as state pie to the blueberry). A similar sandwich cake is beloved in the Southern states where they are called moon pies.

Either way, the most basic beginning of the whoopie or moon pie was probably a quick cake-cum-cookie made with a simple or even leftover batter. One of the most comprehensive websites on food history, Foodtimeline.org, reports a Victorian birth date, but finds no evidence of whoopie pies in early Pennsylvania cookbooks. Their emergence into the mainstream seems to have been gradual, perhaps livened up by a feature on *Oprah* in 2003 which covered a new business making and selling them under the name Wicked Whoopies. Soon they were to be found in coffee shops all over the place, only to sink again within a year or two (a few signature flavours can still be found on the menu at Magnolia). It seems most likely, however, that their rise was based on the same new receptiveness to novelty baked goods which stoked and then sustained the cupcake. Add to this their sense of heritage and childishness and you have a winning combination. What better claim to the latter than the story of how the whoopie pie got its name: from the cry of delight of children finding one in their lunch box.

The next pretender to the cupcake crown, the macaron (not to be confused with the larger, coconut-flavoured and considerably less elegant macaroon), has a certain amount in common with the whoopie pie. Both are sandwiches of cake, filled with a buttercream or mallowy centre. There the resemblance ends, however. If the whoopie pie is pure fun – the joy of childhood in a few messy bites – the macaron is an elegant morsel for adults. It is the epitome of sophistication, down to its delicate colouring and single-bite size (compared with the whoopie, which can be a gargantuan four inches across). It is more demanding of the baker too: the macaron is made from an egg white and ground almond mixture which must be piped into the requisite neat discs and baked in the perfect conditions to create a lightly mounded disc with a shiny exterior. While the outside should be a little crisp, the inside should be chewy and soft, almost melting in the mouth. Where each cakey half meets the filling should be the signature of a well-made macaron: a textured bottom layer known as the 'foot'.

While the whoopie pie was always a home-baked treat with much of its appeal lying in its invitingly unsophisticated appearance, the macaron is shop-bought Parisian perfection. As we've already learned, macarons are a type of petit four, from the category known as dry or 'sec'. Just like so many of the other prized cakes we have met along this journey, there are many claims to be the originator of the macaron. There are several tales of nuns who set up bakeries variously within convents or without, after the suppression of religious orders during the French Revolution, and one which places their arrival in France with Catherine de' Medici from Italy in the sixteenth century – like profiteroles (the name may come from the Italian *macaron* or meringue, and an antecedent certainly seems to have come from Italy). Several French cities lay claim to distinctive versions today, from the sturdy, grainily textured and single-layered *macarons d'Amiens*, to the much more famous Parisian versions, which are the lightly coloured sandwiches filled with ganache or cream in a matching hue so popular today. There is also a similar Swiss version called *Luxemburgerli*, or 'little Luxembourgers' (after the origins of their creator).

If cupcakes are paired in popular culture with New York and Magnolia Bakery, then the macaron is forever linked with Ladurée, whose flagship store is on the fashionable Champs-Élysées in Paris, and which seems to have been one of the first to serve two macarons joined by a filling, rather than simply fused together by their bottoms. The family also set up one of the first *salons de thé*, where respectable women could go to sip tea, catch up on gossip and nibble on a petits fours with their honour unimpugned. Ladurée macarons are highly sought after as dinner party gifts, and offer a changing range of speciality flavours (though they seem to have resisted the inevitable lure of the quixotic: American food writer and Paris resident David Leibowitz reported meeting the only cake he has ever refused to taste, in a foie gras and chocolate macaron from competitor Pierre Hermès). The opening of a new Ladurée store on Madison Avenue, New York City in 2011 brought the ubiquitous queue around the block – the unmistakable sign of the current trend in novelty baked goods. At the other end of the spectrum, you can currently buy a macaron at McDonald's in France, Germany or Australia. But beware – one list of baking trends for 2015 has them on the 'going down' list. You might think that with the sophisticated macaron at their disposal, the French might spurn the less-elegant whoopie pie. In fact, they embraced them, which just goes to show again that novelty goes a long way when it comes to cake.

Some of the other small cakes emerging in recent years have been more specialist items created specifically for a short attention span and thirst for novelty. First, the cake pop, which is cake meets lollipop. The person who turned them from novelty to craze (albeit unintentionally – she had no idea of the attention her invention would attract) was Angie Dudley, author of the now hugely popular American blog, Bakerella.com. In the blog post which sent the cake pop viral in January 2008, she said that she had seen something similar at a party and decided to challenge herself to recreate it. That post had received 384 comments up to November 2014. She has now written several thousand blog posts, multiple cookbooks, and made appearances on national TV shows including *The Martha Stewart Show* for Cupcake Week in 2008.

The appeal of a cake pop is all in its delightfully cute appearance, perched on its stick high above all those ground-level bakes. Underneath that inviting look, however, are several hours of dedicated work, almost entirely invested in the decoration. Dudley actually recommends using a cake mix for the cake, and a tub of ready-made frosting to bind the crumbs together into the requisite balls. But the decoration (including several hours set aside for covering the balls with melted candy coating, and 'tapping' them to ensure an even appearance) is where the skill and, ultimately, the consumer appeal are. They are the ultimate in cute, appealing to children and easily themed to specific purposes, from film releases to cancer awareness campaigns. To continue a theme we have seen emerging quietly through all these fashionable small cakes, however, they seem to be more appealing to women and children than to men. When I bought Dudley's first book, intrigued to find out more about cake pops, my two-year-old son spent a happy half hour looking at the pictures and deciding what he wanted us to make. My partner, meanwhile, was unimpressed at the idea of a cake which sacrificed size and heft for appearance. We will continue with this line of thought shortly, but suffice to note that while Dudley does not suggest anywhere that her book is aimed at women, it does tend to be women who first find these sorts of detailed and intricate cute bakes appealing and, second, are prepared to take the time to make them for friends and family.

Dudley did not create the cake pop, she popularised it. The researchers at Foodtimeline.org found similar lollipop cookies in cookbooks from the 1960s (two cookies sandwiched together with a lolly stick in between), although nothing called a 'pop' until the early twentieth century, and nothing on any scale until the famous Bakerella blog post in 2007. They were made even more ubiquitous by Starbucks, who launched a range of cake pops in 2011 as part of their 'Petites' range (which also included mini cupcakes). What Bakerella did do was cross two trends to create the *cup*cake pop just a few days after her original cake cop. The cupcake pop was an instant hit because it combined three current crazes: for small, impossibly cute, and new. These are possibly even more taxing to a novice baker than a cake pop, as they must be moulded into the cupcake shape before dipping, and also have to be dipped into two different colours of melted candy to get the 'cake' and 'paper liner' effects. The 'cupcake bite' is one notch lower as it requires no moulding and is not mounted on a stick (the cake can thus be dipped in candy coating rather than 'tapped' on its stick). The cake pop and the cupcake pop may be the ultimate in kitschy perfection; they are also very high on the domestic goddess stakes for the same reason. Home-made cake pops are certainly not a rational choice for a small business-person; the price tag would have to be huge to account for the time spent. Perhaps that is why bakers tend to stick to cupcakes.

The last of the latest baking crazes marked the start of a new zeitgeist in the trendy baking world: the portmanteau bake, where one type of treat meets and embraces another. This trend has also been a much more self-conscious attempt by individual bakers and bakeries to create a signature novelty. It all started when noted French-American chef Dominique Ansel, named America's best pastry chef in 2013, launched the (trademarked) cronut on 10 May 2013. It went viral in the way that only a novelty baked good from a fashionable bakery can in today's linked-up world, and the croissant-doughnut hybrid sold out within fifteen minutes. Ansel's official cronut website reports that it took two months of testing and ten different recipes to get the perfect laminated croissant-like dough which could be shaped into a doughnut-like ring, fried and then filled with flavoured cream, rolled in sugar, and glazed. The process takes up to three days, and quality assurance meant that only small batches were available each day: the first 200 consistently sell out within a couple of hours of the bakery opening.

The frenzy and exclusivity surrounding the cronut have led to it being taken very seriously, certainly by the bakery which produces it. Ansel advises eating your cronut (should you be lucky enough to lay hands on one) immediately, cutting it with a serrated knife to keep the delicate layers intact, never refrigerating it (it causes sogginess), and serving it at room temperature, never warmed up. Each cronut sells for $5 from the bakery, but there is a two-cronut limit per customer (pre-orders can be placed for up to six). Queues begin forming up to an hour before opening at 8 a.m., and the bakery has to keep a sharp eye out for 'scalpers' who sell them for vastly inflated prices. Ansel has subsequently shared a 'bake at home' version which also requires three days' preparation, and is rated at an 'extreme' level of difficulty. Ariel Knutson of the Kitchn blog reported her attempts at making them in October 2014, having managed to be first in the queue on the day of the cronut's official launch. She was successful, but posted ten important things a baker should know before starting, one of which was the need to visit a speciality baking shop to get all the ingredients and equipment, which includes a specified piping tip. Other bloggers have reported their own simplified versions, but it seems that the amateur bakers of the world are not falling over themselves to try the original recipe at home.

The cronut is not Ansel's first foray into the world of hybrid bakes; he is also known for a soufflé-brioche combination, although it did not achieve the renown of the cronut. Since its launch he has been responsible for a veritable and inevitable flood of (unendorsed) copycats and spin-offs. Since the name 'cronut' is trademarked, tributes are sold under a variety of catchy titles, including the CroNot, the zonut and the dosant (some, it should be said, claim an earlier birth date than the cronut). Waffles Café in Chicago then launched the wonut – a waffle-doughnut cross (essentially a deep-fried and sugar-dipped waffle). The UK bakery chain Greggs, whose are best known for their sausage rolls and pasties, launched a 'Greggsnut' in September 2013, retailing at just £1.25 each. It was described as a doughnut made from layers of pastry, not unlike that other British favourite, the yum yum. Since then, things have gone, frankly, quite mad. We now have crookies, brookies, duffins, and cruffins, all mash-ups of familiar treats (cookies, tarts, brownies, doughnuts, croissants and muffins respectively). It seems likely that each will be just a flash in the deep-fryer, but they illustrate once again how single-portion baked (or fried) treats have been absorbed into our search for novelty and excitement – even at $5 a go, and a week's worth of calories.

The cronut and the other deep-fried offspring it has spawned seem to appeal to men and women alike. In fact, the sheer decadence of these newest goodies, plus the fact that they are not exactly diminutive in size, takes them out of the realm of 'feminine treat' and into 'man-sized snack'; even 'macho challenge'. And here we really need to tackle head on the assumptions promoted and bought into by producers and customers alike: that cute, small cakes are made for, eaten by, and baked by, women. What is it about the cupcake and its ilk which is inextricably linked to femininity? And is this, ultimately, a good thing or not?

The American writer Caitlin Flanagan wrote in her 2006 book, *To Hell With All That: Loving and Loathing Our Inner Housewife*, about the intrinsic love many women have for pretty things. She used it to explain the power of the Martha Stewart empire; her many books and magazines peddle projects and images which are beautiful to the point of being impractical – eye candy rather than items you actually have any need for. At the heart of this, Flanagan says, is the much overlooked fact that women are attached to homemaking and housekeeping even in an era when these things are not fashionable or expected of liberated and career-capable women.

The ongoing mania for cupcakes fits into this idea very neatly. Cupcakes are pretty, and in a way thought of as traditionally female: neat and beautifully made-up. Men often think them overly fussy and small, with too much emphasis on sugar frosting and not enough on cake. They are also a relatively manageable bake-at-home project which lends itself to the sort of decoration that both impresses and demonstrates motherhood (think of those children's parties). Their one-portion size makes them ideal for the body-conscious, a facet of womanhood which has endured through the years. Lastly, shop-bought gourmet cupcakes are a sure signifier of modern good taste and disposable income; another attribute which makes them appealing to women in particular, who still make most of the spending decisions when it comes to household, and particularly kitchen, matters.

However, these same traits can also make disheartening reading for those who hope to divorce female identity from all of these trappings of beauty, slimness and restraint: the assumption that femininity goes with the colour pink and things that are cute and glittery, and that ties women to a consumer culture which elevates baking and providing sweet treats to a high order. Second-wave feminists in the 1960s worked hard to reject housework and domesticity as the lot of women; their modern counterparts may now ask if we are now sliding back to a position where domesticity is being fetishised without any thought to what else that implies about women's status. Have the cupcake, the cake pop and them played their part in this?

The first way to answer these questions is to say that the biggest difference for women choosing to bake (or buy) cakes today is just that: they choose to do so, just as they choose whether or not to embrace the domestic goddess image. There may be circles where there is pressure to provide home-made cupcakes for children's birthdays (high-profile CEO Katya Andreson confesses that she, in a moment of what she now considers to be madness, scraped the frosting off a batch of store-bought cupcakes in order to replace it with something that looked more home-made before sending them to school for her daughter's birthday), but on the whole, women are no longer expected to spend time in the kitchen producing beautiful baked goods for friends and family if they don't want to. If they don't like baking cakes, they can buy them; if they don't like pink frosted cupcakes, they can provide something else. There is a case for saying that the act of choosing to bake may actually be part of a new form of post-feminist femininity in which women have a huge amount of freedom in crafting their identity. This is exactly what Nigella Lawson, the First Lady of Domestic Goddesses, is getting at when she talks about baking being a feminist act – and also the reason that she attracts criticism. Her positive embodiment of women who enjoy spending time in the kitchen creating confections for others makes uneasy reading for those who think women should not aspire to a return to domestic drudgery. It seems uncomfortably close to a pre-feminist view of women who were defined by their domestic roles. Yet it's an ideal which rings true for many women. Baking, knitting and other home crafts are no longer only associated with older generations; it is younger women who take part in Clandestine Cake Clubs, the newer urban form of the Women's Institute, the 'WI-lite' and who join sewing bees and knitting clubs. For them, these crafts are part of finding a way to express creativity and female companionship. These are the women who embrace and aspire to the term domestic goddess even while not necessarily taking it very seriously. To criticise the results for being twee or cute seems a little unsisterly.

So far, so positive. Cupcakes and the other diminutive cakes we have met in this chapter are a little different though. Their size, shape and appearance all promote a view of femininity which similarly dwells on size, shape and appearance. Women do buy cupcakes in proportionately greater numbers than men; even the supposedly 'male' cupcakes baked by the American Butch Bakery whose lines have names like the 'Driller' and the 'B-52', and which feature ingredients like beer-infused buttercream, crumbled bacon, and crushed pretzels (their owner, David Arrick, believes that the 90 per cent of his female customers buy them as gifts for men; it would be interesting to know how many are actually bought for women). The very fact that there is such a thing as 'male cupcakes' says a lot about the way that these cakes are marketed more generally – although also a sign that actually, men can like them too.

The simple truth is that women are *not* hardwired to need or even desire foods that are small, cute, pretty or sugary; that they often do so is the result of cultural conditioning going back hundreds of years. 'Women's food' consists either of low-calorie and dainty foods like salads, or alternatively, of treats which are seen as emotional crutches – like cupcakes. They are contrasted with hearty meaty fare sought out by men to fill them up and to assert their manly status of consumers of hunted rather than foraged food. In the last few decades, however, this seems to have crystallised into a gender stereotype which men and women buy into in equal measure (is it any coincidence that there are a huge number of children's books with the word 'cupcake' in the title, almost all featuring girl characters and pink covers?). Critiques of the cupcake industry (men and women) often dwell on the overblown cutesiness and lack of substance of the little cakes, their frivolity and shorthand for a type of moneyed female lifestyle. When Hillary Clinton declared that number nine of her top ten campaign promises in her 2007 bid for the Democratic presidential nomination was that everyone should get a cupcake on her birthday, she was saying something about her empathetic qualities as a female candidate (although not as a home baker: in 1992 she is reported to have said that she had deliberately eschewed staying at home and baking cookies in order to have a career). By the time of her bid in 2015, she was staying silent on the issue of sweet treats, instead making a much stronger statement about gender equality. All this sounds like a big charge against a small cake, but it's something we need to address. Put simply, do such treats infantilise the women who are their primary market?

There is a big group of women who would answer this question with a resounding 'no'. For them, cupcakes are symbols of femininity which women should be free to enjoy with unbridled pleasure – ironic as much as delightful. The Canadian-born Mellissa Morgan, aka Ms Cupcake, owner of a London vegan cupcakery and author of a book subtitled *The Naughtiest Vegan Cakes in Town* – 'naughty' because of their decadent ingredients – is one. Ms Cupcake is a successful businesswoman with a high profile on the baking scene and in social media. For her, being an independent career woman should not be incompatible with baking. In fact, she told me that baking for her was an empowering act, as much about exerting control and creativity at a time of economic downturn as about the creation of cake *per se*, although that is her passion. Her cakes deliberately eschew pink, sprinkles, flowers and hearts, and in their sheer variety aim to appeal to men and women alike. Nonetheless, she agrees that there is something about the image, the colour and the whole experience of entering a cupcake bakery which does appeal particularly to women. There are hundreds of applicants for every job vacancy at her bakery, of whom the vast majority are female.

Another interesting aspect of the fondness for baking and other traditional domestic crafts is its coupling with the aesthetic of the 1950s, and particularly the style of clothing and hairdressing of the period. Ms Cupcake's bakery is decorated in a 1950s style, and it is not unusual to see the staff of cupcake bakeries and food stalls (as well as those interested in other 'vintage' crafts) dressed this way. This is where cupcake feminism is harder to square with the original aims of second-wave feminism, which was striving to escape from all of the kitchen-bound lack of choice laid down by a patriarchal society. Again, though, cupcake feminists (a term used as much pejoratively as with pride) might say that they have cherry-picked those of the values of the 1950s which speak to femininity and reclaimed them. There are a number of burlesque clubs in London and elsewhere which serve cupcakes and afternoon teas, deliberately repossessing the romantic and feminine ideal of beauty of the 1950s and updating it for the modern day. It is probably also no coincidence that the grandmothers who are called on with such regularity to explain the attachment of the younger generation to cupcake baking were doing their primary homemaking in the 1950s. Furthermore, as Ms Cupcake reminded me, in North America the decade did not have the same overtones of austerity and narrowing of domestic boundaries as it did in Britain. There, it was an era of new freedoms, youth culture and less restrictive fashions; the fifties touches in her bakery's décor are all about bright colour and the new materials that were emerging at that time. The fondness for the fifties thus has two aspects, both positive for those who embrace it: first an ideal of female empowerment and a celebration of beauty, colour and choice; and second, a nostalgia for family-oriented home baking – values which many young women feel they lack today. In Britain at least, cupcake nostalgia is also a form of national identity. The smaller type of dainty British cupcake comes out in force on all occasions when Britishness is being celebrated: the Queen's diamond jubilee; the royal wedding; the Olympics. This can be read as another form of idealised nostalgia for the community of times past. Yes, all this might overlook the restrictions on women of the period (although we should not forget that there were many women active in psychology, art, science and many other fields in the 1950s); but should this stop us celebrating a sense of shared history and values which seem to be peculiarly summed up in the cupcake? Feminist writers have not traditionally paid much attention to how and whether homemaking can be squared with feminism; perhaps this is what the current wave of cupcake-baking young women are achieving.

Another factor which complicates the equating of cupcakes with femininity is the fact that men are getting in on the act. If we go back to *The Great British Bake Off* for a moment, we may note that a very large proportion of finalists and winners have been men, and they have excelled in cake baking and decorating as much as in the more traditional male field of bread-making. While the finals in 2011 and 2013 both featured three female bakers, the one in 2012 was all male. The fact that women completely dominated two out of those three years can also be read as a statement about female equality given that this is a highly competitive show where 'male' qualities such as precision and keeping one's nerve under pressure can do as well as 'female' ones like intuition and inherited knowledge. French pâtissier Eric Lanlard (aka Cake Boy) is popularising all sorts of cake-making for men, while Yotam Ottolenghi's delis regularly appear on lists of top cupcake eateries in London. And just to balance out the gender stereotypes, the male-owned Butch Bakery has a counterpart in the female-led Prohibition Bakery in New York, which features, among other alcohol-spiked offerings, pretzel and beer cupcakes, which one hopes are as popular with female customers as male.

But what is really undeniable is that the mania for both baking and eating cupcakes, especially the fancy 'gourmet' sort, is very much bound up with affluence. Despite the fact that cupcakes apparently rode the wave to popularity on the economic recession, they are still an expensive treat. Baking a batch of cupcakes at home is not as cheap as buying them from the supermarket. If you are genuinely 'trading down' to save money, you look elsewhere for a sweet treat. Almost all of the high-profile bakers of these little treats are white, middle-class women, and almost all of the rest are white, middle-class men. The cupcake is not only a female dainty, it is a white, middle-class one, and that probably ought to give us as much food for thought.

*

Another truth we need to acknowledge is that what all these small treats are not, is nutritious, or kind to the teeth. Cupcake denigrators frequently refer to the ratio of frosting to cake; several of the highest-profile bakeries have had damning reviews citing a dry and poorly executed cake, which seems to be simply a vehicle for a huge twist of flavoured buttercream. At the same time the cupcake has grown and grown. The now defunct Crumbs range scaled from 'Taste' (one inch), 'Classic' (2.5 inches), 'Signature' (4 inches and 6 ounces in weight) and 'Colossal' (6.5 inches in both width and height, and designed to serve eight). Just by way of contrast, Irma Rombauer's recipe for yellow cupcakes made twenty-eight 2-inch cakes.

All this has a lot to do with our seemingly unquenchable desire for sweetness. Originally an evolutionary advantage (it allowed our ancestors to store energy in the form of fat through lean winters), our addiction to sugar has grown and grown, giving us energy in large quantities but little in the way of the more useful major nutritional building blocks like protein or vitamins. Moreover the carbohydrate it contains is of the 'quick release' variety which is less useful to the body, while all that energy is easily stored as fat. It is released into the blood stream where it contributes to raised blood pressure and the risk of Type 2 diabetes, and it busily goes to work on our teeth enamel too. It is absolutely no coincidence at all that rates of obesity, tooth decay, diabetes and hypertension have all risen in the developed world just as sugar has crept into more and more of our foods and drinks.

The average American now eats 22.7 teaspoons of sugar per day, equating to 95 grams or 3.4 ounces, which sits uncomfortably against the American Heart Association's recommendation of 9 teaspoons for men and 6 for women. America is not even in the top five consumers of refined sugar in the world, however; that honour goes to Brazil at 122 pounds per person per year in 2011, followed by Russia at 88 pounds. Still, the majority of those American 22.7 teaspoons are from sucrose – the refined sugar used for baking.

All this sugar means that cupcakes have been in the firing line when it comes to healthy eating. When Mintel surveyed cake-buying habits in Britain in June 2013, they found that sugar and fat levels were the biggest concern among consumers (a third of those surveyed). But the health conscious have an uphill battle to fight if they want to persuade us to cut down on sugary treats. In 2007 one professor of nutrition in America coined the term 'cupcake problem' – not to refer to the number of cakes being eaten, but instead to explain the furore from parents when schools tried to restrict the snacks available to children on the premises, including treats sent in on birthdays. The 'problem', it seems, lay in the emotional load a cupcake represents for parents as much as children. The state of Texas went ahead with a ban on 'junk food' in schools in 2004 but faced so much opposition from parents that it had to pass a 'Safe Cupcake Amendment' in 2005 (aka 'Lauren's Law', named after the daughter of a local Republican politician who took her father to task on the matter), to protect the right of children to take cupcakes and other treats to school for celebrations. When the issue was raised again in a press conference with the new agricultural commissioner for Texas in 2015 (when healthy eating in school was again being promoted as part of Michelle Obama's wellness policy, and the new 2014 'Smart Snacks in Schools' guidelines), it was still the cupcakes which were singled out as a now protected part of childhood celebrations. It is hard to imagine a clearer summing up of the place cupcakes occupy in adults' emotional memory; so much so that they will fight for their right to keep it part of their children's childhood, even when they know the toll it takes on their health.

America is not the only place where sweet snacks are being limited in schools, although nowhere else have cupcakes come in for such special treatment. The UK's School Food Plan, issued by the Department of Education and effective from 2015, bans all snacks except seeds, nuts, vegetables and fruits across the whole school day. Desserts, cakes and biscuits are allowed only at lunchtime. The Ontario School Food and Beverage Policy of 2010 does not permit the sale of any baked goods with more than 10 grams of fat per serving, or more than 2 grams of saturated fat, or less than 2 grams of fibre (just for reference, a red velvet cupcake from Magnolia Bakery contains 22.8 grams of fat and 442 calories). The guidelines note that this includes most croissants, danishes, cakes and pies. Even the classic Canadian doughnut gets no exemption, although the provincial government has left room for the sort of celebration mourned by Texan parents: every school has ten discretionary 'special event days' where the guidelines may be waived.

Cupcakes and other baked goods are not the worst culprits here; the highest sugar intake for children comes from sugary drinks, fruit juices and confectionery – but they do play a significant part. Cakes, muffins, scones and cake-type desserts are the top type of snack consumed by Australian children. Buns, cakes, pastries and fruit pies are responsible for 7 per cent of British adults' sugar intake, 6 per cent of that of teens, 9 per cent of those aged 4 to 10, and 6 per cent of those aged 1½ to 3. And with portion sizes growing, cupcakes deliver an undeniably heftier sugar kick now than they did in the past, thanks to the now ubiquitous combination of cake, frosting and adornments. The UK School Food Plan recommends cake portion sizes of 40 to 50 grams for 4–10 year olds – that's 1.4 to 1.8 ounces, which is about the size of a standard Tesco chocolate cupcake. A chocolate cupcake with frosting from Magnolia, meanwhile, weighs in at 152 grams or 5.3 ounces. Currently, all age groups in the UK eat more sugar than they should (the recommended limit is 10 per cent of the average energy intake or 11–14 teaspoons per day, although this is in the process of being revised downwards), and in 2012 almost a third of 5 year olds in England had tooth decay. One Texan food blogger and mother recently pointed out that the impact of her child eating one cupcake for each of the possible 20 term-time birthdays in their school class could be a gain of 10 pounds in weight over the course of their elementary school career. Texas, meanwhile, already suffers an obesity problem. And don't let's get started on some of the industrially manufactured small treats we met in Chapter 6: author Steve Ettlinger discovered on close enquiry that a Twinkie is made from 25 different *types* of ingredients (he considered all of the soy, corn and phosphate derivatives together), that it contains as much sugar as flour, and that it features fourteen of the twenty most common chemicals made in the United States.

Cupcakes are, then, making their own contribution to a severe health problem in the developed world. But on the other hand, they are beloved as treats and expressions of family and childhood. As they grow ever larger and spawn even unhealthier offspring like the saturated-fat-laden cronut, they move further and further away from childhood treat and closer to the sort of adult qualities which often typify modern culture: that we 'deserve' a treat and hang the dietary consequences; that we don't want to share; and that we are always after a newer and racier experience. Perhaps instead we need a campaign for the fairy cake to be the new cupcake. And also for more children to learn their cupcake baking at their father or grandfather's side.

Small treats like cupcakes, whoopie pies and macarons have many different roles to play. Like their larger cake relations they serve the tea table well; in fact, they are custom built for the traditional English afternoon tea, with its tiered plate of small morsels. When we spoke, Ms Cupcake noted the novelty of the 'complete treat just for me' which goes with buying a cupcake rather than a slice from a large cake. Some of the other small bakes we have met are more of a novelty snack with no fixed occasion to anchor themselves to; one can't imagine the cake pop, for example, having the gravitas to grace a tea table, although they would certainly be welcomed at a high-end children's party. This was, of course, the original hangout of the cupcake, but all of the cakes we've considered here have a big following among adults too. And while the macaron really needs a tea table, worthy of its French origins, many others are well suited to be eaten on the move, cream oozing from their paper bag, leaving fingers to be licked as the wrapper is thrown away, just like the medieval 'fairing' cakes we met in Chapter 2.

One of the other key themes to come out of this consideration of the small and the cute of the cake world is the growing inter-nationalisation of tastes and culinary fashions. The whoopie pie, the macaron and the cupcake itself were all originally rooted in particular cultures, but have now been embraced across the world, sometimes intact, sometimes acquiring new attributes along the way. While the cupcake means childhood to an American or a Briton, it means fashion and Western culture to someone in Dubai or Beijing. On the other hand, bakeries in London and New York now offer matcha-flavoured cupcakes and rosewater-tinted macarons, so taste influences work both ways. One taste forecaster in 2015 predicted that Middle Eastern flavours like zaatar and harissa would soon be making their way into Western cupcakes. The next small treat is supposed to be the *merveilleux*, another French/Belgian export, consisting of layers of light meringue, filled with cream and shaped into a chocolate-coated, beehive-like dome. They are named for the female dandies who proliferated in Paris at just the time that Antonin Carême was starting his rise to culinary superstar. The first shop devoted to them in the States opened in New York in 2013. Meanwhile, the cronut, the macaron and the whoopie pie are supposedly on the way down, their moment in the limelight past (others disagree – the cronut is apparently set for a gourmet make-over with new flavours and fillings). Perhaps this explains the enduring popularity of the cupcake; it is really a vehicle to reflect new tastes. Any number of flavour combinations and additions can be accommodated in its batter-and-topping format – and boy, have they been.

So whether you love a gourmet cupcake, would queue for a cronut, sigh over a cake pop or none of the above, whether you embrace the pretty pink cupcake or wish you could send it back to the 1950s patriarchy, you probably have happy memories of small cakes from somewhere in your life. And on that note, you'll have to excuse me – I have some robot cake pops to make. Yum-yum.

Epilogue

A SLICE OF HISTORY

Let's end by going back to where we began: the Great British Snowball controversy of 2014. The judges in that tribunal were essentially being asked a very simple question: what is a cake? After much deliberation they came up with a definition which focused on the occasions on which cakes were eaten, and more than that, the *sense* of occasion they brought. A cake was eaten from a plate, possibly with cutlery; certainly not on the move or with the fingers. A cake, then, was something above a regular snack, and something with a bit of a sense of refinement.

Our survey of the long history of these bakes has shown that there's a bit more to it than that, though the judges were certainly right about a cake's status as a special sort of snack. If we go far enough back in time, though, we've seen that the principal defining characteristics of a cake was actually its shape. Lindow Man's last meal was nothing particularly special, but it is referred to by archaeologists as a cake of the most staple sorts of food at the time: grains. In its earliest guise, then, cake predates bread, although neither was in the form we know it today.

By the time of the sophisticated culture of the Egyptians, cake had certainly taken on its guise of sweet and 'special'. Even in the legends of the 'Dark Ages' of King Alfred's Mercia, cake was very specifically not bread, and producing it was women's work – not something it behoved a warrior king to be messing about with. A cake contained extra ingredients which made it sweeter and richer than the regular, staple foodstuffs. It was also already accompanying special occasions, from the passing of the shortest day and the festive Christmas period, and eventually on to birthdays, weddings and, finally, baby showers, graduations and almost any other occasion you care to name. It even makes a cup of tea an occasion; more than that, it's a symbol of national culture – from the British and their afternoon teas to the Germans and their *kaffeeklatsch*.

Our account has shown that a lot of the other modern characteristics of cake were slow in coming. A cake was not always baked in a tin, as it usually is today. Centuries' worth of bakers would have been baffled at the idea that cake is baked in an oven, let alone one in your own home, which baked to a specified temperature. They would have marvelled at the idea that a dash of powder could replace an hour's worth of beating eggs, or that a specialised piece of equipment would eclipse the bundles of twigs and perforated spoons of yore. Would they have laughed to see that many of us keep a designated cake tester in our kitchen drawers (it will usually have slipped underneath the cutlery rack when you want it) instead of a broom splinter or a knife? And what on earth would they have made of the cake mix?

All of this underplays the sheer variety of modern cakes. There are parts of the world where cakes are still much more likely to be fried or steamed than baked. There are cakes which do not contain sugar, or eggs, or which feature cola, tinned soup, beetroot or salad oil. There are those which stand proudly tall, others which fall in on themselves with the weight of chocolate. Cake, then, is a much more varied and adaptable beast than we might think as we make our choice in a bakery. And while some cake lovers' preferences are based on taste and appearance, others are grounded in the way they make them feel in a broader sense: a sense of attachment to a family, community or heritage. For those people, the first taste evokes much more than the simple endorphin response to sugar, fat and carbohydrate.

These thoughts bring us to another distinctive part of the history of cake: the contrast between the simple pleasure of baking and eating, and the much wider history which underpins it. We have met many, many instances in these pages where the arrival of our favourite bakes has depended utterly on revolutionary developments in technology, international trade and communication, migration, printing, and the building of communities. Cake is an expression of the way that society forms its ideas about childhood, motherhood, sweetness and celebration. Big claims for a small pleasure, eh?

And this brings us on to another consideration: the relationship between cake and the various aspects of femininity. For centuries it was legions of women who did the regular home baking and who used it as an expression of love, maternal joy and – let's not rose-tint our view too much – duty. At times this became an expression of skill and worth; at others it came to represent oppression and lack of opportunity. For much of history it was simply a reflection of a dominant system of patriarchy. But cake-making can be distinguished from the routine tasks of cookery and homemaking because for most of its history, it has meant more than providing nutrition. Instead, it has signified hospitality, love and celebration. That's not to say that women always enjoyed producing it, or that it was always an easy task, but it meant that cake-bakers contributed to an economy of gifting and nurture which we haven't always appreciated as much as the more male-dominated one of hard cash and sustenance.

More than that, cake-making was the literal making of many women: witness the burgeoning market for cookbooks and household manuals written by female authors. It was not even necessary to have much experience of baking or running a household if you could achieve the right combination of authority, simplicity and trustworthiness. Elizabeth Raffald combined writing a bestseller with a business making cakes and other goods; Catherine Beecher's cookbook was a product of her career promoting female education. For Irma Rombauer, writing about baking and cooking was her lifeline from a widowhood spent in poverty. Writing a cookbook was one of the first ways that women could acceptably cross the divide between the private world of the home and the public one of the professional expert.

But what of the ingrained assumption that it is women who particularly like *eating* cake? I hope that I've shown that this is a notion we can throw out. Women like cake; children like cake; men like cake. It's full of sweetness, fat and stodge: it's there to be liked. The association of women with cakes – and especially the cute and pretty sort like the cupcake and the macaron – tells us a lot more about societal constructions of gender than about women's biology, tastes, abilities, relationship with sugar or the kitchen – or cakes. The winner of *The Great British Bake Off* in 2015, Nadiya Hussain, is a stay-at-home mum from a Bangladeshi Muslim family who rapidly found that she was expected to fly the flag for multi-cultural Britain. But the role she was happiest promoting was that of the full-time homemaker. It is very pleasing that she was also loved by the British public for her wit and skill. A look at the bestseller lists on Amazon strongly suggest that Nadiya and her ilk – amateurs with high standards, considerable imagination and a love of baking – are our new domestic gods and goddesses.

For cake today in today's Western world is nothing if not democratic. It's cheap enough that anyone who fancies it can eat it; they can buy it or make it; share it with family and friends; or send it out to the world of social media. They can bake and donate to charities;

use it to make a political statement, break records or declare their resignation – and people have done all of those things just in the last few months of writing. The modern cake is created by men and women; it's bespoke, colourful and fun. It can be cheap and cheerful in a plastic wrapper, or queued for for hours and carried home in a beautiful box.

It's true that cake is also once again a sign of accomplishment as it had arguably not been for some decades, but it's the sort of accomplishment that goes beyond gender, social background or professional training. My friends with young children talk about whether they can bake or not – one recently set herself the task of learning, but admits that making her daughter's birthday cake made her tummy ache with stress. I am also a baker who enjoys making homey recipes, not state-of-the-art sculptures (a side note: the robot cake pops were a disaster).

The fact is that in the process of all the research for this book, and all the conversations I've had with friends and family as a result, I have never heard anyone speak disparagingly or negatively about cake. Their affection for it may vary; they may not have a sweet tooth and may hate baking, but almost everyone has a cake they are fond of and which means something to them.

As I wind up this epilogue, I am somewhat distracted by thoughts of the Minion cake my son has requested for his third birthday party. I have scoured Pinterest and bought a ton of eggs, sugar, butter and fondant icings in the requisite colours of yellow and blue. The pressure is on to get it looking right: my friends are very forgiving but it's a joint birthday party and there will be two other birthday cakes on display too. I want my Minion to hold its own (though by midnight tonight I may settle for it just being recognisable). But I'm also looking forward to going home and baking it with my son: trying to keep the sugar off the counter and his fingers out of the bowl. He's mainly in it for the batter-laden spoon at the end, but then that's one of the chief baker's perks. The one thing I have not hesitated over is the recipe itself: the same one which produced my childhood birthday cakes and my sister's wedding cake: Great Aunt Queenie's chocolate cake.

Acknowledgements

Huge thanks first to James Barr, who made the vital introductions and gave me lots of invaluable advice. Also to Sally Holloway of Felicity Bryan Associates Literary Agency, who saw enough in my proposal to put me on her 'quirky' list, and Zoë Pagnamenta who did the same in the States. Then to Simon Thorogood of Headline, for taking it on and being so supportive, along with his marketing and copy-editing teams, and Jessica Case of Pegasus for doing the same with the American edition. I'd also like to thank Mellissa Morgan (aka Ms Cupcake) for being so generous with her time and thoughts on baking, and the staff at the Bodleian Library, the Special Collections at Oxford Brookes University and the Mass Observation Archive at the University of Sussex.

My friends, family and colleagues have given me huge amounts of support and encouragement. At Oxford Brookes, Joanne Begiato, Jane Stevens Crawshaw, Glen O'Hara and David Nash in particular, and at home, Rich above all, and my parents, siblings and friends, especially those who read very early drafts – Mum, Dad, Sue, Hannah, Carys, Nic, Roisin and Rosie – and Zoe for the tax ruling on Snowballs.

And finally, since a lot of this book is about the childhood joys of baking and eating cake, my icing and wonky sweeties on the top are Alex and the cousins and friends we bake for: Owen, Oliver, Eve, Luke, Henry, Parker and Emily; Caitlin, Lizzie, Will, James, Jenson, Theo and Thomas.

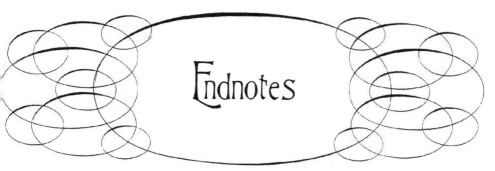

Endnotes

INTRODUCTION

What exactly, then, makes a cake a cake?: This description is based on the report from the First-tier Tribunal Tax Chamber *Lees of Scotland Ltd & Thomas Tunnock -v-HMRC* [2014] UK FTT. Retrieved from http://www.financeandtaxtribunals.gov.uk/judgmentfiles/j7837/TC03754.pdf. See also http://www.hmrc.gov.uk/manuals/vfoodmanual/vfood6260.htm (both retrieved 22 September 2015).

More than three-fifths of British adults baked at home at least once in 2013: Several recent reports have highlighted the rise in home baking. For a summary of this particular report see http://www.telegraph.co.uk/culture/tvandradio/great-british-bake-off/11059161/How-The-Great-British-Bake-Off-became-a-beast.html (retrieved 22 September 2015).

If the flour is mixed in too heavy-handedly: See Alan Davidson, *The Oxford Companion to Food* (Oxford: Oxford University Press, 1999), p. 124; Barbara Maher, *Cakes* (Harmondsworth: Penguin, 1984), pp. 28–38; also www.guardian.co.uk/science/blog/2010/jun/09/science-cake-baking-andy-connelly. For more on food and baking science see Harold McGee, *On Food and Cooking: The Science and Lore of the Kitchen* (Scribner: New York City, 1984; a revised edition was published in 2004).

CHAPTER 1

He is the only English king to be known as 'Great': There are many books devoted to Alfred's life. Readers interested in the cake story in particular could consult David Horspool's *Why Alfred Burned the Cakes* (London: Profile Books, 2006).

An encyclopaedia published in 1382: This usage is noted in the *OED* entry on cake.

The Abbot of Peterborough: The facts on dietary intake and on the Abbot of Peterborough are both from D. J. Stone, 'The consumption of field crops in late medieval England', in C. M. Woolger, D. Serjeantson and T. Waldron (eds), *Food in Medieval England: Diet and Nutrition* (Oxford: Oxford University Press, 2006), pp. 11–26. For more on the diet of medieval England see Peter Brears, *Cooking and Dining in Medieval England* (Totnes, Devon: Prospect Books, 2012).

All ten miscreants in this case were put in the pillory: For more on this see http://www.british-history.ac.uk/manchester-uni/london-lay-subsidy/1332/pp19-34#fnn17 and Reay Tannahill, *Food in History,* rev. ed. (London: Penguin, 1988), p. 163.

Once humans started to cultivate grain crops around 8000–7000 BC: This section draws on Tannahill, *Food in History*, pp. 72–3, and Tom Standage, *An Edible History of Humanity* (London: Atlantic Books, 2009), Chapter 1.

Even after all this the grain still needed long cooking: See C. Anne Wilson, *Food and Drink in Britain from the Stone Age to Recent Times* (Harmondsworth: Penguin, 1973).

Once the grains had finally been ground, sifted and bolted: See Tannahill, *Food in History*; for more on harvest cakes see Krystina Castella, *A World of Cake: 150 Recipes for Sweet Traditions from Cultures Near and Far* (North Adams, MA: Storey Publishing, 2010), pp. 262–3. For French traditions see Steven Laurence Kaplan, *The Bakers of Paris and the Bread Question, 1700–1775* (Durham and London: Duke University Press, 1996), pp. 24–5.

The Greeks and the Romans took up this culinary example: An excellent reference work on all matters to do with food in this long period is Andrew Dalby's *Food in the Ancient World from A to Z* (London and New York: Routledge, 2003). Many of the details in this section are drawn from this book.

Elizabeth David reported: Elizabeth David, *English Bread and Yeast Cookery* (Harmondsworth: Penguin, 1979), p. 157. For more on these general topics see the works by Tannahill and Wilson already cited.

In fact, the Anglo-Saxon word for 'lady': Ann Hagan, *A Handbook of Anglo-Saxon Food Processing and Consumption* (Pinner, Middlesex: Anglo-Saxon Books, 1992), p. 10.

The word 'pandemaine': See David, *English Bread Cookery*, pp. 329–40, and Hagan, *Handbook*.

These alternative flours: These details are from David, *English Bread Cookery*.

At this stage it was scarce enough: Brears, *Cooking and Dining*, p. 343.

As might be expected from its cost and scarcity: For more on the British use of sugar in this period see Brears, *Cooking and Dining*, pp. 343–64.

Over the next few centuries: The best work on the rich variety of English baking is David, *English Bread Cookery*.

'I shouldn't wonder, in these dark, nameless, perplexing times': *Home and Country* volume 24, issue 2 (February 1942), p. 20.

CHAPTER 2

In 1714 a young Englishman: *Spectator* No. 597, 22 September 1714, available at http://www.gutenberg.org/files/12030/12030-h/SV3/Spectator3.html#section597 (retrieved 3 January 2012)

For the first time, baking hoops: Elizabeth David, *English Bread and Yeast Cookery* (Harmondsworth: Penguin, 1979), pp. 212–3.

Their name is something of a misnomer: John Ayto, *An A to Z of Food and Drink*, new ed. (Oxford: Oxford University Press, 2002), p. 142.

Early British recipes: David, *English Bread Cookery*, p. 340. For more on gingerbread generally, see Peter Brears, *Cooking and Dining in Medieval England* (Totnes, Devon:

Prospect Books, 2012), p. 348, and C. Anne Wilson, *Food and Drink in Britain from the Stone Age to Recent Times* (Harmondsworth: Penguin, 1973), pp. 223, 237; also the article 'English Gingerbread Old and New' at http://recipes.hypotheses.org/660.

Benjamin Franklin recorded buying gingerbread: Amelia Simmons, *The First American Cookbook. A Facsimile of 'American Cookery', 1797*, Mary Tolford Wilson's introductory essay, p. xv.

Reims, in the Champagne-Ardenne region: See http://dijoon.free.fr/pepicehistoire.htm. Julia Child's recipe is in Julia Child and Simone Beck, *Mastering the Art of French Cooking*, vol. II (New York: Alfred A. Knopf, 1970), p. 481.

In Germany: There are several good websites offering histories of German gingerbread, and recipes. See, for example, http://germanfood.about.com/od/adventandchristmas/ss/nuernberger_lebkuchen.htm and www.germanfoodguide.com/lebkuchen.cfm (retrieved on 17 February 2014).

Part of that involved communal celebration: The information in the sections which follow draws on the excellent studies of the ritual year by Ronald Hutton, *The Stations of the Sun: a History of the Ritual Year in Britain* (Oxford: Oxford University Press, 1996) and Dorothy Gladys Spicer, *Yearbook of English Festivals* (Westport, Conn: Greenwood Press, 1954).

In 1838 a man was indicted: Details of this case can be found at Tim Hitchcock, Robert Shoemaker, Clive Emsley, Sharon Howard and Jamie McLaughlin *et al.*, *The Old Bailey Proceedings Online, 1674–1913* (www.oldbaileyonline.org, version 7.2, consulted 3 September 2015).

One traditional children's rhyme: This rhyme is cited in the entry under 'cake' in the *Oxford English Dictionary*. The information on the Scotch black bun is from Alan Davidson, *The Oxford Companion to Food* (Oxford: Oxford University Press, 1999), pp. 79–80.

Another bready cake . . . is the German stollen: For details on stollen and other German cakes, see Wilfred J. Fance (ed.), *The International Confectioner: Confectionery, Cakes, Pastries, Desserts and Ices* (London: Virtue & Company Ltd, 1968).

Scottish Hogmanay was a time for cakes: An excellent overview of traditional New Year cakes can be found in Krystina Castella, *A World of Cake: 150 Recipes for Sweet*

Traditions from Cultures Near and Far (North Adams, MA: Storey Publishing, 2010), pp. 249–51. The note on Bury St Edmunds is from Spicer's *Yearbook*.

Easter is another key point: This section draws on information from Hutton, *The Stations of the Sun*, Castella, *A World of Cake*, and David, *English Bread Cookery*.

The tradition is continued to this day: Spicer, *Yearbook*.

The now-unknown tansy cakes: Spicer, *Yearbook*.

But it was the spices . . .: On spices, see Tom Standage, *An Edible History of Humanity* (London: Atlantic Books, 2009) and Reay Tannahill, *Food in History,* rev. ed. (London: Penguin, 1988). Also the entries on individual spices in Alan Davidson, *The Oxford Companion to Food* (Oxford: Oxford University Press, 1999).

A seventeenth-century recipe: Gervase Markham, *The English Huswife,* 1615.

Similar traditions existed in other countries too: Castella provides an overview of cakes made for mourning and the celebration of life in *A World of Cake*, p. 74.

Simon Charsley: Simon R. Charsley, *Wedding Cakes and Cultural History* (London: Routledge, 1992).

Elizabeth Raffald: Elizabeth Raffald, *The Experienced English Housekeeper,* 1769.

Prince William famously had his own cake: For the recipe Prince William enjoyed as a child see http://www.dailymail.co.uk/home/you/article-3064097/Recipes-fit-prince-two-Chocolate-biscuit-cake.html (retrieved on 17 February 2015).

In Norway . . .: Castella gives another excellent overview in her *A World of Cake*, pp. 296–9.

CHAPTER 3

Meanwhile, the adoption of the whisk: The *Oxford English Dictionary* lists the first recorded use of a whisk as an implement to beat eggs in 1666, but does not record what it was made from.

The first published recipe: Gervase Markham, *The English Huswife*, 1615.

Vanilla, meanwhile . . .: There is an excellent overview of the cultivation and culinary use of vanilla in Alan Davidson's *The Oxford Companion to Food* (Oxford: Oxford University Press, 1999). Two instructive attempts at recreating Simmons' pound cake can be found at http://historicalfoodways.com/category/pound-cake-project/ and http://www.americantable.org/2012/08/recipe-pound-cake-1796/ (retrieved 15 July 2014).

In the words of British food writer and cook Nigel Slater: Nigel Slater, *Eating for England* (London: Harper Perennial, 2007), p. 219.

It was still being used by nearly half of British housewives: Nicola Humble, *Culinary Pleasures: Cookbooks and the Transformation of British Food* (London: Faber & Faber, 2005), Chapter 1.

It is an integral part of the traditional afternoon tea: 'Tea', in Solomon H. Katz and William Woys Weaver (eds), *Encyclopedia of Food and Culture* (New York and London: Scribner, 2003), vol. III, pp. 389–94.

In Nigel Slater's words again: Slater, *Eating for England*, p. 21.

Fuller's Walnut Cake: See http://www.kzwp.com/lyons2/fullers.htm (retrieved 29 September 2015).

The lightness of the pound cake also relies on the correct proportion of sugar to flour: Barbara Maher, *Cakes* (Harmondsworth: Penguin, 1984), pp. 28–38.

In 2014 the American Butter Institute reported: http://www.nmpf.org/latest-news/articles/american-butter-institute-takes-new-direction-2014 (retrieved 21 May 2014).

The 'butter mystique': M. Visser, *Much Depends on Dinner: the Extraordinary History and Mythology, Allure and Obsessions, Perils and Taboos, of an Ordinary Meal* (Harmondsworth: Penguin, 1986), p. 84.

The author Jane Austen: V. Jones, *Jane Austen: Selected Letters* (Oxford: Oxford University Press, 2004), p. 18 (the letter was written over the two days from 1–2 December 1798).

In the north-eastern United States it was not until 1910 . . .: 2010 Census of Population and Housing, CPH-2-5 (Washington DC: US Government Printing Office, 2012), pp. 13–29. Available at www.census.gov/prod/cen2010/cph-2-1.pdf. (retrieved 29 September 2015).

By 1902 the highest social classes in England: These figures were calculated by the Statistical Society of England based on a survey of their own members – who did cover a fairly large portion of the population, although not the very poor. They found that 'wage-earners' consumed 15 pounds of butter per year compared with 41 pounds by the upper classes. Reported in John Burnett, *Plenty and Want: a Social History of Diet in England from 1815 to the Present Day* (Harmondsworth: Penguin, 1968), p. 202.

Oleomargarine – or, as we know it today, margarine: A useful history of margarine is J. H. Van Stuyvenberg (ed.), *Margarine: An Economic, Social and Scientific History, 1869–1969* (Liverpool: Liverpool University Press, 1969).

Martha Stewart unequivocally backs the flavour of butter: See http://www.marthastewart.com/266183/butter-or-margarine (retrieved 30 April 2014).

Crisco first appeared on the market . . .: Marion Harris Neil, *The Story of Crisco* (Cincinnati: The Procter & Gamble Company, 1913). This can be found at http://www.gutenberg.org/files/13286/13286-h/13286-h.htm.

An experiment in the 1970s: Lloyd M Beidler, 'The Biological and Cultural Role of Sweeteners', in National Academy of Sciences, *Sweeteners: Issues and Uncertainties* (Washington DC: National Academy of Sciences, 1975), p. 13.

In 1550 there were five sugar plantations . . . they also brought huge wealth: Reay Tannahill, *Food in History,* rev. ed. (London: Penguin, 1988), p. 218.

In the early nineteenth century only half of the raw sugar . . .: *A Century of Sugar Refining in the United States, 1816–1916.* Retrieved from http://archive.org/stream/cu31924003621046/cu31924003621046_djvu.txt 15 July 2015.

Nowadays, the whole process is mechanised: Sydney W. Mintz, *Sweetness and Power: the Place of Sugar in Modern History* (Harmondsworth: Penguin, 1985), pp. 190–1, and Chapter 2 generally on production. Mintz's book is an excellent overview of the history and meanings of sugar.

Nonetheless, beet sugar only accounts for one-fifth . . .: See W. R. Aykroys, *Sweet Malefactor: Sugar, Slavery and Human Society* (London: Heinemann, 1967), pp. 96–101.

In the words of sugar historian Sidney Mintz: Mintz, *Sweetness and Power*, p. 148.

In medieval times it was so expensive that it was often kept under lock and key: These figures are based on inflation rates since 1520 (see Lawrence H. Officer and Samuel H. Williamson, 'Purchasing Power of British Pounds from 1270 to Present', Measuring Worth, 2015, http://www.measuringworth.com/ppoweruk/). Using relative average incomes (based on GDP) it would be worth upwards of £783.80 or US$1,320. Peter Brears, 'Tudor England', in Peter Brears, Maggie Black, Gill Corbishley, Jane Renfrew and Jennifer Stead, *A Taste of History: 1,000 Years of Food in Britain* (London: English Heritage with the British Museum Press, 1993), p. 143.

Jane Austen wrote to her sister Cassandra: Jones, *Jane Austen*, p. 143 (letter written 24 May 1813).

The rapidly dropping price of sugar: Carole Shammas, *The Pre-industrial Consumer in England and America* (Oxford: Oxford University Press, 1990), p. 81; 'Sugar and Sweeteners', in Katz and Woys-Weaver, *Encyclopedia of Food and Culture*, vol. III, p. 361. For American figures see references at http://blissfulwriter.hubpages.com/hub/How-Much-Sugar-Do-We-Eat (retrieved 30 June 2014).

Britons were consuming an average of 49 pounds per head: G. W. Johnstone, 'The Growth of the Sugar Trade and Refining Industry', in Derek J. Oddy and Derek S. Miller, *The Making of the Modern British Diet* (London: Croom Helm, 1976), p. 60. This contrasts with a per capita consumption per year of 4 pounds in 1700–1709, and 18 pounds in 1800–1809. By 1949–59 consumption stood at 99.4 pounds per head per year. The figures they are citing are from Noel Deer's two-volume *The History of Sugar* (London: Chapman and Hall, 1950).

A government report on the ill-fated attempt at derationing: 'Personal Points Rationing 1949–50', Appendix V, p. 3. This file is held at the National Archives at Kew, London, under reference MAF 223/93.

It is now about 18 per cent . . . The WHO recommends . . .: Mintz, *Sweetness and Power*, p. 133; http://grist.org/industrial-agriculture/2011-04-05-american-diet-one-chart-lots-of-fats-sugars/ (retrieved 22 May 2014).

Pearl ash was an effective raising agent . . . Baking powder . . .: Davidson, *Oxford Companion*, pp. 50, 73.

The relevant entry in the modern *Encyclopaedia of Food and Culture*: 'Baking', in Katz and Woys-Weaver, *Encyclopedia of Food and Culture*, vol. 1, p. 154.

By which time, of course, cakes were also being baked in metal or wooden hoops: Humble, *Culinary Pleasures*, pp. 10–23; 'Cake and Pancake', in Katz and Woys-Weaver, *Encyclopedia of Food and Culture*, vol. I, pp. 288–92; 'Cake', in Davidson, *The Oxford Companion*, pp. 122–4.

Bringing reliable stoves within the range of the domestic user: Maggie Black, 'Victorian Britain', in Brears et al., *A Taste of History*, pp. 275–7.

CHAPTER 4

President Rutherford B. Hayes: Poppy Cannon and Patricia Brookes, *The Presidents' Cookbook* (New York: Funk & Wagnalls, 1968), p. 293–301. There is an entry on the favourite foods of US presidents at the comprehensive history of food site www.foodtimeline.org/presidents.html.

From *The Boston Cooking School Cookbook* of 1884: http://www.foodtimeline.org/foodcakes.html#angelfood (retrieved 28 October 2015).

'Not being a domestic goddess exactly': Nigella Lawson, *How to Be a Domestic Goddess: Baking and the Art of Comfort Cooking* (London: Chatto & Windus, 2000), p. vii.

Barr's official website: http://www.roseanneworld.com/

But, like Nigella, Roseanne attracts negative attention . . .: Kathleen K. Rowe, 'Roseanne: Unruly Woman as Domestic Goddess', *Screen* 31:4 (1990), pp. 408–19.

Isabella Beeton was actually a young woman: For an excellent biography of Isabella Beeton see Kathryn Hughes, *The Short Life and Long Times of Mrs Beeton* (London: Fourth Estate, 2005), from which many of these details are drawn.

Food historian Nicola Humble: Nicola Humble, *Culinary Pleasures: Cookbooks and the Transformation of British Food* (London: Faber & Faber, 2005), pp. 7–20.

It is estimated that she lifted over a third of her 972 recipes: Hughes, *Short Life*, p. 206, and pp. 198–217 generally on the works from which Mrs Beeton 'borrowed'.

Food writer Elizabeth David: Elizabeth Ray (ed.), *The Best of Eliza Acton*, with an introduction by Elizabeth David (Harmondsworth: Penguin, 1968), pp. xxvii, xixx.

The British publishing industry reacted quickly: Jennifer Stead, 'Georgian Britain', in Peter Brears, Maggie Black, Gill Corbishley, Jane Renfrew and Jennifer Stead, *A Taste of History: 1,000 Years of Food in Britain* (London: English Heritage with the British Museum Press, 1993), pp. 227–8.

A report of the use of pearl ash . . .: Amelia Simmons, *The First American Cookbook. A Facsimile of 'American Cookery', 1797*. Introductory essay by Mary Tolford Wilson.

This American vision, which has been referred to as a cult of womanhood: See Laura Shapiro, *Perfection Salad: Women and Cooking at the Turn of the Century* (New York: North Point Press, 1995). The key article on the cult of womanhood in America was Barbara Welter's 'The Cult of True Womanhood, 1820–60', *American Quarterly* 18:2, pp. 151–174 (available at https://webstorage.worcester.edu/sites/thangen/web/Shared%20Documents/Welter.CultTrueWomanhood.pdf). It has been much discussed since its publication and the ideas extended and updated by other scholars.

The reference to 'your saleratus sifted': 'Baking Powder' in Andrew F. Smith, *The Oxford Encyclopedia of Food and Drink in America* second edition, (New York: Oxford University Press, 2013), 3 vols, vol. I, pp. 109–11; Elizabeth David, *English Bread and Yeast Cookery* (Harmondsworth: Penguin, 1979), pp. 515–17.

What one author has called 'recreational cooking': Anne Mendelson, *Stand Facing the Stove: the Story of the Women who Gave America The Joy of Cooking. The Lives of Irma S. Rombauer and Marion Rombauer Becker* (New York: Henry Holt and Co, 1996), p. 117. Mendelson is ambivalent about the impact of this development, noting that it also degraded and juvenilised the status of baking to a certain extent as it was, instructionally speaking, a dead end.

Hardly any American households owned one in 1918: Julie A. Mattaei, *An Economic History of Women in America: Women's Work, the Sexual Division of Labor, and the*

Development of Capitalism (New York: Schocken Books, 1982), p. 239, quoting the 1960s work of Kathryn Walker on domestic economics.

The new modern ovens were not quite as self-regulating: E. Silva, 'The Cook, the Cooker and the Gendering of the Kitchen', *Sociological Review*, 48:4, 2000, pp. 612–28.

Survey figures show: Mattaei, *Economic History of Women*, pp. 120–1, citing Walker. These figures show that women were spending 51.1 hours per week on homemaking in urban areas in 1926–7, 51.8 hours in 1952 and 67 hours in 1967/8 (p. 168).

The new modern ovens were not quite as self-regulating: Silva, 'The Cook'.

The name most intimately connected with 'joyfulness' in the kitchen . . .: Much of the information on Rombauer is drawn from http://www.thejoykitchen.com/all-about-joy/history-joy-cooking (retrieved 20 May 2015) and Mendelson, *Stand Facing the Stove*.

10,000 copies were printed, and 6,838 were sold: These sales figures were retrieved from http://www.oldcooksbooks.com/master_book_by_let_search.php?passed_book_id=10937 (retrieved 28 May 2015).

Her book was the only cookbook to feature: http://www.harvardsquarelibrary.org/biographies/irma-rombauer/ (retrieved 2 June 2015).

In 1996 Irma's biographer estimated: Mendelson, *Stand Facing the Stove*, p. 413.

Food historian Laura Shapiro describes her: See www.bettycrocker.com; Laura Shapiro, *Something from the Oven: Reinventing Dinner in 1950s America* (Harmondsworth: Penguin, 2005), p. 180.

As the preface to the first edition of the Big Red Cookbook stated: *Betty Crocker's Picture Cook Book* (New York: McGraw-Hill, 1950).

The reality, as historian Laura Shapiro has shown: Shapiro, *Something from the Oven*.

Her most popular offering currently being the 'Supermoist': Data retrieved from http://www.statista.com/statistics/277449/us-households-most-used-brands-of-dry-cake-mixes/ (retrieved 20 May 2015). This line of mix was bought by 32.1 per cent of respondents in 2013–14.

A 2013 review of cake mixes in the *Guardian*: 'Cake Mix Review: the Best Packets', *Guardian*, 25 July 2013 (http://www.theguardian.com/lifeandstyle/2013/jul/25/cake-mix-review-packet-test, retrieved 27 May 2015).

Even the Cake Mix Doctor herself: Retrieved from http://www.cakemixdoctor.com/books/the-cake-mix-doctor/, 27 May 2015.

It was launched in 1949 by the Pillsbury flour company: Shapiro gives an excellent analysis of this contest in *Something from the Oven*.

The first winner . . . the only male winner . . .: The recipes can all be found on the Pillsbury website at http://www.pillsbury.com/recipes/bake-off/dessert/cake.

The culinary role models for this new generation: More information on all of these women can be found in Joanne Hollows, 'The Feminist and the Cook: Julia Child, Betty Friedan and Domestic Femininity', in Emma Casey and Lydia Martens (eds), *Gender and Consumption: Domestic Cultures and the Commercialisation of Everyday Life* (Aldershot, Hants: Ashgate, 2007), pp. 33–48; and Steve Jones and Ben Taylor, 'Food Writing and Food Cultures: the Case of Elizabeth David and Jane Grigson', *European Journal of Cultural Studies*, 4:2, 2001, pp. 171–88.

While writing about gingerbread in *British Cookery*: Reproduced in *The Enjoyment of Food: the Best of Jane Grigson*, (London: Michael Joseph, 1992), pp. 63–4, 66–7.

Food technologists in the 1930s . . . The angel food cake soon donned a range of party frocks: 'Cake: Overview', in Smith, *Oxford Encyclopedia of Food and Drink in America*, vol. 1.

CHAPTER 5

In 1942, Nancy Biglin, aged nine: Agnes Nancy Biglin, born 1933. Interview from the Imperial War Museum Sound Archive, 13557 (http://www.iwm.org.uk/collections/item/object/80013266, last retrieved 29 September 2015).

The weekly ration per person: See Ina Zweiniger-Bargielowska, *Austerity in Britain: Rationing, Controls and Consumption 1939–1955* (Oxford: Oxford University Press, 2000), pp. 12–18.

When the polling agency Gallup: George H. Gallup (ed.) *The Gallup International Public Opinion Polls*, 2 vols, (New York: Random House, 1976), vol. 1, p. 48. Forty per cent of people said they had experienced some difficulties; 40 per cent said not, and 17 per cent did not know.

This was an organisation . . .: Tom Jeffery, *Mass Observation: A Short History* (Occasional paper, University of Birmingham No. 55 (1978)). There are several published collections of Mass Observation diaries, including *Our Hidden Lives: the Remarkable Diaries of Post-War Britain*, and *Private Battles: How the War Almost Defeated Us*, both edited by Simon Garfield (London: Ebury Press, 2004 and 2007), which have provided some of the material cited here. Nella Last's diaries are published as *Nella Last's War: the Second World War Diaries of Housewife, 49*, edited by Richard Broad and Suzie Fleming (London: Profile Books, 2006).

She wrote in her diary: *Nella Last's War*, pp. 116–17: 11 April 1941.

Pam Ashford: Garfield, *Private Battles*: Pam Ashford, 31 May 1941, p. 122; 5 October 1942, p. 299; 7 July 1942, p. 264; 16 July 1942, p. 268.

Meanwhile, a Lyons tea shop menu: I came across this Lyons menu from February 1940 in the Mass Observation collection (MO TC67 Box 2). The Mass Observation archive is held at the University of Sussex (http://www.massobservation.amdigital. co.uk/Home/index).

A Mass Observation report in 1942 found: *Food Tensions in 1942*, MO (Mass Observation) File Report 1155.

Another survey found that 12 per cent of those questioned: Central Office of Information, *The Social Survey. Food: An Inquiry into a Typical Day's Meals and Attitudes to Wartime Food in Selected Groups of the English Working Population* (The National Archives, Kew, London, RG 23/15), pp. 3–6.

By the next year the numbers were even higher: *The Social Survey: Manufactured Food Inquiry*, Part II, December 1942 (The National Archives, Kew, RG 23/31).

Similarly, three quarters of those who said they didn't have enough cooking fat: ibid., pp. 45–7.

As one leaflet put it . . .: Ministry of Food advert, 'The Lighter Side of Cooking', reproduced in a file on Advertising, The National Archives, Kew, MAF 223/21, 1945.

Cookbook authors became quite innovative in 'making do': For more on wartime cookbooks, see Nicola Humble, *Culinary Pleasures: Cookbooks and the Transformation of British Food* (London: Faber & Faber, 2005), Chapter 3.

Cookbook author Constance Spry, on the other hand: Humble, *Culinary Pleasures*, p. 98.

A 'flower cake': Barbara Maher, *Cakes* (Harmondsworth: Penguin, 1984), p. 7.

In April 1943 the tea bar in the Fulham branch of Woolworth's: 'People's Homes', Mass Observation File Report 1641, April 1943, p. 456.

The migrants on the westward pioneer trails in America: Jacqueline Williams, *Wagon Wheel Kitchens: Food on the Oregon Trail* (Lawrence, Kan.: University Press of Kansas, 1993), pp. 131–48 and 172–6. Another useful book on this topic is Reginald Horsman, *Feast or Famine: Food and Drink in American Westward Expansion* (Columbia and London: University of Missouri Press, 2008).

One child pioneer of the 1850s: http://www.foodtimeline.org/foodcakes.html# pioneerbirthdaycake (retrieved 3 July 2015).

By 1870 a thousand miles of railway had opened in eastern Australia: Michael Symons, *One Continuous Picnic: A Gastronomic History of Australia*, (Adelaide: Duck Press, 1982), p. 97.

The answer was canning: For more on canning and the developments outlined below, see Tom Standage, *An Edible History of Humanity* (London: Atlantic Books, 2009), pp. 159–63; Williams, *Wagon Wheel Kitchens*, p. 119; Theoldfoodie.com/ 2006/11/condensed-milk-man.html (retrieved 6 July 2015).

They built a 'flying kitchen': http://www.foodtimeline.org/foodcakeshtml#highaltitude (retrieved 8 July 2015).

Chapter 6

Even wheat flours are not created equal: Elizabeth David, *English Bread and Yeast Cookery* (Harmondsworth: Penguin, 1979), p. 45. 'Hard' wheats can have a gluten content of 12–15 per cent, while soft ones have 8–10 per cent.

Pillsbury started to manufacture it in 1932: 'Pillsbury', in Andrew F. Smith, *The Oxford Encyclopedia of Food and Drink in America*, second edition, (New York: Oxford University Press, 2013), 3 vols, vol. 3, pp. 1–2.

'Foodways': For an overview, see 'Foodways', in Smith, *Oxford Encyclopedia of Food and Drink in America*, vol. 2, pp. 817–8.

As Hasia Diner has written: Hasia R. Diner, *Hungering for America: Italian Irish and Jewish Foodways in the Age of Migration* (Harvard: Harvard University Press: 2001), p. 1.

Around thirty million Europeans went to America: Diner, *Hungering*, pp. 1–2.

Manhattan was taken over by the British in 1664: 'Dutch Influences on American Food', in Smith, *Oxford Encyclopedia of Food and Drink in America*, vol. 1, pp. 661–3.

More than a tenth of Americans spoke German: 'German-American Foods', in Smith, *Oxford Encyclopedia of Food and Drink in America*, vol. 2, pp. 98–105.

Inventories of personal goods from the seventeenth century: Sheilagh Ogilvie, Markus Küpker and Janine Maegraith, 'Women and the Material Culture of Food in Early Modern Germany', *Early Modern Women: An Interdisciplinary Journal* (2009), vol. 4, pp. 149–59.

The influence of the French and Spanish in America: See the entries on Iberian, French and Mexican influences on American food in Smith, *Oxford Encyclopedia of Food and Drink in America*.

The Twelfth Night Revelers: Mardigrastraditions.com/best-new-orleans-king-cake/ (retrieved 3 July 2015).

Several stories pinpoint its origins: Krystina Castella, *A World of Cake: 150 Recipes for Sweet Traditions from Cultures Near and Far* (North Adams, MA: Storey Publishing, 2010), p. 93.

Only about 200,000 of the country's 4 million inhabitants were *not* farm-dwellers: 'Advertising Cookbooklets and Recipes' in Smith, *Oxford Encyclopedia of Food and Drink in America*, vol. 1, p. 10.

Certainly, American bakers did not remain wedded to their British heritage: This section draws on the entry on 'Cakes: Overview' in Smith, *Oxford Encyclopedia of Food and Drink in America*.

The first Betty Crocker Big Red Book of 1950 stated: *Betty Crocker's Picture Cook Book* (New York: McGraw-Hill, 1950), p. 105.

Chocolate had not been incorporated into cake batters before the middle of the nineteenth century: See the entry on 'Chocolate in Cookery', Alan Davidson, *The Oxford Companion to Food* (Oxford: Oxford University Press, 1999).

In 1828 a Dutch chemist called Casparus van Houten: 'Chocolate' in Smith, *Oxford Encyclopedia of Food and Drink in America*, vol. 1, pp. 396–400.

In fact, the earliest 'chocolate cakes': See the entries on 'Chocolate' and 'Brownies' in Smith, *Oxford Encyclopedia of Food and Drink in America*. (vol. 1, pp. 396–400 and vol. 1, pp. 220–1).

Creating a whole new type of non-stick bakeware as it did so: Examples from the company who made this pan are now in the collection of the Smithsonian Museum, so great is their influence on baking in America deemed to be. The pan itself leaped to fame after a Bundt cake called the 'Tunnel of Fudge' won the Pillsbury Bake-Off in 1966 (Jean Anderson, *American Century Cookbook: the Most Popular Recipes of the 20th Century* (New York: Clarkson Potter, 1997), p. 458.

The layered orange and lemon Robert E. Lee cake: whatscookingamerica.net/History/Cakes/RobertLeeCake.htm (retrieved 25 June 2015).

Also the Lane Cake: www.encyclopediaofalabama.org/article/h-1340 (retrieved 25 June 2015).

One classic example is the hummingbird cake: Castella, *A World of Cake*, p. 62.

It was often they who held the knowledge: See the introduction and contributions to Anne L. Bower (ed.), *African-American Foodways: Explorations of History and Culture* (Urbana and Chicago: University of Illinois Press, 2007); and Herbert C. Covey and Dwight Eisnach, *What the Slaves Ate: Recollections of African-American Foods and Foodways from the Slave Narratives* (Oxford: Greenwood Press, 2009).

The highest profile black cook of the antebellum era: 'African-American Food', in Smith, *Oxford Encyclopedia of Food and Drink in America*, vol. 1, pp. 26–39 (this reference on p. 28).

Even the name Aunt Jemima came from a song: For example, see Alice A. Deck, '"Now Then, Who Said Biscuits?" The Black Woman Cook as Fetish in American Advertising, 1905–1953', in Sherrie A. Inness (ed.), *Kitchen Culture in America: Popular Representations of Food, Gender, and Race* (Philadelphia: University of Pennsylvania Press, 2000), pp. 69–93; 'Aunt Jemima', in Smith, *Oxford Encyclopedia of Food and Drink in America*, vol. 1. p. 97.

The author Maya Angelou: Anne Yentsch, 'Excavating the South's African-American Food History', in Bower, *African-American Foodways* p. 82.

Started to invest heavily in brand advertising: 'Advertising Cookbooklets and Recipes', in Smith, *Oxford Encyclopedia of Food and Drink in America*, vol. 1, pp. 10–17.

Pineapple upside-down cake got a boost: *whatscookingamerica.net/Cake/pineapplecake.htm* (retrieved 28 June 2015).

A revolutionary new cake which featured salad oil: whatscookingamerica.net/History/Cakes/ChiffonCake; http://www.foodtimeline.org/foodcakeshtml#chiffoncake (both retrieved 28 June 2015).

Cola drinks . . . 'mystery cake' . . .: http://www.foodtimeline.org/foodcakeshtml#colacake; http://www.foodtimeline.org/foodcakes.html#mystery (both retrieved 28 June 2015); Anderson, *American Century Cookbook*, p. 448.

Campbell's Soup was another savvy marketer: 'Advertising Cookbooklets and Recipes', in Smith, *Oxford Encyclopedia of Food and Drink in America*, vol. 1, p. 15.

CHAPTER 7

The online pinboard site Pinterest: www.pinterest.com

Birthday cakes only really became popular . . .: For a good overview of the history of birthday cakes see http://www.foodtimeline.org/foodcakes.html#birthdaycake (retrieved 25 June 2015); also 'Birthdays', in Andrew F. Smith, *The Oxford Encyclopedia of Food and Drink in America* second edition, (New York: Oxford University Press, 2013), 3 vols, vol. 1, pp. 164–7; 'Birthday foods', in Solomon H. Katz (editor in chief), *Encyclopedia of Food and Culture* (New York: Thomson Gale, 2003), 3 vols, pp. 212–14.

A new and growing aspect of the rituals marking the important events of childhood: For example, see Viviana A. Zelizer, *Pricing the Priceless Child: the Changing Social Value of Children* (New York: Basic Books 1985); for one case study see Daniel Thomas Cook, *The Commodification of Childhood: The Children's Clothing Industry and the Rise of the Child Consumer* (Durham: Duke University Press, 2004).

The original 1980s edition of the same *Australian Women's Weekly*: https://www.facebook.com/groups/2356371047/?ref=ts&fref=ts#_=_

The Australian news site news.com.au: http://www.news.com.au/lifestyle/food/the-best-book-ever-written-in-this-country/story-fneuz8zj-1227258065852 (retrieved 29 September 2015).

Articles on putting together a school tuck box: 'Don't Forget the School Tuck Box', *Good Housekeeping*, VIII:I (September 1925), pp. 82, 90. The WI's magazine included an article titled 'An Economical Tuck Box Much Appreciated by Small Boys' in May 1927 (*Home and Country*, IX: 5, May 1927, p. 209.

An article on 'cakes for the party': 'Cakes for the Party', *Good Housekeeping*, January 1928, XII:5, pp. 75 and 88–9.

Mothers and wives had more time to spend on baking: This is a recurring theme in Laura Shapiro's *Something from the Oven: Reinventing Dinner in 1950s America* (Harmondsworth: Penguin, 2005).

'Hedgehog cakes': Dorothy Hartley, *Food in England* (London: MacDonald, 1969),

p. 216; see also http://researchingfoodhistory.blogspot.co.uk/2012/06/hedgehogs. html, retrieved 4 August 2015.

'Haunch of lamb glacé en surprise': Alexis Soyer, *The Gastronomic Regenerator*, 1846. Available at http://www.gutenberg.org/ebooks/47444.

One study of 200 families: Nickie Charles and Marion Kerr, *Women, Food and Families: Power, Status, Love, Anger* (Manchester: Manchester University Press, 1988), p. 32.

According to cake historian and baker Krystina Castella: Krystina Castella, *A World of Cake: 150 Recipes for Sweet Traditions from Cultures Near and Far* (North Adams, MA: Storey Publishing, 2010), pp. 156–7 and 228–9.

Richmal Crompton's *Just William*: Richmal Crompton, *More William*, 90 year anniversary reprint, (Basingstoke: Macmillan Children's Books, 2009), 'William's Burglar', 'The Knight at Arms'.

According to her erstwhile personal chef: http://www.theroyalchef.com/2012/04/ happy-birthday-your-majesty/ (retrieved 29 July 2015).

Where she gave him the glacé cherry from the top of her cake: http://www. englishmonarchs.co.uk/windsor_3.htm (retrieved 29 July 2015).

A three-foot high, five-tier creation: http://royalcentral.co.uk/residences/hampton-court-palace-celebrates-its-500th-birthday-with-brilliant-bespoke-cake-44838 (retrieved 29 July 2015).

That seal recently went on auction: http://www.ha.com/heritage-auctions-press-releases-and-news/-happy-birthday-mr.-president-1962-jfk-birthday-cake-decoration-held-by-detective-s-family-for-50-years-readies-for-public-auction-in-dallas.s?releaseId=1912 (retrieved 29 July 2015).

More than 15,000 people attended JFK's party that year: Laura Fitzpatrick, 'Presidential Birthdays', http://content.time.com/time/nation/article/0,8599,1914439, 00.html (retrieved 29 July 2015).

His favourite birthday cake was an old-fashioned fruit cake: There are a number of excellent food history websites which have collected information detailing many of the cakes in this chapter. Two key examples are http://www.foodtimeline.org, and http://www.whatscookingamerica.net. For details on Roosevelt's cakes see http://www.foodtimeline.org/presidents.html#troosevelt, citing Henrietta Nesbitt's *The Presidential Cookbook: Feeding the Roosevelts and Their Guests* (Garden City, NY: Doubleday & Co.), 1951.

Bill Clinton's 50th party: Fitzpatrick, 'Presidential Birthdays'.

It was an orange-spiked vanilla cake: http://carlanthonyonline.com/2012/11/14/mamie-queen-of-cakes-a-first-lady-who-showed-a-nation-how-to-birthday-party/ (retrieved 29 July 2015).

There are cakes named for Washington, Lincoln and Jefferson: http://www.theoldfoodie.com/2015/04/presidential-cakes.html (retrieved 29 July 2015).

We can fondly speculate . . .: All of these examples are from Cannon and Brooks, *Presidents' Cookbook*, via http://www.foodtimeline.org/presidents.html (retrieved 29 July 2015).

The *Sachertorte* . . .: For the *Sachertorte* story, see http://www.whatscookingamerica.net/History/Cakes/Sachertorte.htm (retrieved 3 August 2015); Alan Davidson, *The Oxford Companion to Food* (Oxford: Oxford University Press, 1999), p. 679.

The Dobos torte: Castella, *A World of Cake*, p. 172.

The American speciality German chocolate cake: http://www.whatscookingamerica.net/History/Cakes/GermanChocolateCake.htm (retrieved 4 August 2015).

The Lamington, on the other hand, has a much more secure history: http://australianlamingtons.blogspot.co.uk/p/history-of-world-famous-australian.html, and http://www.fast-ed.com.au/a-brief-history-of-lamingtons/ (both retrieved 30 July 2015).

A possibly more plausible alternative: http://www.foodtimeline.org/foodcakes.html#lamingtons (retrieved 30 July 2015).

There are many other cakes named for specific national heroes: Castella. *A World of Cake*, pp. 173–4. Also http://www.india-forums.com/forum_posts.asp?TID=270785 on Bobby Deol's cake (retrieved 30 July 2015).

Food historian Ivan Day . . . more research on the Battenberg cake: See http://foodhistorjottings.blogspot.co.uk/2011/08/battenburg-cake-truth.html; http://foodhistorjottings.blogspot.co.uk/2011/12/battenburg-cake-revisited.html; and http://foodhistorjottings.blogspot.co.uk/2012/04/battenburg-cake-history-again.html (all retrieved 30 July 2015).

Mr Kipling: http://brandingsource.blogspot.co.uk/2012/07/mr-kipling-brand-history.html; http://www.mrkipling.co.uk/about-us (both retrieved both 27 July 2015).

McVitie's: http://www.mcvities.co.uk/about (retrieved 27 July 2015).

One of the most popular brands in Britain: http://www.scotsman.com/lifestyle/heritage/mcvitie-s-among-uk-s-most-trusted-brands-1-2918802. McVitie's products are bought an average of 12.7 times a year by 87.6 per cent of the population (retrieved 3 August 2015).

A real market presence is said to be difficult to establish: http://www.just-food.com/interview/premier-foods-sets-sights-on-overseas-markets_id128256.aspx (retrieved 3 August 2015).

Leandra Palermo . . . asked readers about their favourite snack foods: The initial post asking for suggestions for favourite snack cakes appeared at http://sweets.seriouseats.com/2014/02/snack-attack-open-thread-whats-your-favorite-snack-cake.html, and the subsequent 'Very Unofficial Snack Cake Field Guide' at http://sweets.seriouseats.com/2014/03/a-very-unofficial-snack-cake-field-guide.html.

The Twinkie: 'Twinkies', in Smith, *Oxford Encyclopedia of Food and Drink in America*, vol. 3, p. 507; Steve Ettlinger, *Twinkie, Deconstructed* (London: Plume, 2008).

Also allegedly true is the legend . . . Ohio Zoo . . . Jimmy Carter: Jean Anderson, *American Century Cookbook: the Most Popular Recipes of the 20th Century* (New York: Clarkson Potter, 1997), p. 446; David Mansour, *From Abba to Zoom: A Pop Culture Encyclopedia of the Late 20th Century*, (Kansas City, MO: Andrews McMeel, 2005), p. 502.

The 1999 Millennium Time Capsule: See http://clinton5.nara.gov/Initiatives/Millennium/capsule/index.html (retrieved 5 August 2015).

The Hostess CupCake: 'Hostess', in Smith, *Oxford Encyclopedia of Food and Drink in America,* vol. 2, p. 285.

Hostess Brands filed for Chapter 11 bankruptcy: http://www.forbes.com/sites/quora/2012/11/21/did-hostess-go-bankrupt-in-2012-because-people-no-longer-find-twinkies-appealing/ (retrieved 3 August 2015).

It was actually the second brush with the bankruptcy courts for Hostess: http://hostesscakes.com/Products 3 Aug 2015; http://www.adweek.com/news/advertising-branding/hostess-twinkie-relaunch-brands-treats-dude-food-151734 (retrieved 3 August 2015).

Drake's: 'Drake's Cakes', in Smith, *Oxford Encyclopedia of Food and Drink in America,* vol. 1, pp. 650–1.

Ring Dings: http://www.drakescake.com/www/docs/102/ring-dings (retrieved 5 August 2015).

The Tasty Baking Company: 'TastyKake', Smith, *Oxford Encyclopedia of Food and Drink in America,* vol. 3, pp. 418–9; http://www.tastykake.com/history (retrieved 5 August 2015).

Little Debbie: http://www.littledebbie.com/6/who-we-are (retrieved 5 August 2015).

'Snackfood nationalism': Steve Penfold, *The Donut: A Canadian History* (Toronto: University of Toronto Press, 2008).

Sociologist Pierre Bourdieu: Pierre Bourdieu, *Distinction: A Social Critique of the Judgment of Taste* (London and New York: Routledge, 1984).

CHAPTER 8

The inaugural 1.200-kilometre Paris to Brest cycle race: The details given here are drawn principally from the series of reports in *Le Petit Journal*, which can be read online, starting at http://gallica.bnf.fr/ark:/12148/bpt6k6109779.zoom (retrieved 19 August 2015). There are good histories of the event at http://www.randonneurs.bc.ca/pbp/books-collections/journal-IR-1989/mccray-hist/1891.html; and in Bill Bryant's 'A Short History of Paris–Brest–Paris': http://www.rusa.org/pbphistory.html; http://

www.paris-brest.fr/durand_et_fils_createur_du_paris-brest_depuis_1909/historique.
html (all retrieved 19 August 2015).

The original recipe is a secret: http://www.paris-brest.fr/durand_et_fils_createur_
du_paris-brest_depuis_1909/Createur_du_Paris-Brest_Durand_et_fils.html (retrieved
30 September 2015).

The old French *guastrel* . . . **the word** *gâteau*: 'Gâteaux', in Alan Davidson, *The
Oxford Companion to Food* (Oxford: Oxford University Press, 1999), pp. 332–3.

In 1740 French bakers were forbidden to use flour to make gâteaux des rois:
Steven Laurence Kaplan, *The Bakers of Paris and the Bread Question, 1700–1775*
(Durham and London: Duke University Press, 1996); Jean-Louis Flandrin and
Massimo Montanari (eds), *Food: A Culinary History* (New York: Columbia University
Press, 1999); Jules Gouffé, *The Royal Pastry and Confectionery Book (Le Livre de
Pâtisserie)* (London: Sampson Low, Marston, Low, & Searle, 1874).

Choux pastry was invented in the sixteenth century: See http://www.foodtimeline.
org/foodpies.html#pastry (retrieved 5 August 2015).

**The French Revolution of 1789 left many renowned chefs kitchen-less . . . return
of the aristocracy and monarchy**: Edward B. Page and P. W. Kingsford, *The Master
Chefs: a History of Haute Cuisine, from the Egyptians and Ancient Greeks to Escoffier*
(London: Edward Arnold, 1971), pp. 75–6.

Antonin Carême: The details on Carême's life and career which follow draw on Ian
Kelly, *Cooking for Kings: the Life of Antonin Carême the First Celebrity Chef* (London:
Short Books, 2004); Page and Kingsford, *The Master Chefs*.

Carême delighted in showing off his prowess: Kelly, *Cooking for Kings*, pp. 19–20.

Jules Gouffé . . . wrote in his own book *Le Livre de Pâtisserie*: Gouffé, *The Royal
Pastry and Confectionery Book*, pp. 8–9.

Another famous French chef, Alexis Soyer: There are several accessible biographies
of Soyer; many of the details cited here are from Ruth Brandon, *The People's Chef:
Alexis Soyer, a Life in Seven Courses* (Chichester, West Sussex: Wiley, 2004); Ruth
Cowen, *Relish: the Extraordinary Life of Alexis Soyer, Victorian Celebrity Chef* (London:
Phoenix, 2007).

George Auguste Escoffier: Page and Kingsford, *The Master Chefs*.

A perusal of any master pâtissier's reference work: There are countless books by master pâtissiers even if the reader is confined to English. For this survey I examined *Desserts* by Pierre Hermé (London: Little, Brown and Company, 1999); Gaston Lenôtre, *Lenôtre's Desserts and Pastries* (New York: Barron's 1977); Richard Bertinet, *Pâtisserie Maison: Simple Pastries and Desserts to Make at Home* (London: Ebury Press, 2014); Murielle Valette, *Pâtisserie: a Step-by-Step Guide to Baking French Pastries at Home* (London: Constable & Robinson Ltd, 2013). These works, together with Wilfred Fance's comprehensive *The International Confectioner: Confectionery, Cakes, Pastries, Desserts and Ices* (London: Virtue & Company Ltd, 1968) provided many of the details on individual cakes in this chapter.

Pâtisserie is now one of the very few courses at the Culinary Institute of America which is split evenly: Beverly Russell, *Women of Taste: Recipes and Profiles of Famous Women Chefs* (New York: John Wiley and Sons Inc, 1997).

A 2011 list of the top French pâtisseries in the *Guardian*: http://www.theguardian. com/travel/2011/may/06/top-10-french-rench-patisseries-paris (retrieved 5 August 2015).

Beverly Russell's 1997 study of influential female chefs: Russell, *Women of Taste*.

The White House announced that it was employing its first female pastry chef: http://www.nytimes.com/politics/first-draft/2014/11/21/white-house-taps-first-female-pastry-chef/ (retrieved 9 August 2015).

Sarabeth Levine: Russell, *Women of Taste*.

The first recipient of its Grande Dame award: http://www.ldei.org/index. php?com=aboutus (retrieved 5 August 2015).

Viennese 'Intangible Cultural Heritage': http://immaterielleskulturerbe.unesco.at/ cgi-bin/unesco/element.pl?eid=71&lang=en (retrieved 11 August 2015).

Trotsky, Klimt and Herzl . . . Hotel Sacher: There is more historical background at https://www.wien.gv.at/english/culture-history/viennese-coffee-culture.html (retrieved 10 Aug 2015); see also Josephine Bacon, *Pâtisserie of Vienna* (London: Macdonald Orbis, 1988).

One book on German confectionery: Fance, *The International Confectioner*.

Black Forest gâteau, or *Schwarzwälder Kirschtorte*, described by Alan Davidson: Davidson *Oxford Companion*, p. 80.

The town of Ribeauvillé in Alsace hosted a *kugelhopf* fête: David, *English Bread Cookery*, p. 508.

It seems clear that the baba came first . . . not created until after his death: http://behind-the-french-menu.blogspot.co.uk/2012/08/what-is-rum-baba-or-baba-au-rhum-what.html (retrieved 27 Aug 2015).

Seventy-one per cent of French people bake their own cakes at home: Cited in http://www.bbc.co.uk/news/world-europe-24609525 (retrieved 19 August 2015).

CHAPTER 9

According to Ivan Day, food historian and blogger at 'Food History Jottings': http://foodhistorjottings.blogspot.co.uk/2011/09/queen-cakes-and-cup-cakes-1.html, with parts 2 and 3 following in the two subsequent posts (retrieved 27 August 2015).

A Mintel survey of 2013: http://www.mintel.com/press-centre/food-and-drink/uk-cakes-market-trend; http://store.mintel.com/cakes-and-cake-bars-uk-may-2013 (retrieved 27 April 2015).

The bakery was opened in 1996 by two friends . . . Moscow, Abu Dhabi, Beirut, Kuwait City and Doha: http://www.nytimes.com/2003/11/05/dining/05CUPC.html; http://www.magnoliabakery.com/about-us/ (both retrieved 30 September 2015).

Sixty-one cupcake bakeries in New York City alone at the time of writing: http://cupcakestakethecake.blogspot.co.uk/ (last accessed 30 September 2015).

Current record for the world's largest cupcake: http://www.guinnessworldrecords.com/world-records/largest-cupcake-fairy-cake/ (retrieved 11 June 2015).

Hummingbird, which first opened in Notting Hill: www.primrose-bakery.co.uk/; https://hummingbirdbakery.com/.

They are making inroads into China: See reports available at http://www.bakery andsnacks.com: 'Something like a phenomenon: Bakery in China' and 'Mooncake Festival 2014: The Biggest Event in Asia's Cake Calendar', both by Kacey Culliney (2014) (retrieved 15 June 2015).

Katherine Kallinis Berman and Sophie Kallinis LaMontagne . . . Grandma Babee: Katherine Kallinis and Sophie Kallinis LaMontagne, *The Cupcake Diaries: Recipes and Memories from the Sisters of Georgetown Cupcakes* (New York: Harper Collins, 2011).

Susan Sarich: https://www.susiecakes.com/about/susies-story/ (retrieved 11 June 2015).

They got up at 4 a.m. to bake 500 Cupcakes: Kallinis and Kallinis LaMontagne, *Cupcake Diaries*.

Daniel Gross had predicted such a shift in the market: http://www.slate.com/ articles/business/moneybox/2009/09/the_cupcake_bubble.html (retrieved 15 June 2015).

As Joshua M. Brown . . .: http://thereformedbrokercom/2014/07/08/r-i-p-cupcake-bubble-2009-2014/ (retrieved 25 June 2015).

Sales have been slowing slightly in recent years: http://www.forbes.com/sites/ maurapennington/2013/04/17/as-cupcake-bubble-pops-will-college-education-be-the-next-craze-to-collapse/ (retrieved 25 June 2015).

Forbes.com called the cupcake 'a fanciful luxury': http://www.cnbc.com/ id/46752522 (retrieved 11 June 2015).

Sustained a high level of interest throughout the period 2012–14: All information on internet searches is from Google Trends. All data are shown relative to the highest point of interest in that term, rather than in absolute numbers.

It is said to be a traditional Amish treat . . . Moon Pies: http://www.foodtimeline. org/foodcookies.html#whoopiepies (retrieved 10 June 2015).

There are several tales . . .: http://www.slate.com/articles/life/food/2011/11/macarons _macaroons_and_macaroni_the_curious_history.html (retrieved 11 June 2015). There is a light-hearted historical overview at http://www.seriouseats.com/2007/10/ introduction-to-french-macarons.html (retrieved 11 June 2015).

The macaron is forever linked with Ladurée: https://www.laduree.com/en_gb/#!brand/history (retrieved 10 June 2015).

David Leibowitz reported meeting the only cake he has ever refused to taste: http://www.davidlebovitz.com/2008/12/the-macaron-i-wouldnt-eat/ (retrieved 10 June 2015).

One list of baking trends for 2015 has them on the 'going down' list: http://kernpack.co.uk/wp-content/uploads/2015/03/Baking-Trends-2015-Infographic.jpg (retrieved 10 June 2015).

The person who turned them from novelty to craze . . . *The Martha Stewart Show* for Cupcake Week: The original Cake Pop post can be found here: http://www.bakerella.com/dont-lick-bite%E2%80%A6/; see also Angie Dudley, *Cake Pops* (San Francisco: Chronicle Books, 2010), and for more historical background, http://www.foodtimeline.org/foodcakes.html#cakepops (both sites retrieved 10 June 2015).

Cross two trends to create the *cupcake* pop: http://www.bakerella.com/chocolate-cupcake-pops/ (retrieved 10 June 2015).

Dominique Ansel . . . launched the (trademarked) cronut . . . the first 200 consistently sell out: http://dominiqueansel.com/cronut-101/ (retrieved 15 June 2015).

Ariel Knutson of the Kitchn blog: http://www.thekitchn.com/10-things-you-need-to-know-before-making-a-cronut-211530 (retrieved 15 June 2015).

High-profile CEO Katya Andreson: https://www.linkedin.com/pulse/20130423100032-6200057-my-best-mistake-faking-homemade-cupcakes-not-leaning-in (retrieved 11 June 2015).

Their owner, David Arrick: www.entrepreneur.com/article/207508 (retrieved 11 June 2015).

The now defunct Crumbs range: http://www.crumbs.com/pages/catering-menu (retrieved 30 September 2015).

The average American eats 22.7 teaspoons of sugar . . . majority of those American 22.7 teaspoons are from sucrose: Rich Cohen, 'Sugar Love (A Not So Sweet Story)' *National Geographic* (August 2013), pp. 78–97.

Coined the term 'cupcake problem' . . . Safe Cupcake Amendment: http://www.nytimes.com/2007/09/23/weekinreview/23kershaw.html (retrieved 11 June 2015).

When the issue was raised again: See, for example, the reporting at http://www.texastribune.org/2015/01/12/commissioner-sid-miller-gives-amnesty-cupcakes/ (retrieved 11 June 2015).

The UK's School Food Plan: http://www.schoolfoodplan.com/standards/ (retrieved 23 June 2015).

The Ontario School Food and Beverage Policy of 2010: Ontario Ministry of Education School Food and Beverage Policy Resource Guide, 2010, available from http://www.edu.gov.on.ca/eng/healthyschools/policy.html (retrieved 23 June 2015).

A red velvet cupcake from Magnolia Bakery contains 22.8 grams of fat: Nutritional information is from www.myfitnesspal.com.

Cakes, muffins, scones and cake-type desserts are the top type of snack consumed by Australian children: http://healthy-kids.com.au/the-top-four-snacks-consumed-by-children/ (retrieved 23 June 2015).

Buns, cakes, pastries and fruit pies are responsible for 7 per cent of British adults' sugar intake: Public Health England paper, 'Sugar Reduction: Responding to the Challenge', available from https://www.gov.uk/government/publications/sugar-reduction-responding-to-the-challenge (retrieved 23 June 2015).

A chocolate cupcake with frosting from Magnolia: Nutritional information from www.myfitnesspal.com.

Currently, all age groups in the UK eat more sugar than they should: 'Sugar Reduction'.

One Texan food blogger: http://www.thelunchtray.com/cupcake-amnestychildhood-obesity-political-divide/ (retrieved 23 June 2015).

A Twinkie is made from twenty-five different types of ingredients: Steve Ettlinger, Twinkie, Deconstructed (London: Plume, 2008).

One taste forecaster in 2015: http://kernpack.co.uk/wp-content/uploads/2015/03/Baking-Trends-2015-Infographic.jpg (retrieved 10 June 2015).

Meanwhile, the cronut, the macaron and the whoopie pie: http://kernpack.co.uk/wp-content/uploads/2015/03/Baking-Trends-2015-Infographic.jpg; https://www.itsabakingthing.com/expert-advice/blogs/the-need-to-know-baking-trends-of-2015/ (retrieved 10 June 2015).

EPILOGUE

And people have done all of those things: In October 2015 British junior doctors and their friends posted pictures of cakes online on the day of *The Great British Bake Off* final, marked with social media hashtags like #notsafenotfair to protest at a proposed restructuring of their hours and pay (one of the three finalists was a junior doctor); in the same month Guinness World Records endorsed the largest ever cake sculpture, baked by professionals in Italy. In May judges ruled that a Northern Ireland bakery had exercised discrimination in refusing to bake a cake for a gay wedding; also in May an American newscaster sent in his resignation letter printed onto the top of a cake (a similar story had made the British press in April 2013 when a man iced his resignation letter onto the top of a cake, saying that he wanted to spend his time launching his cake business instead).

Index